IMAGES
of America

THE COMMUNITIES OF WESTERN AROOSTOOK COUNTY

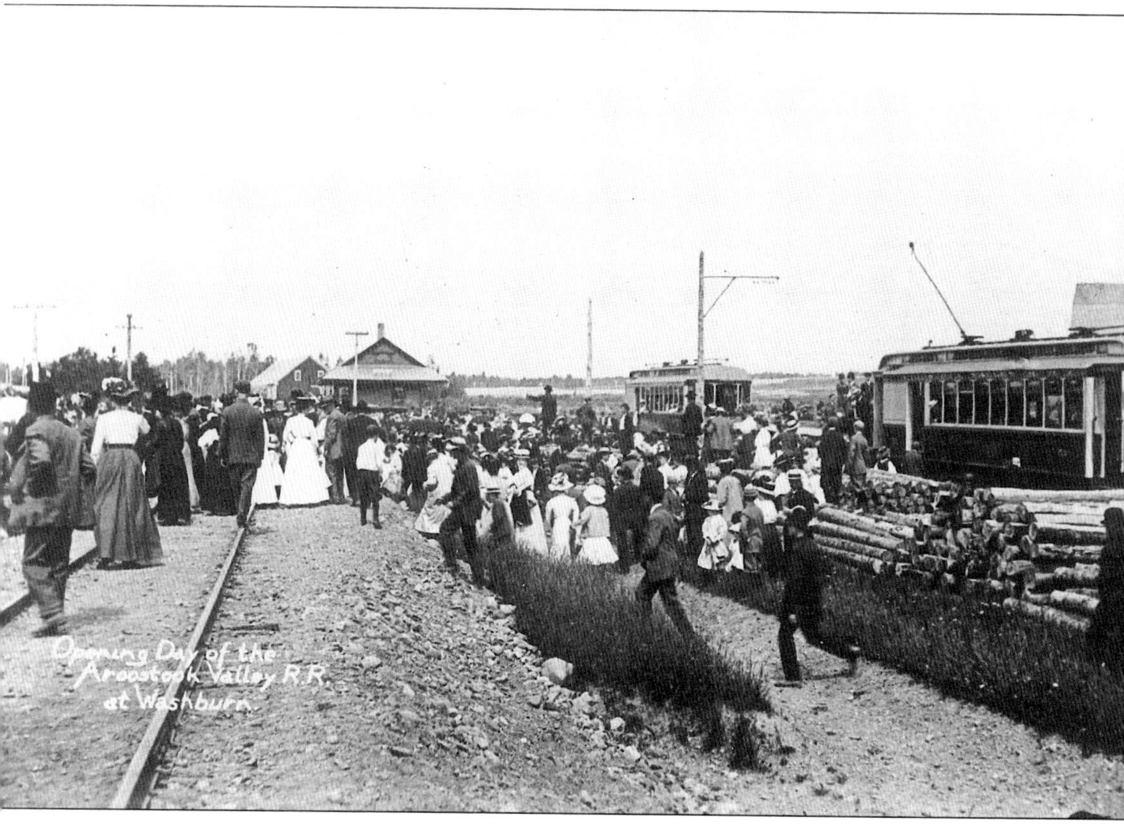
Opening Day of the
Aroostook Valley R.R.
at Washburn

IMAGES
of America

THE COMMUNITIES OF WESTERN AROOSTOOK COUNTY

Jackie Greaves and Christie Cochran

ARCADIA
PUBLISHING

ISBN 978-0-7385-5027-5

Published by Arcadia Publishing
Charleston, South Carolina

Printed in the United States of America

Library of Congress Catalog Card Number: 2007921775

For all general information contact Arcadia Publishing at:
Telephone 843-853-2070
Fax 843-853-0044
E-mail sales@arcadiapublishing.com
For customer service and orders:
Toll-Free 1-888-313-2665

Visit us on the Internet at www.arcadiapublishing.com

Contents

Acknowledgments

Trying to cover the area that this book encompasses would have been a long, slow process without the help of my co-author, Christie Cochran. Her knowledge of its history, her many acquaintances and contacts, and her invaluable advice made the gathering of pictures and information much quicker and more enjoyable. My first thanks goes to you, Christie!

A special "thank you" is extended to Ellsworth Woodman who helped in dating nearly all the automobiles, trucks, airplanes, and even tractors; to Margaret Allen, Paul Blackstone, Arvard Crouse, Norma Hitchcock, and Gaynel Tilley for providing additional and accurate information on photographs; and to Glenna Condon and Donna Martin, our deep appreciation in searching archives for photographs and information.

To the many individuals who generously offered valuable pictures with no hesitation or reservations, we thank Ron McKee, Richard Blanchard, Owen Smith, Garold and Vi Alley, Anna McGrath, Rachael Burden, Norma Hitchcock, Jim Hunter, and Barb Drost.

We are also in debt to the Salmon Brook Historical Society, the Woodland Historical Society, and the Ashland Historical Society. The University of Maine at Presque Isle gave us permission to borrow a few photographs from its *Images of Aroostook* project that was written with a grant from the National Endowment for the Arts.

And to Frank Sleeper: thank you for your help and advice!

Jackie Greaves
June 1995

Introduction

For many people, the mention of northwestern Maine brings to mind its numerous lakes and rivers, its rolling hills and ranging fields, its vast woodlands and hunting grounds. There is beauty and strength in this landscape. Not as visible, but perhaps more important, is a reflection of this fortitude and endurance in the people who came here and claimed sections of the land for themselves and their ancestors.

A well-known Aroostook County banker once said, "It's not the few large depositors who make a bank, but the many small ones." And this was also true of the early settlers—the individuals, families, and small groups who arrived in the western part of Aroostook County in the mid to late 1800s, who allocated their individuality to the region. From near and far they came to make a hard, and sometimes unforgiving, land into settlements, farms, and homes. Traveling from as far away as Sweden and as near as the next village, settlers took root and carved from rugged wilderness a civilization that many refer to as "the last frontier." Loggers, wood cutters, farmers and hired hands, hunters and guides, innkeepers, truckers and teamsters, soldiers, sailors, as well as the mill workers and storekeepers, all arrived and set up their businesses. And most of them took on additional tasks—from barbering to burying.

Unlike the frontier in the western part of the country, they worked with the Indians, learned from the Indians, and helped the Indians. "Recipes" for food, medicines, insect bites, gardening, and birthing were exchanged. Thus began the rich legacy that was left by our forebearers.

At the outset both mental and physical survival demanded self-reliance and innovative thinking. Separated sometimes by miles from the nearest neighbor, the loneliness could be overwhelming. One story is told about a woman and her four young children who were forced to spend their entire first winter alone with no one closer than 4 miles away. Her husband had left in the fall to travel to Bangor for household goods and food. Long periods of rain made the "cow path" impossible to bring wagons and horses back through the mud. This was followed by winter setting in with snow too deep to travel in. By spring the young mother's firewood and provisions were gone. Undaunted, when the family was reunited, they decided to stay. With determination, stamina, and perseverance, such individuals as these hardy souls carved an existence out of their surroundings, and lay the solid cornerstones for further expansion in the area.

Another story involves a man who was working in a sawmill. One day, he accidentally cut off part of his foot. Not wanting to slow or stop operations, he remained on the job! And that evening a doctor tried to repair the damage on the kitchen table at the man's home.

With meager financial assets, these hard workers—who came to build their homes and care for their families, farms, and equipment—made the best of little. Through it all, they maintained their humor, ethnic backgrounds, and their love of the area. Once the land was cultivated, they settled in. From Wade to Oxbow, from Mapleton to Portage, families found themselves woven into a tightly knit "community" made up of several communities—each still separate, but interacting and interdependent on each others' strong points.

They earned not only their livelihoods but a cultural reputation for their individual towns and the geographical area. They raised large families, whose names today immediately bring to mind the legacy of honest, dependable, tenacious, hard-working ancestors. Many times former students of mine who had moved "south" have told me that in applying for a job in their new town, if they mentioned they were from the area, they were hired on the spot. The solid, enduring reputation established for them long ago remains to this day. Ironically, many of these same students return home after spending a short period of time in the cities.

From the early blacksmith shop to the mills and factories to the farms and sawmills, early pioneers probably didn't look on their efforts as being vital to history—but today's generation owes them a great deal.

Jackie Greaves
Christie Cochran

One

The Seekers and Searchers

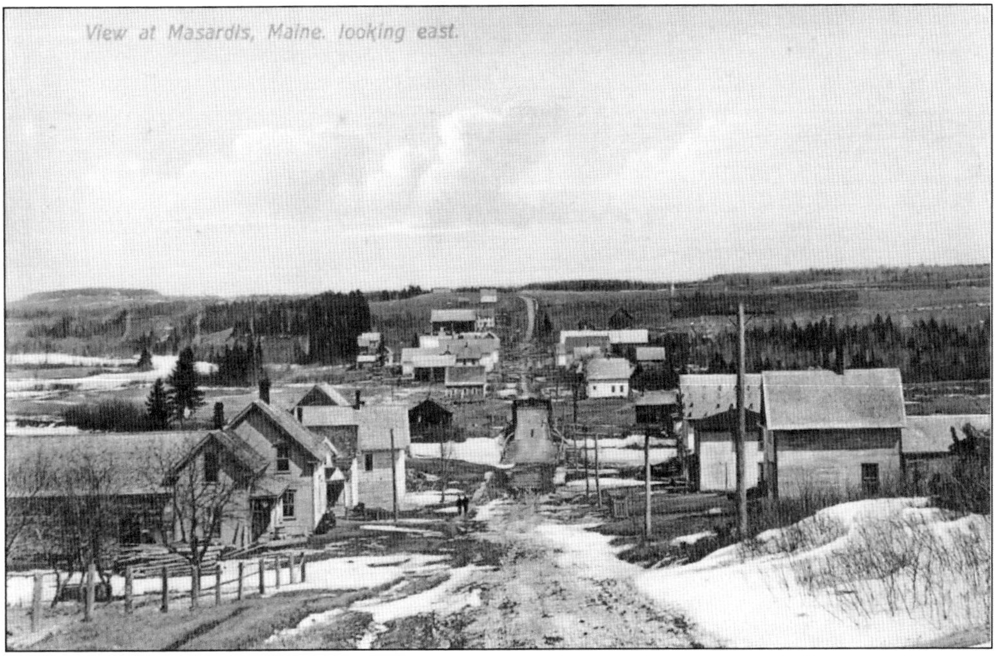

In this c. 1908 photograph, the road through Masardis runs down a long hill, across the river, and up another long hill, just as it does today.

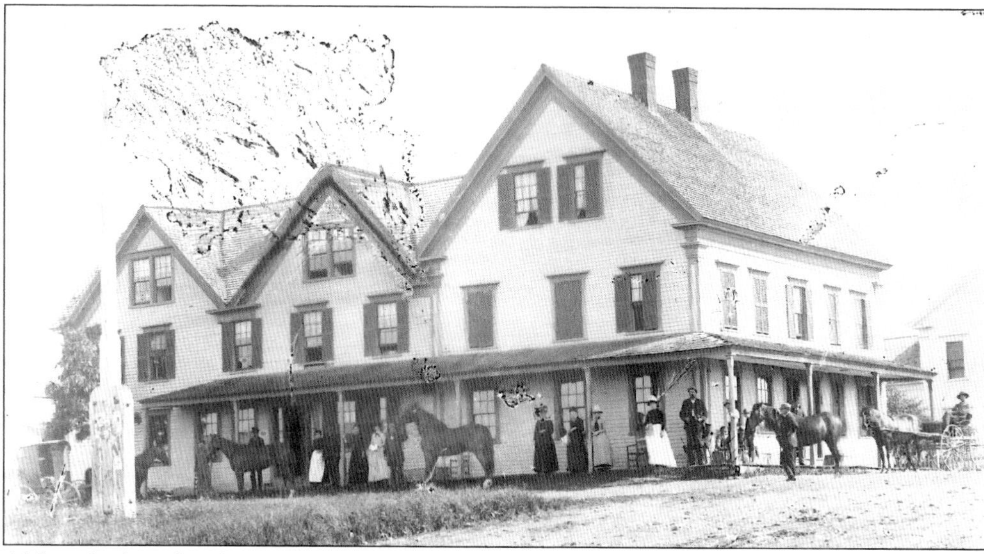

Although there has been some discussion over the name of this old hotel, descendants have confirmed that this building is the old Sperrey Hotel, which was located at the top of Town Hill in Washburn in the late 1800s or early 1900s. It was the town's first hotel. It burned, and another was built on the same location. And that, too, burned.

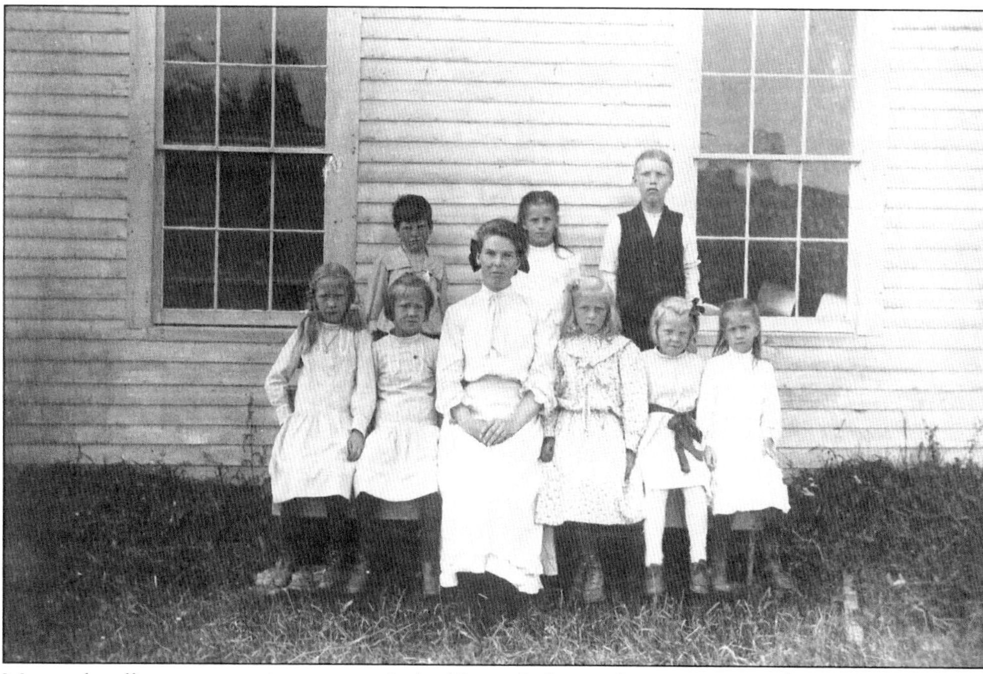

Most schoolhouses contain a great deal of knowledge without ever traveling. This building, however, was moved from Woodland Road in Washburn to Upper Thomas Road and was used by Percy Landeen as a woodshed. It later was moved again to Magnus Monson's farm on Thomas Road and used as a house for farm hands. But, before "taking to the roads," this class picture was procured in the early 1900s. From left to right are: (front row) Gladys Anderson, Lillian Anderson (teacher), Minnie Monson, unknown, Beda Monson, Mildred Anderson, and Laura Henry; (back row) Edwin Thomas, Olive Henry, and Paul Monson.

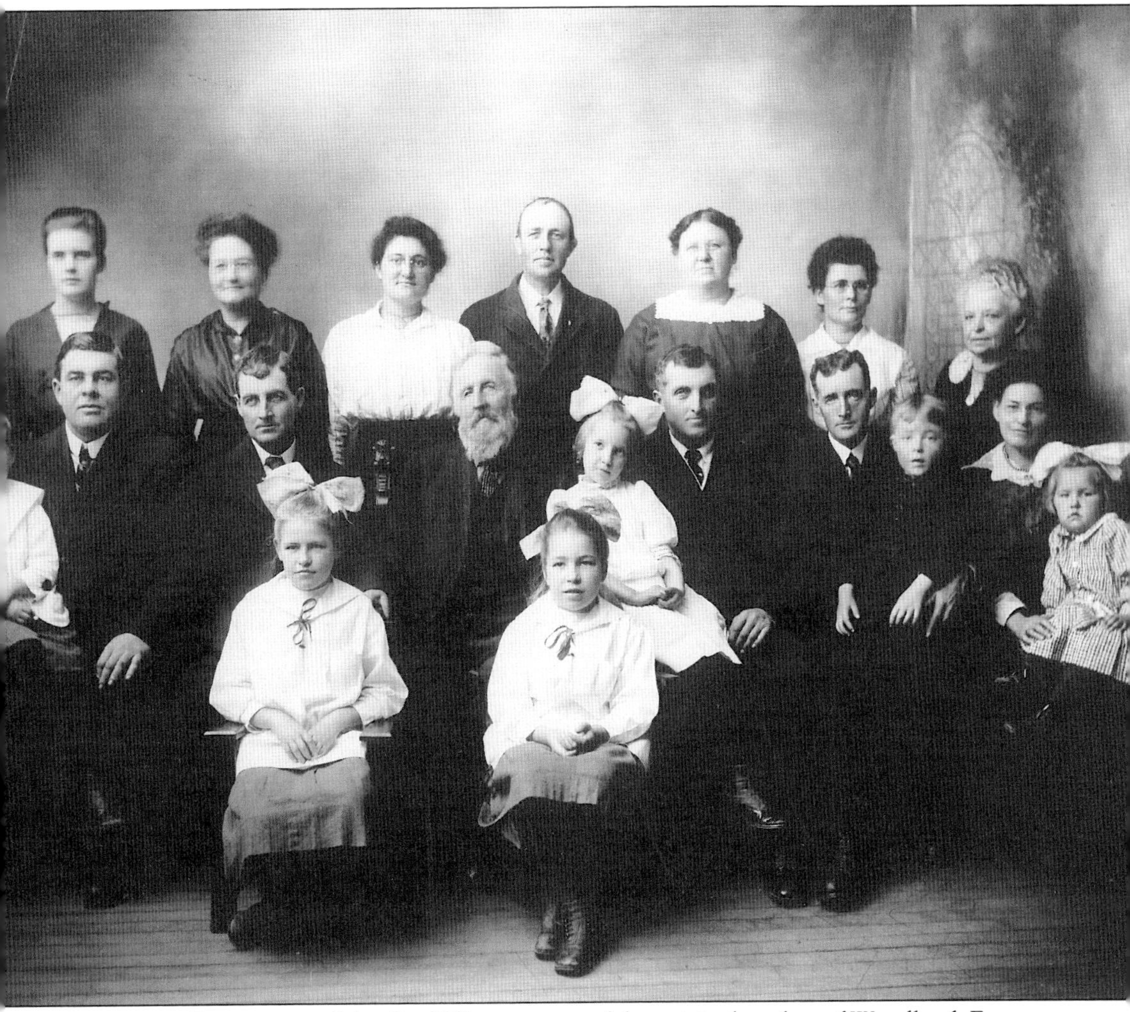

Sullivan Russell, a veteran of the Civil War, was one of the original settlers of Woodland. From left to right are: (front row) Fatima "Fay" and Lovice Currier; (middle row) Russell Currier, Almer Russell, Maurice Russell, Sullivan Russell, Opel Currier, George Russell, Charles Russell, Jesse R. Russell, Irene (Russell) Currier, and Gladys Currier; (back row) Tryphena Russell, Elnora (Tuttle) Russell, Minnie (Nelson) Russell, Charles Currier, Laura (Churchill) Russell, Ida (Barnes) Russell, and Paulina (Beals) Willey.

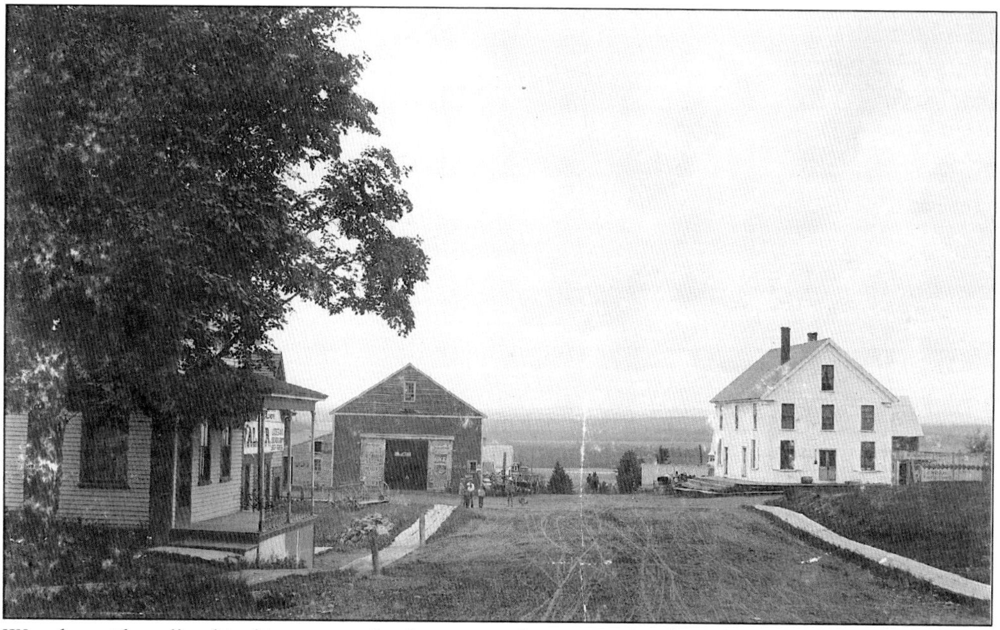

Wooden sidewalks, hitching posts for horses, and wagon-wheel marks reveal the date of this 1897 photograph of Exchange Street in Ashland. Standing on Main Street, friends pass the time of day by swapping news. The large building on the right later became the firehouse; further along the road of time it became the Catholic church.

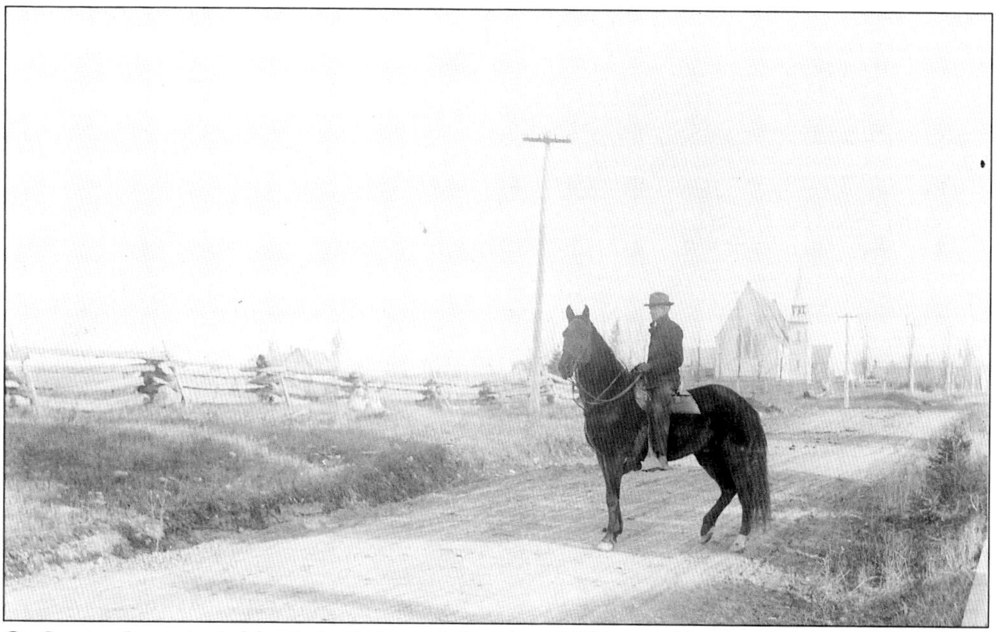

On Station Street in Ashland, the Episcopal church in 1897 waited for worshippers to congregate. And, although the building still stands today, times and the population have brought change, making it a recreation center.

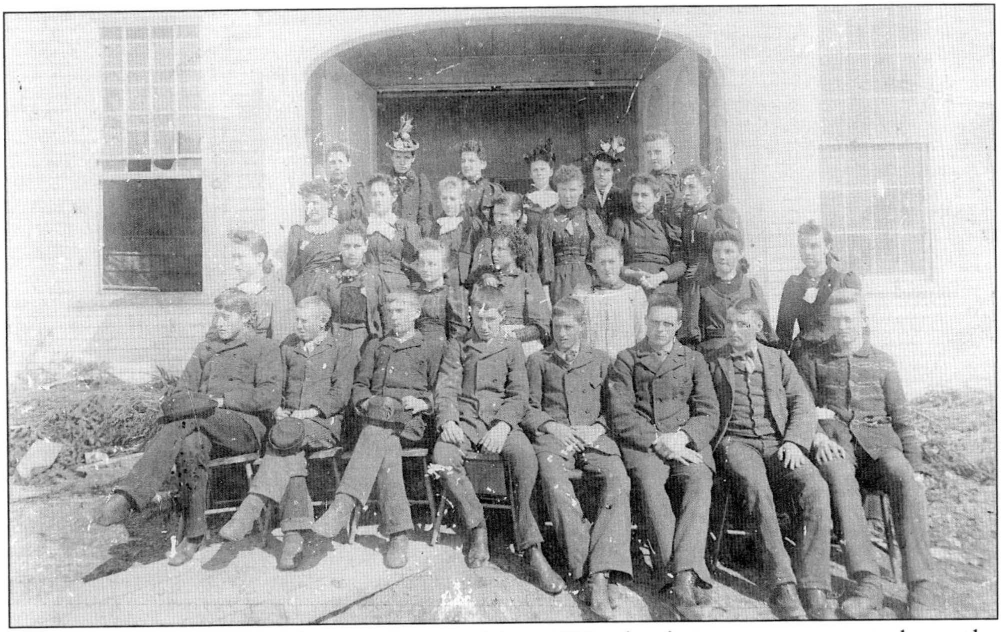

Although the attention of these students in this *c.* 1890 school picture seems not to be on the camera, the picture reflects the attire of the day. The heavy boots and coats the boys have on and the hats two girls have donned belie the open window. From left to right are: (front row) Henry Patten, Frank Seamons, Henry Wilder, Rodney Beckford, Millard Dickinson, Elmer Stoddard, Ernest Rogers, and Allen Smith; (second row) Kate Bugbee, Josie McCubrey, Elsie Tuttle, Jessie Rogers, Martha Kimball, Josie Pelkey, and Hattie Whitten; (third row) Bertha Learnard, Alice Wilder, Stella Munson, Lucy Beckford, Emma Stow, Mamie Willey, and Mary Duncan; (back row) Effie Chase, Rose Rediker, Carrie Sleeper, Maude McCubrey, Bessie Tompkins, and Ivy Clair.

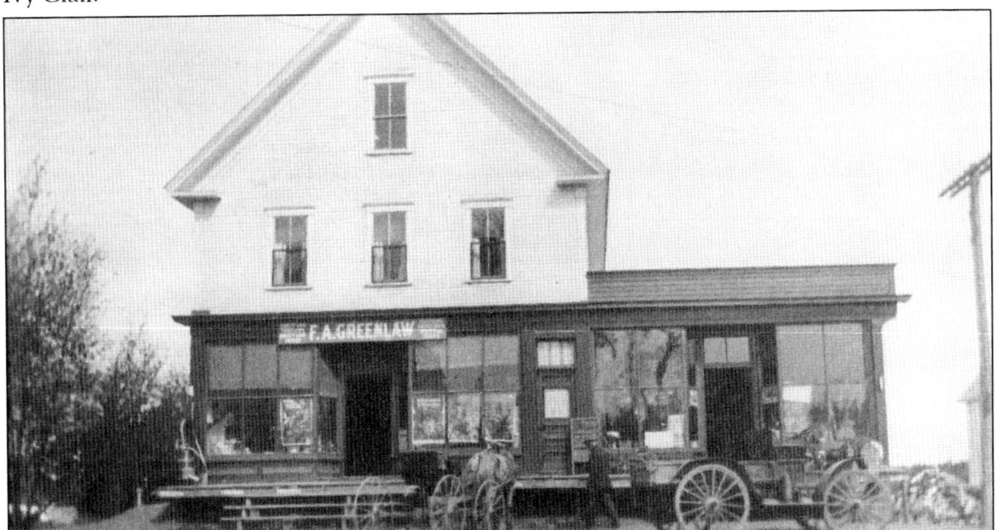

In 1913, through their own ingenuity, the owners of the F.A. Greenlaw General Store in Masardis implemented an old buckboard to make deliveries between the railroad station and the market. It was converted to a "horseless carriage" with wooden wheels that wouldn't slip in the snow.

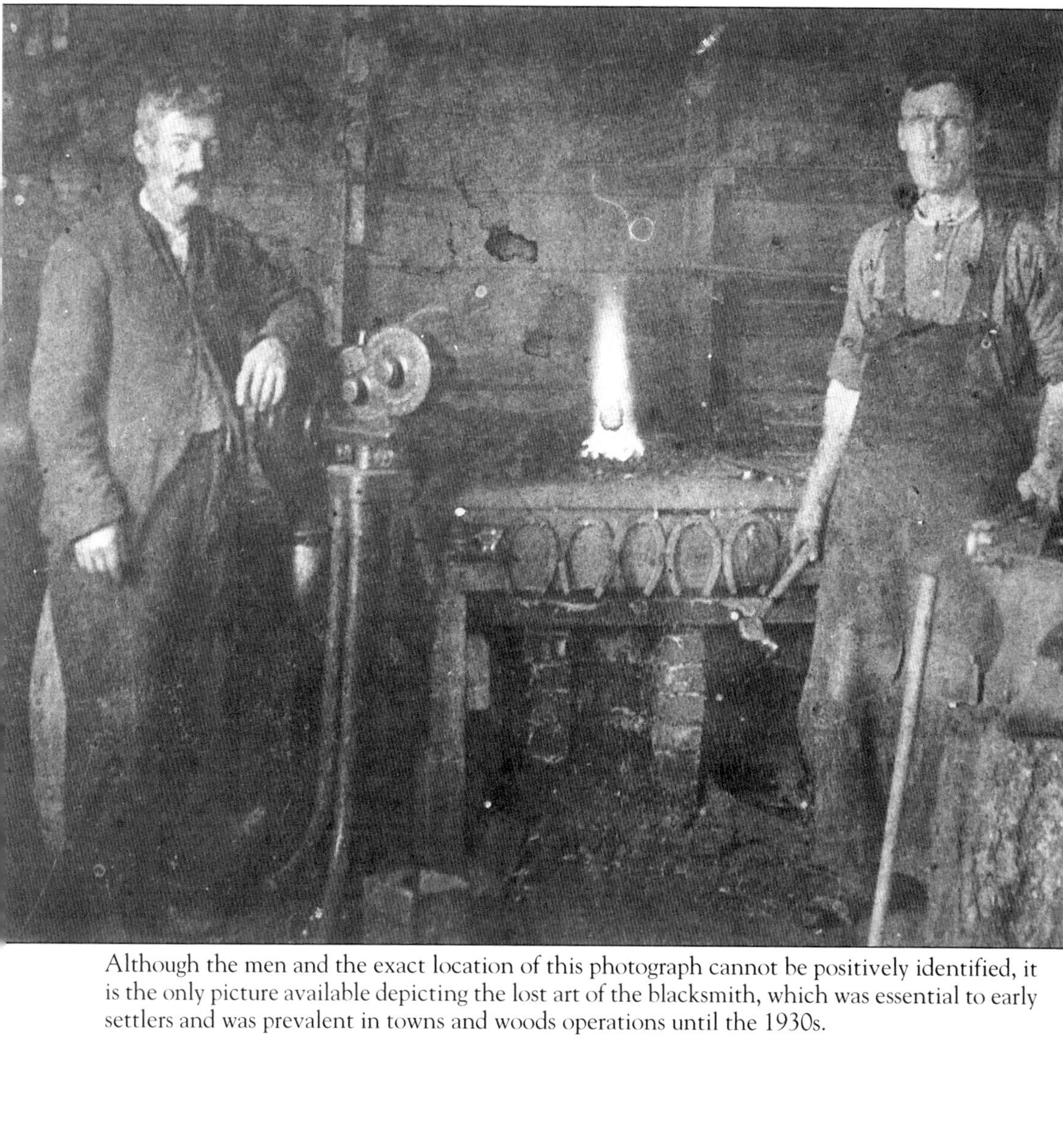

Although the men and the exact location of this photograph cannot be positively identified, it is the only picture available depicting the lost art of the blacksmith, which was essential to early settlers and was prevalent in towns and woods operations until the 1930s.

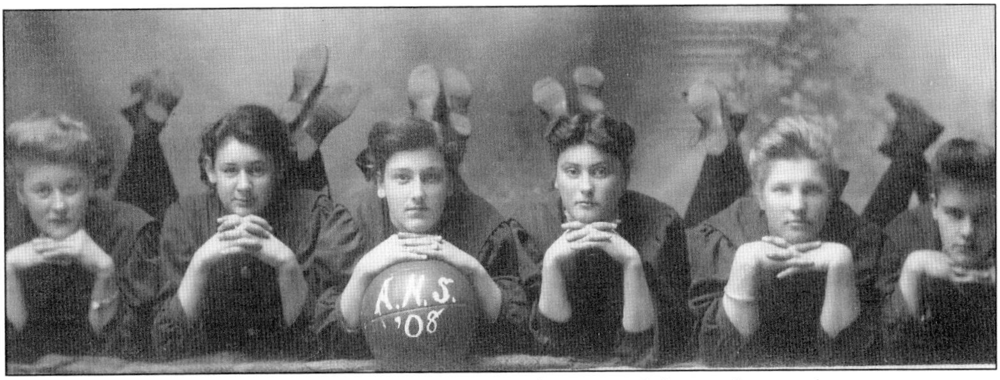

Even though the blouses, bloomers, cotton stockings, and heavy boots that women were required to wear when they played basketball in 1908 were nearly as cumbersome as their long, heavy dresses, these six young ladies from Ashland appear pleased with their accomplishments. From left to right are Fern Dorman, Kate McNally, Alice Coffin, Hannah Clayton, Nina (or Lou) Coffin, and Julia Hews.

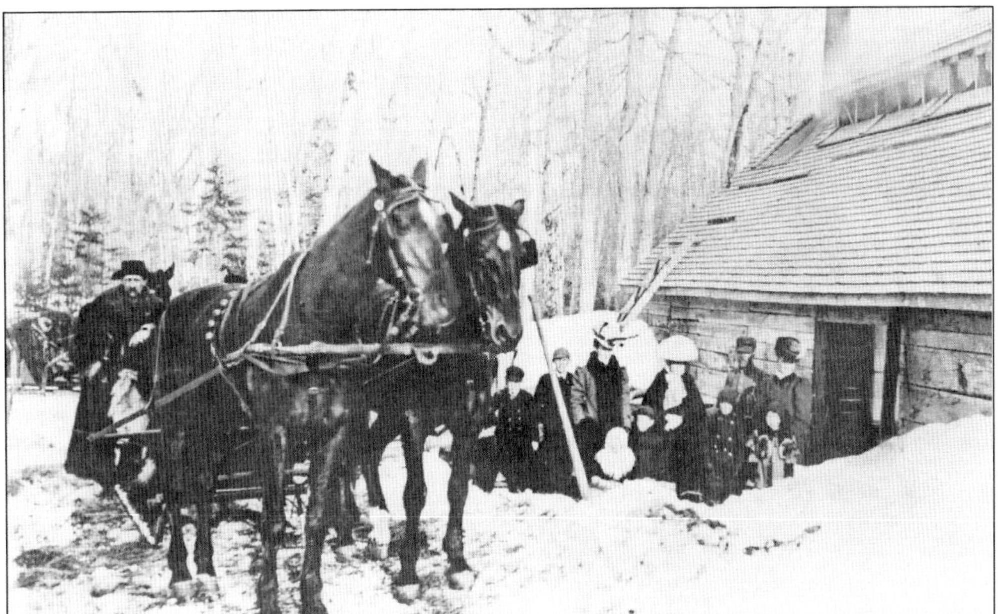

In the early 1900s, the collection of sap from maple trees was the first sign of spring. With snow still on the ground, warm days and cool nights brought out residents eager to help in boiling down the sweet liquid into maple syrup and maple sugar, or just to sample it. Hauling the vats of sap for their driver, Charles Tupper, are the horses, Minnie and Nelson. Waiting are, from left to right: (front row) Hannah Tupper, ? Tupper, Harston Blackstone, and Milford Blackstone; (back row) Lester Tupper, George Tupper, Alice Tupper, Mrs. Charles Tupper, Fayette Blackstone, and his wife Mamie Austin Blackstone.

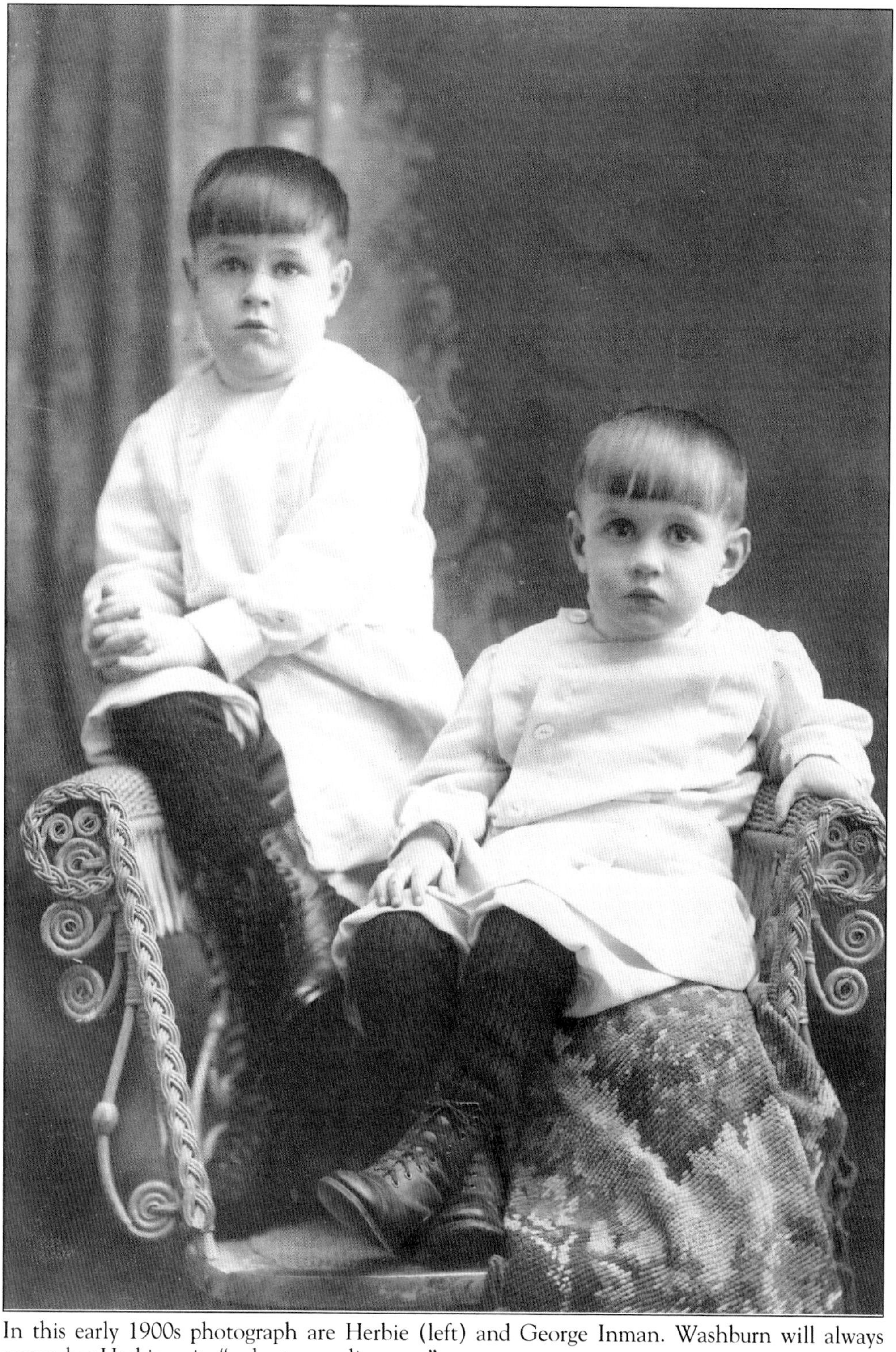

In this early 1900s photograph are Herbie (left) and George Inman. Washburn will always remember Herbie as its "volunteer policeman."

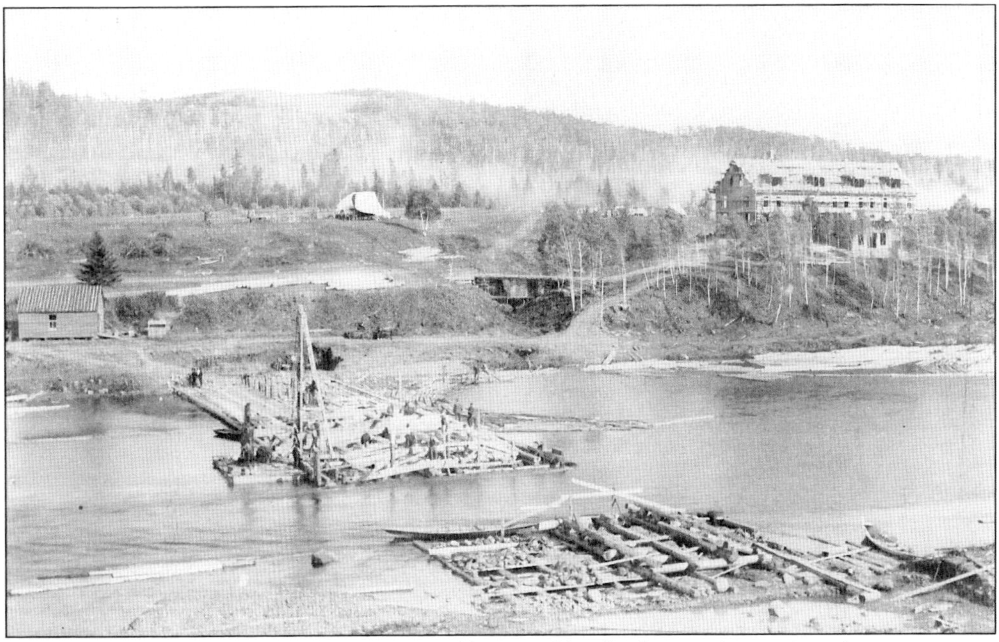

If the Aroostook River could speak for itself, it would tell a history beyond one's imagination; if it could relate the changes it has seen take place or the number of logs that it has floated to sawmills, it would be unbelievable. In 1897 the Sheridan Dam was constructed, beginning a new era for the river.

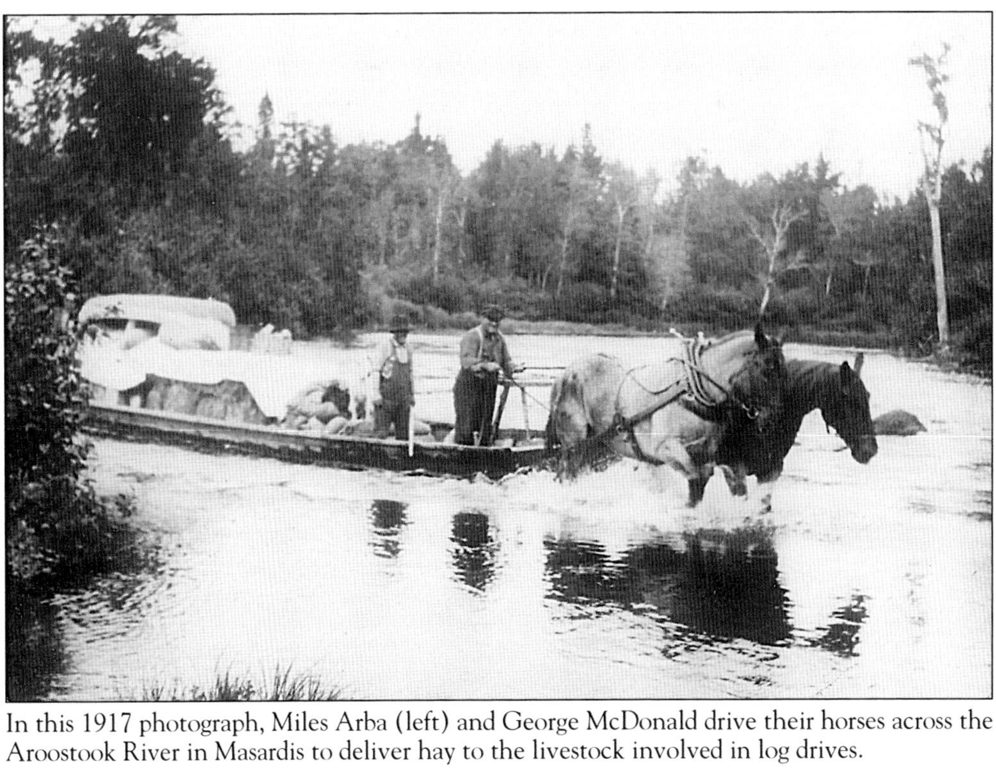

In this 1917 photograph, Miles Arba (left) and George McDonald drive their horses across the Aroostook River in Masardis to deliver hay to the livestock involved in log drives.

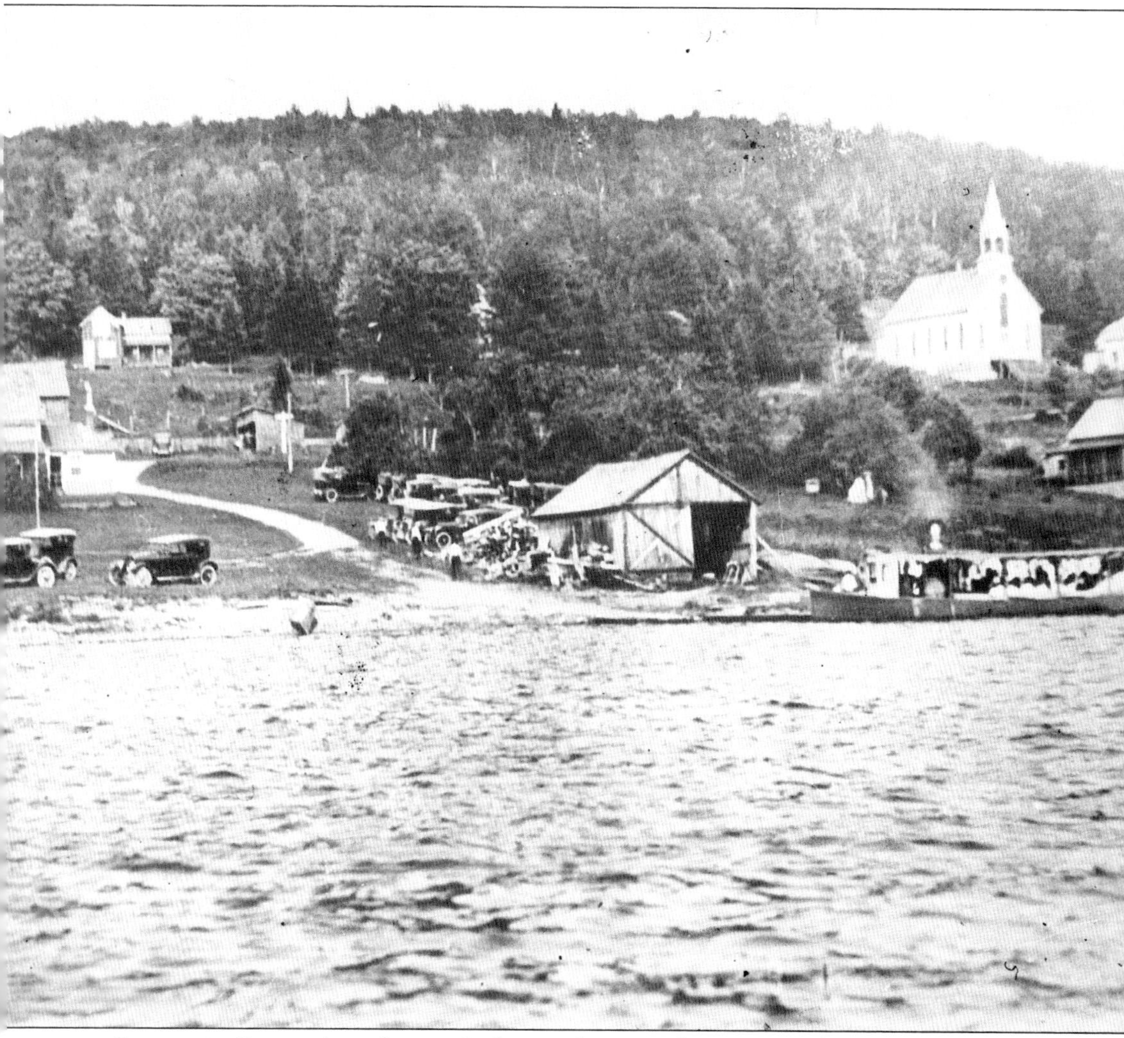

Summer in Portage brought people from miles around to enjoy sight-seeing tours on Portage Lake and the Fish River area. Chauffeurs were left on shore to stay with the cars to wile away the time. Around 1905, Our Lady of the Lake Catholic Church stood proudly, as she did for many years after as a landmark.

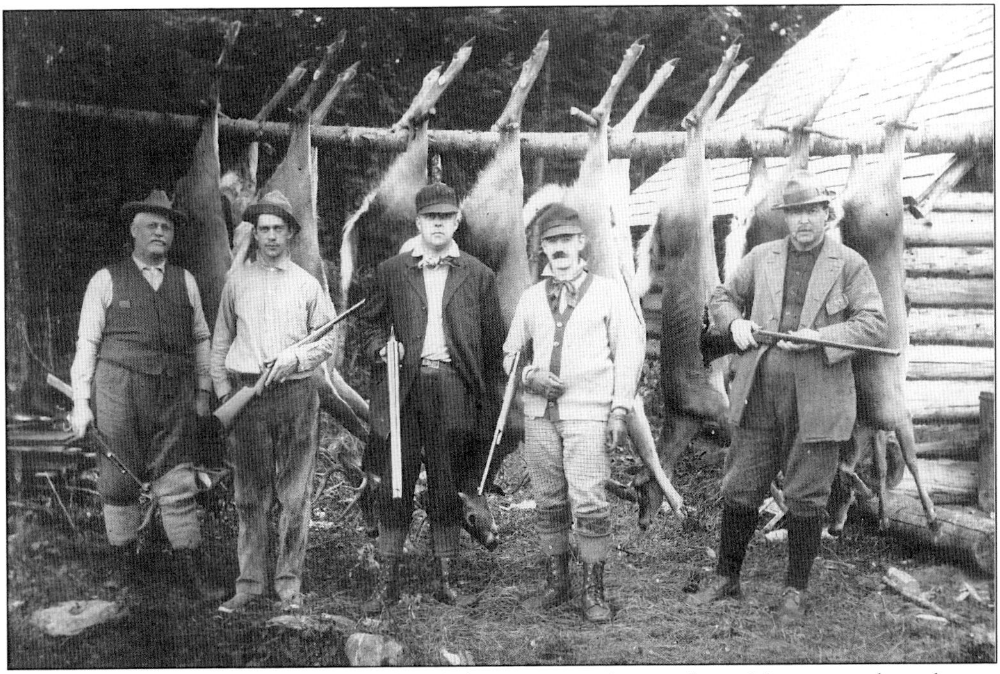

During the early 1920s, sportsmen found their way to the northern Maine woods and were usually successful in their quest for prey. Sporting camps opened, and men who had explored the outdoors for years for their own enjoyment were paid to guide the hunters and fishermen. Emery Swett (fourth from the left) was one of those guides. It is sad to note that one year when he was coming across Millimagassett Lake, loaded down with backpacks, he went through thin ice and drowned.

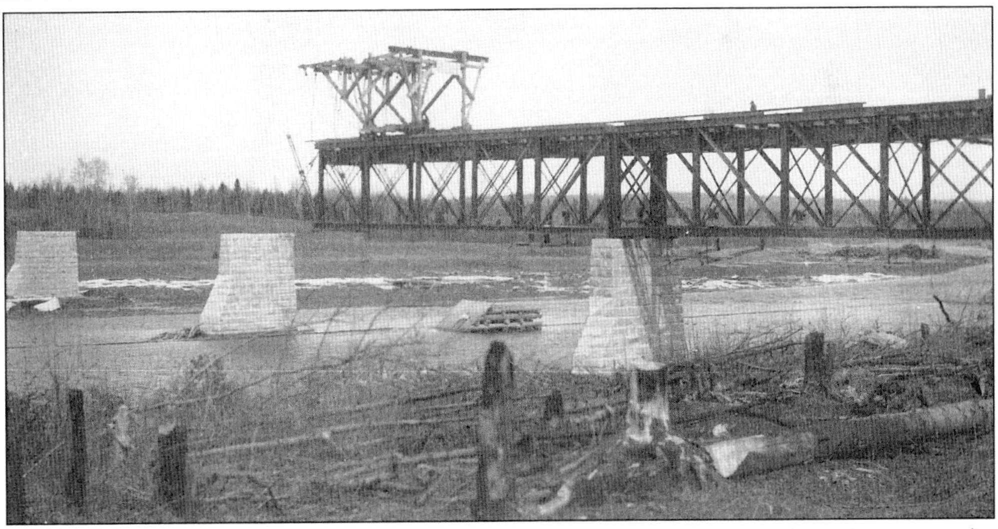

In the early 1900s horse-drawn wagons transporting settlers and wares from Bangor to the southern part of Aroostook County took a minimum of two weeks, and then only if good weather prevailed. The Bangor and Aroostook Railroad, which played a large role in the development of Aroostook Country, found that expansion was frequently in demand. During the first few years of the nineteenth century, a railroad bridge was erected across the Aroostook River at Sheridan.

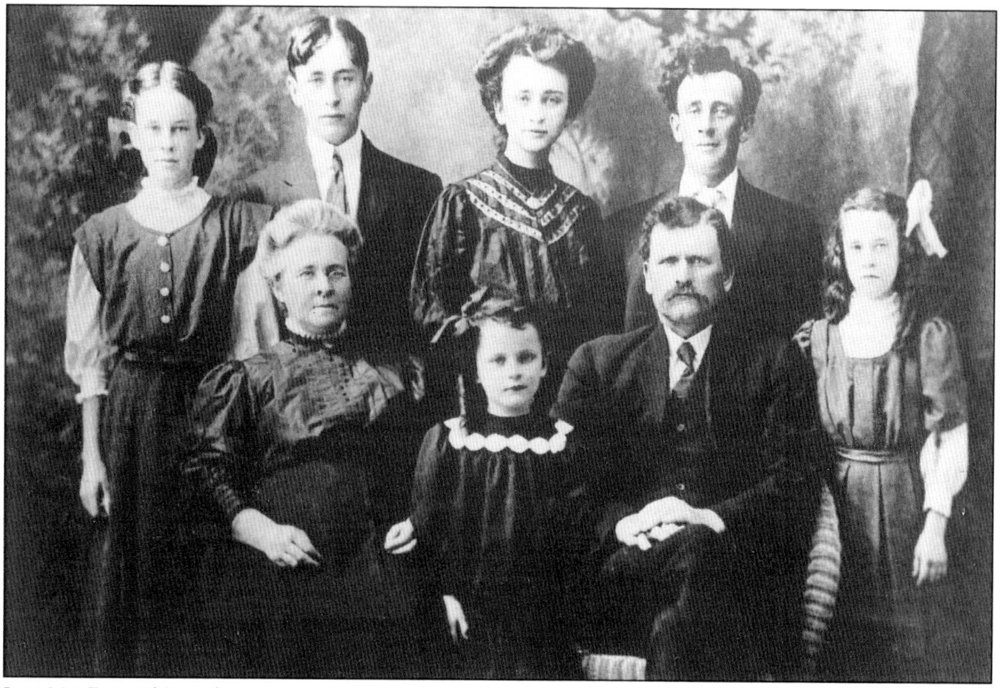

In 1804 Daniel Brooks immigrated from New Brunswick, Canada, to Ashland, where he bought and sold cattle and operated a slaughter house. When he died, his sons continued the business for many years as the Brooks Brothers Store. This family picture, taken in 1907 or 1908, shows, from left to right: (front row) Sarah Harmon Brooks, Mina Brooks Peet, Daniel Brooks, and Annie Brooks Coffin; (back row) Flora Brooks Blanchard, Charles Arthur Harmon Brooks, Georgie Brooks Orcutt, and Lee Brooks.

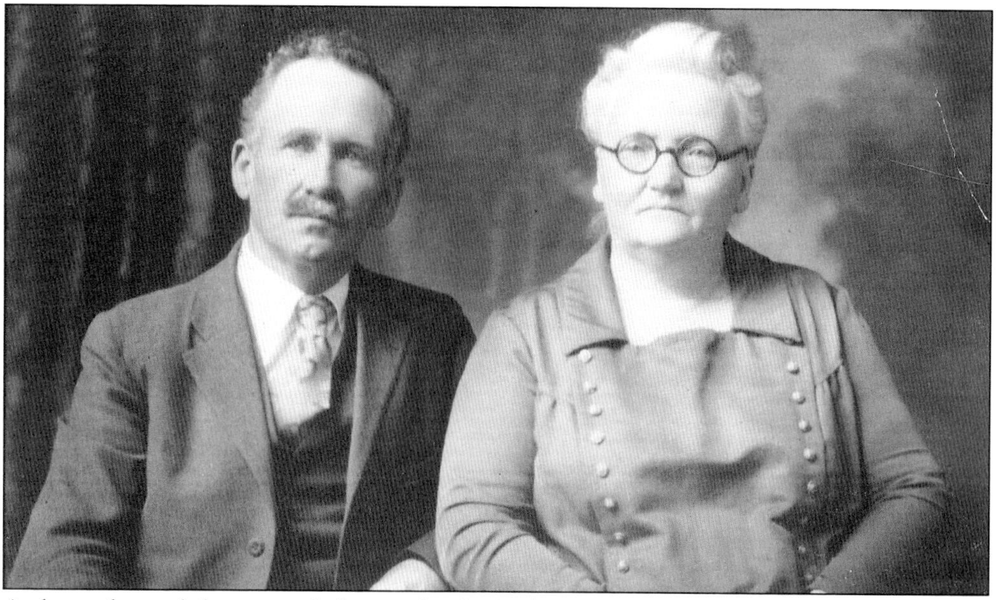

A descendent of the original Crouse family, Wilmot owned and operated the Crouseville Slaughter House and also farmed. Married in 1873, Wilmot and Mamie celebrate their fiftieth anniversary in this 1923 photograph.

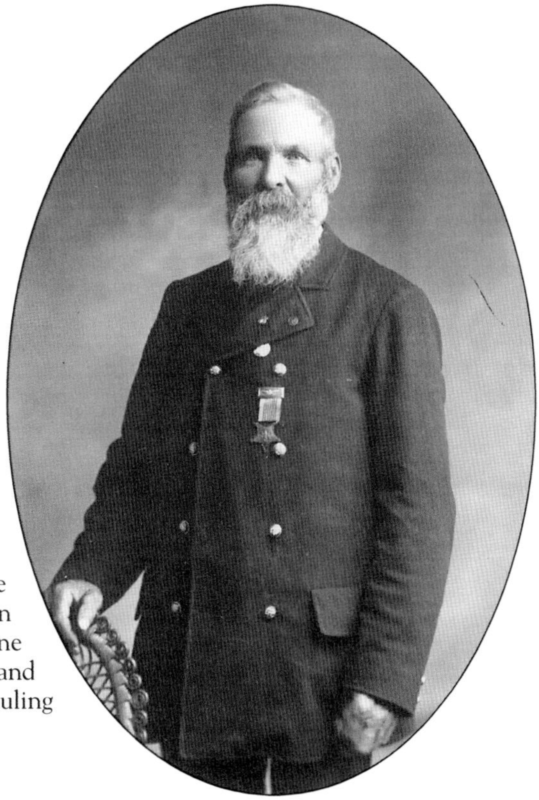

Sam Austin, in 1890, was a member of the Grand Army of the Republic. He began serving in the Civil War with the Maine Volunteers, and transferred to the Rhode Island Lite Artillery Bat. E #1 as an ox-teamer, hauling caissons onto the battlefield.

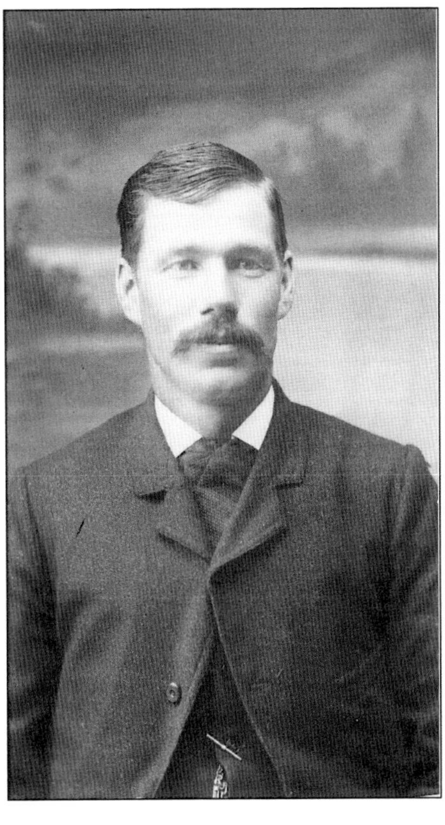

Fred Sylvester was born in Portage Lake in 1871. Moving a few miles southeast to Ashland, he later became known for being one of the first farmers to raise pure bred Guernsey cows. The oldest resident of the town, he was ninety-one years old when he died in 1962.

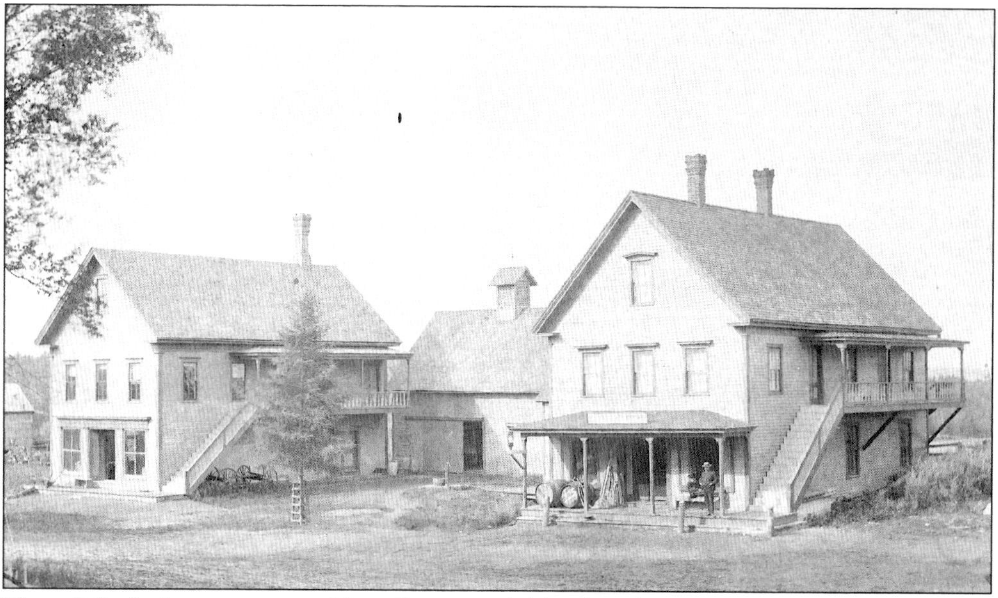

The solidly-built structures on Main Street in Ashland in the late 1800s prove the intended permanency of the town. Today the split-rail fences are gone, as are some of the buildings. The building on the left, however, still remains and is presently Art's Appliance Store.

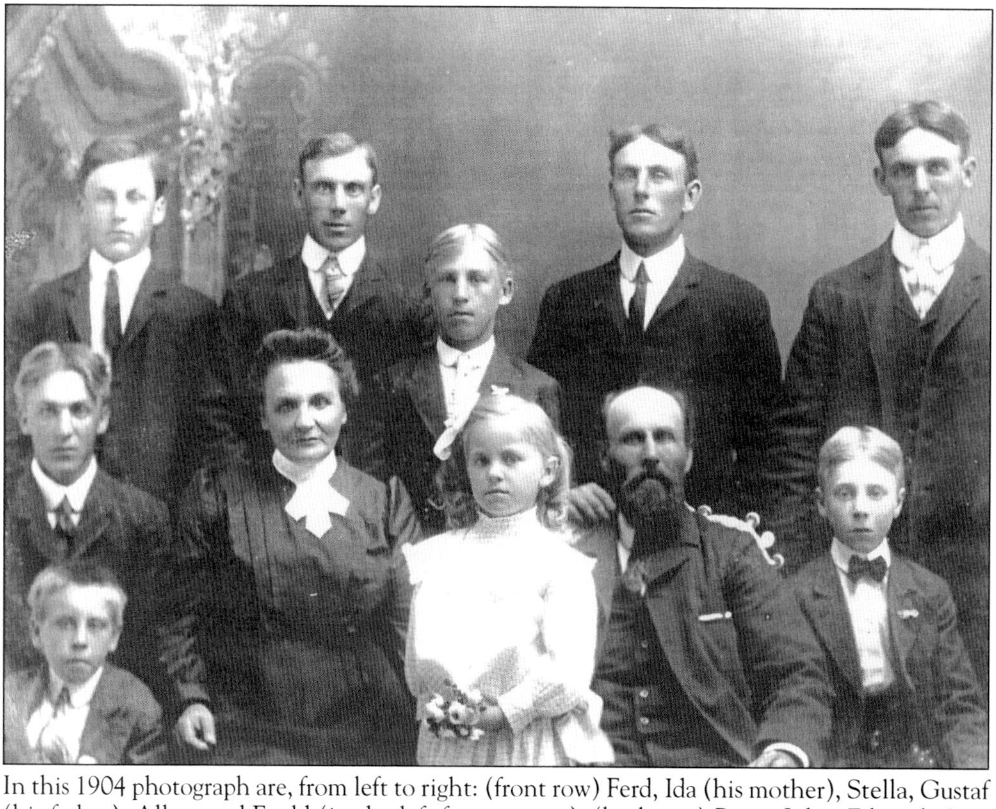

In this 1904 photograph are, from left to right: (front row) Ferd, Ida (his mother), Stella, Gustaf (his father), Allan, and Evald (in the left front corner); (back row) Percy, John, Edward, Guy, and Ricker Dahlgren.

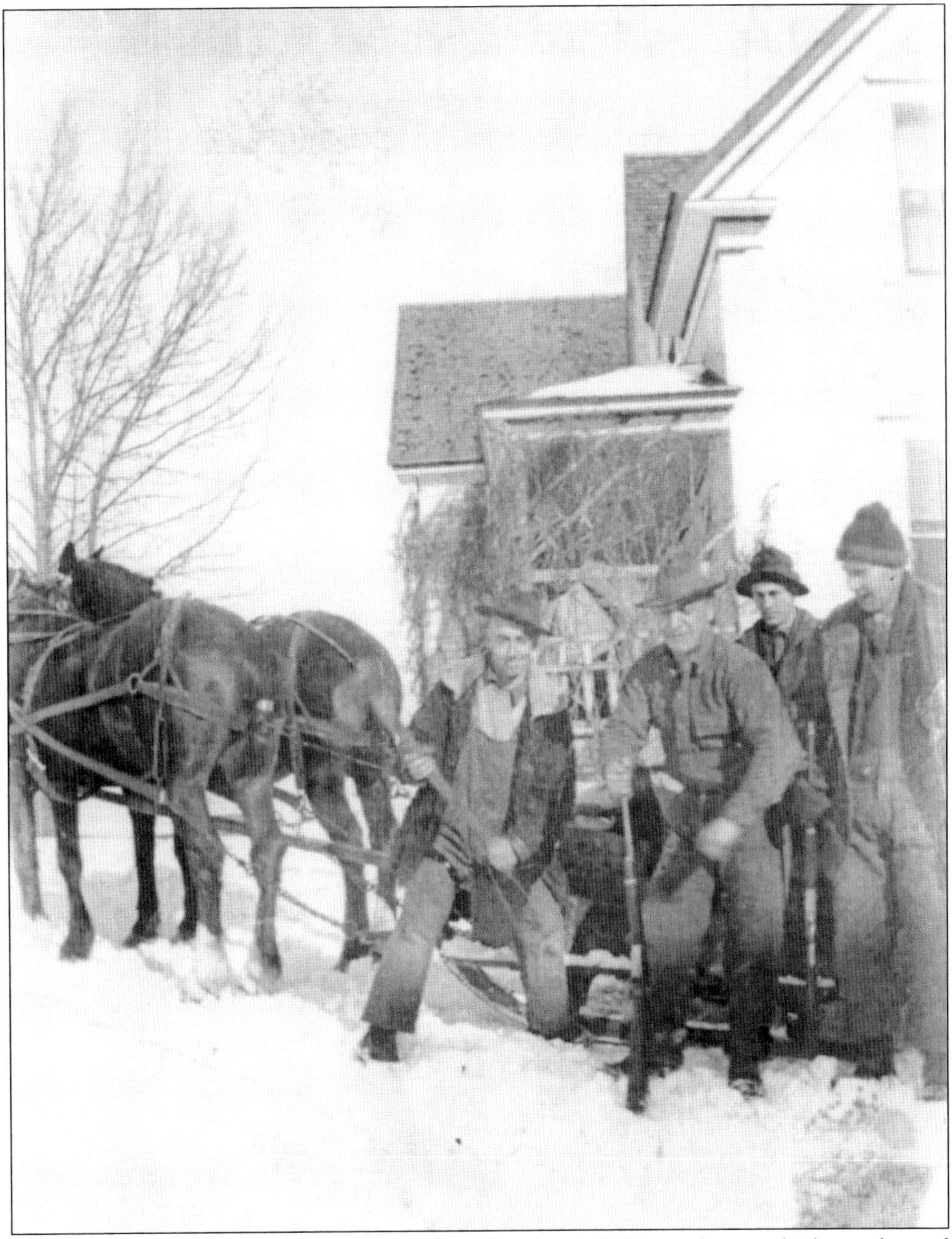

In the background is the old Gustaf and Ida (Sponberg) Dahlgren home which was located in Perham. It burned in 1929. From left to right are Evald Dahlgren, Ferd Dahlgren, Percy Dahlgren, and Otto Dahlgren. Gustaf and Ida were among the first Swedish settlers in Perham.

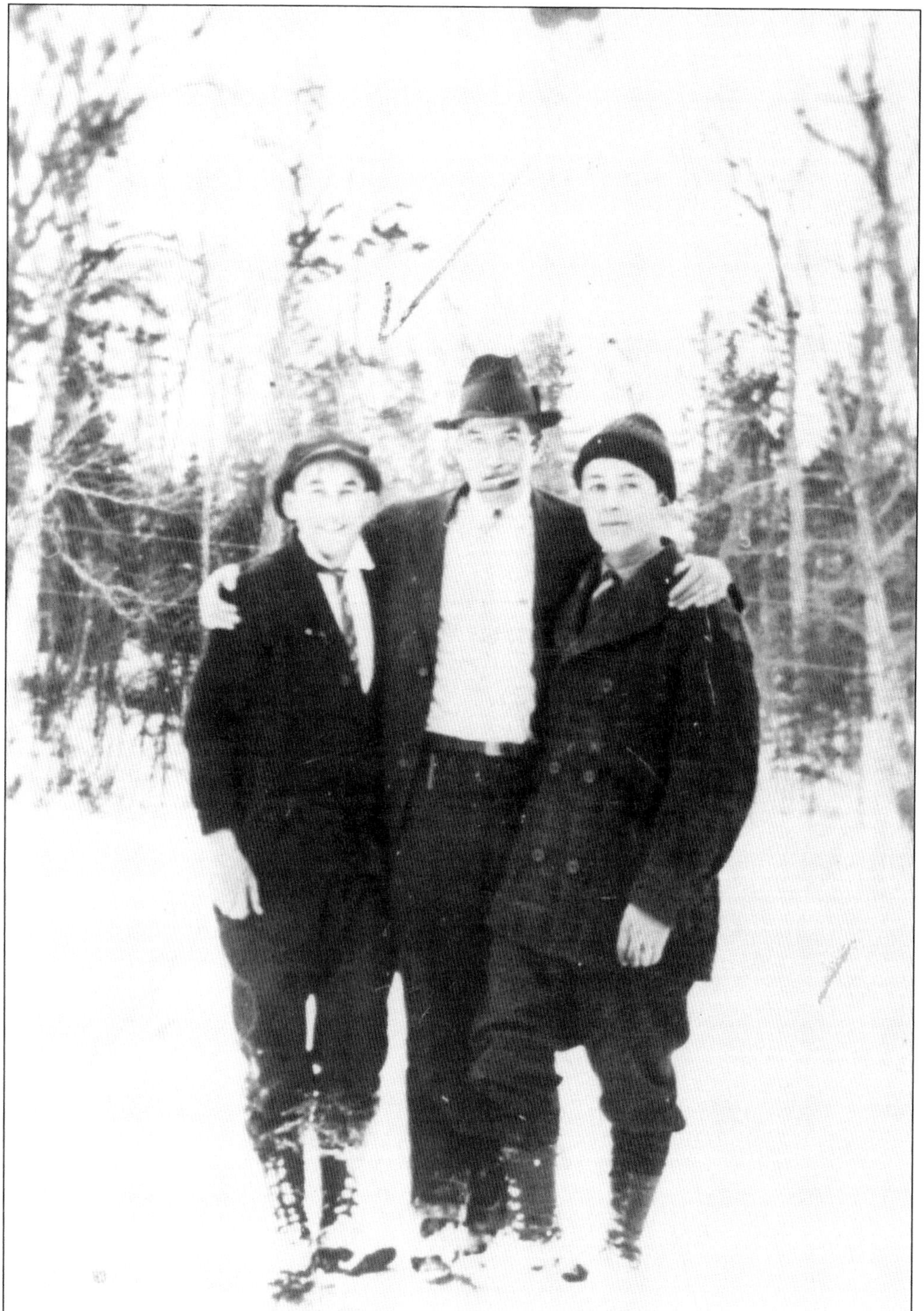

When men went into the vast northern Maine woods to cut trees, they were there for the winter. From left to right in this 1911 photograph are Ernest Smart, Fred Frazier, and Levi Smart, ready to join civilization again.

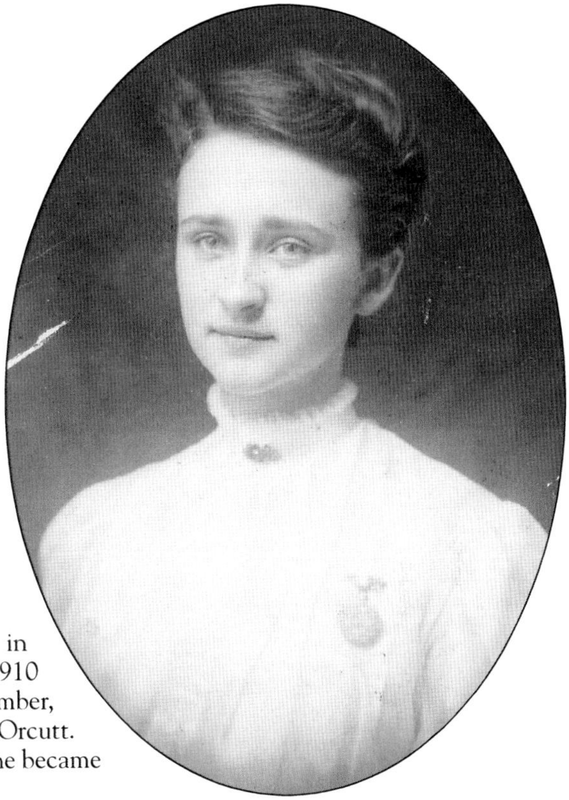

When telephones were first introduced in the Ashland area, sometime between 1910 and 1915, the voice that said, "Number, please" belonged to Georgia Brooks Orcutt. Sought out by the telephone company, she became the town's first telephone operator.

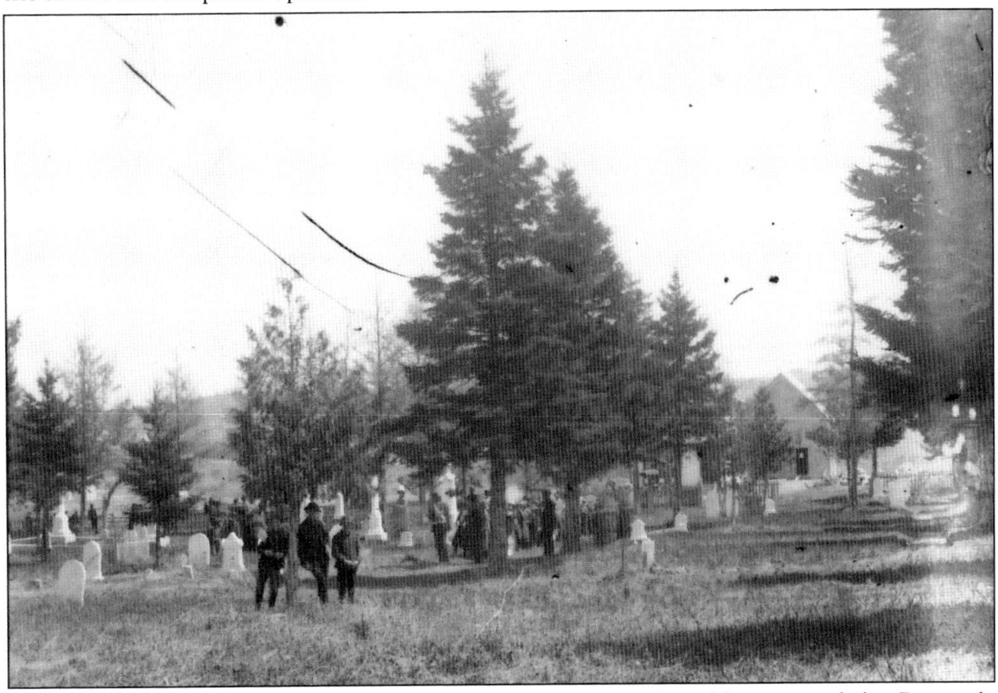

A rare 1909 photograph of a funeral in Washburn shows the oldest part of the Riverside Cemetery. Now closed, the burial ground has been expanded to Crouseville.

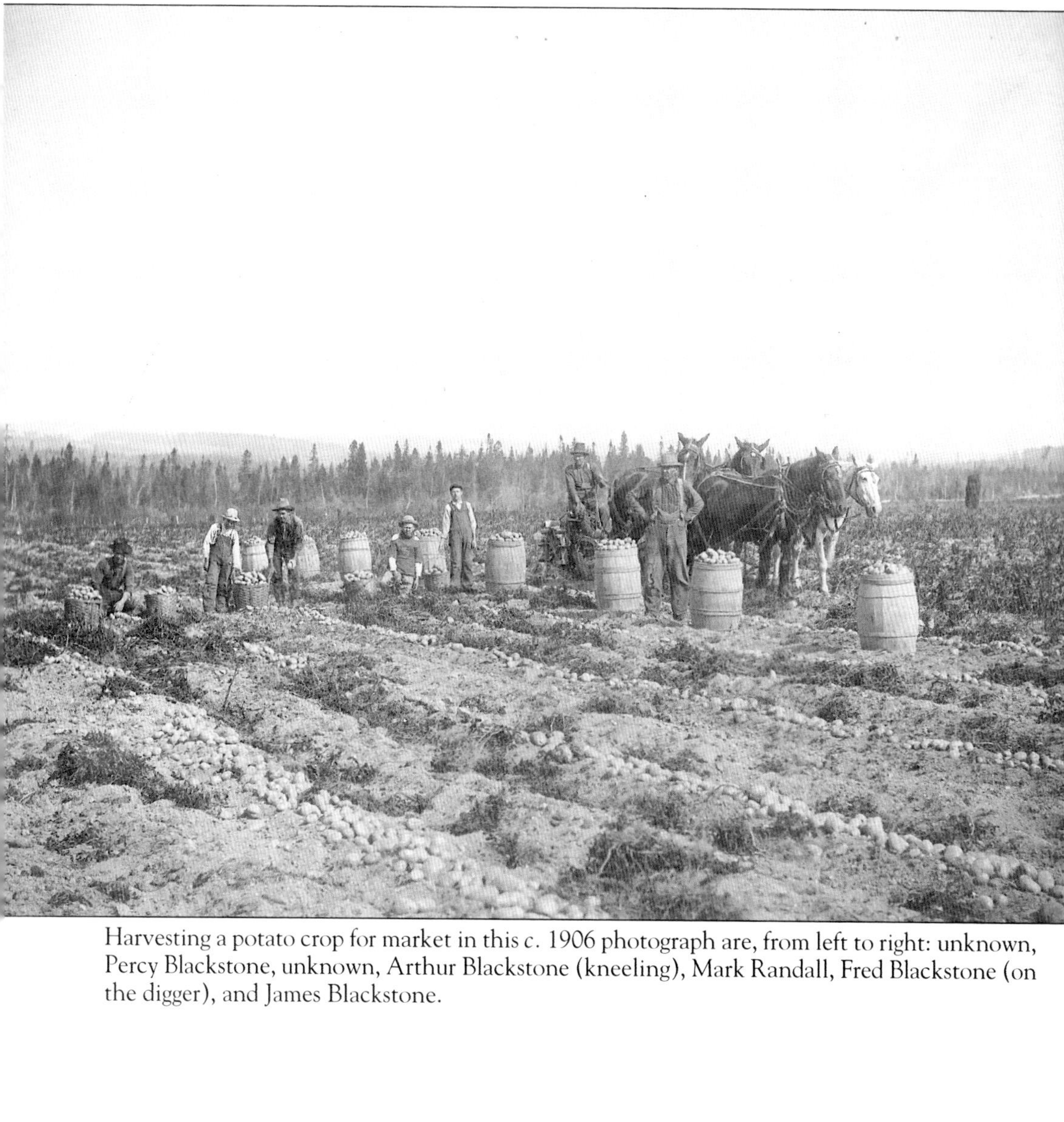

Harvesting a potato crop for market in this c. 1906 photograph are, from left to right: unknown, Percy Blackstone, unknown, Arthur Blackstone (kneeling), Mark Randall, Fred Blackstone (on the digger), and James Blackstone.

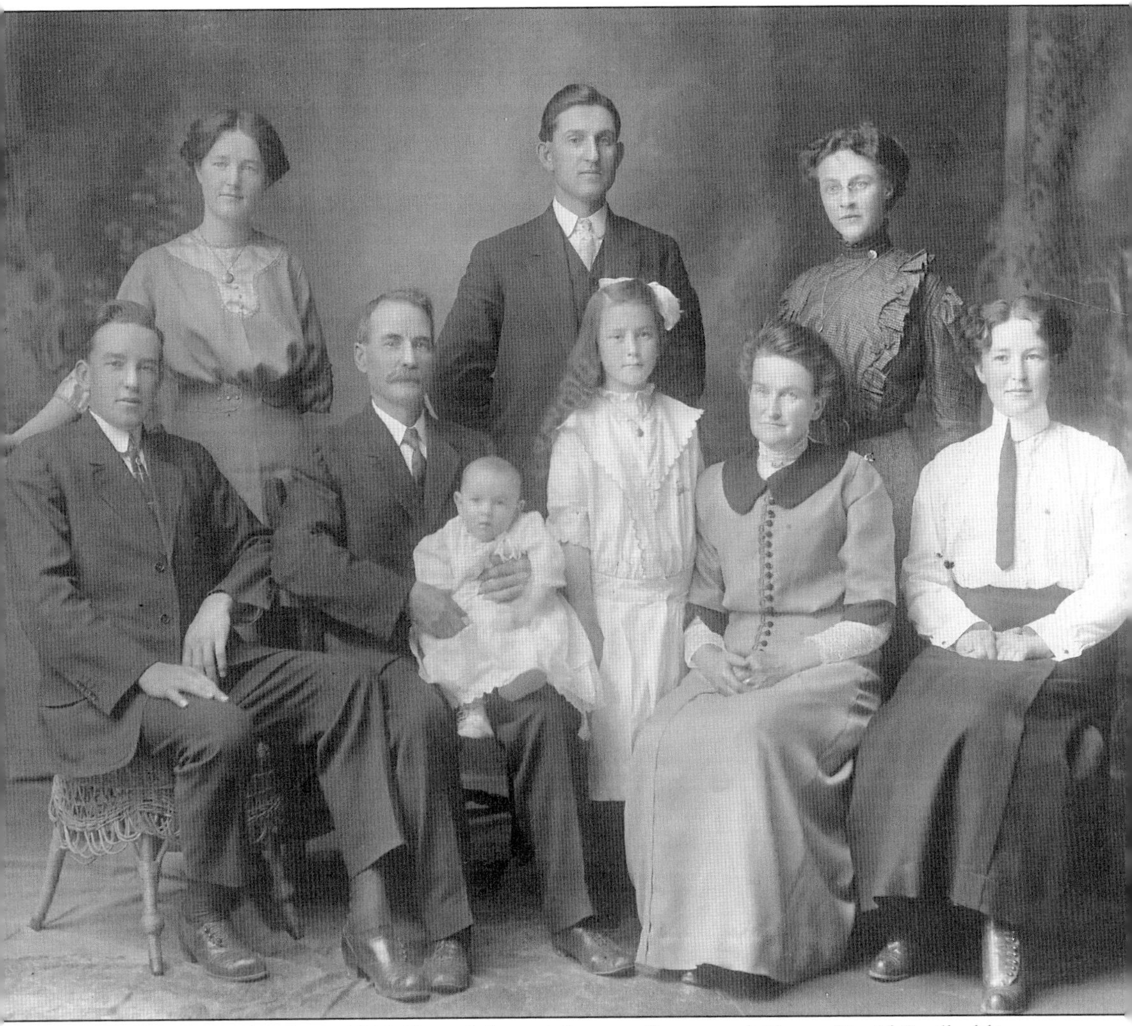

The David Duncan family in 1910. From left to right are: (front row) Harry, David Sr. (holding David Jr.), Mildred, Catherine, and Mary; (back row) Guy Durepo and Annie (Duncan) Durepo.

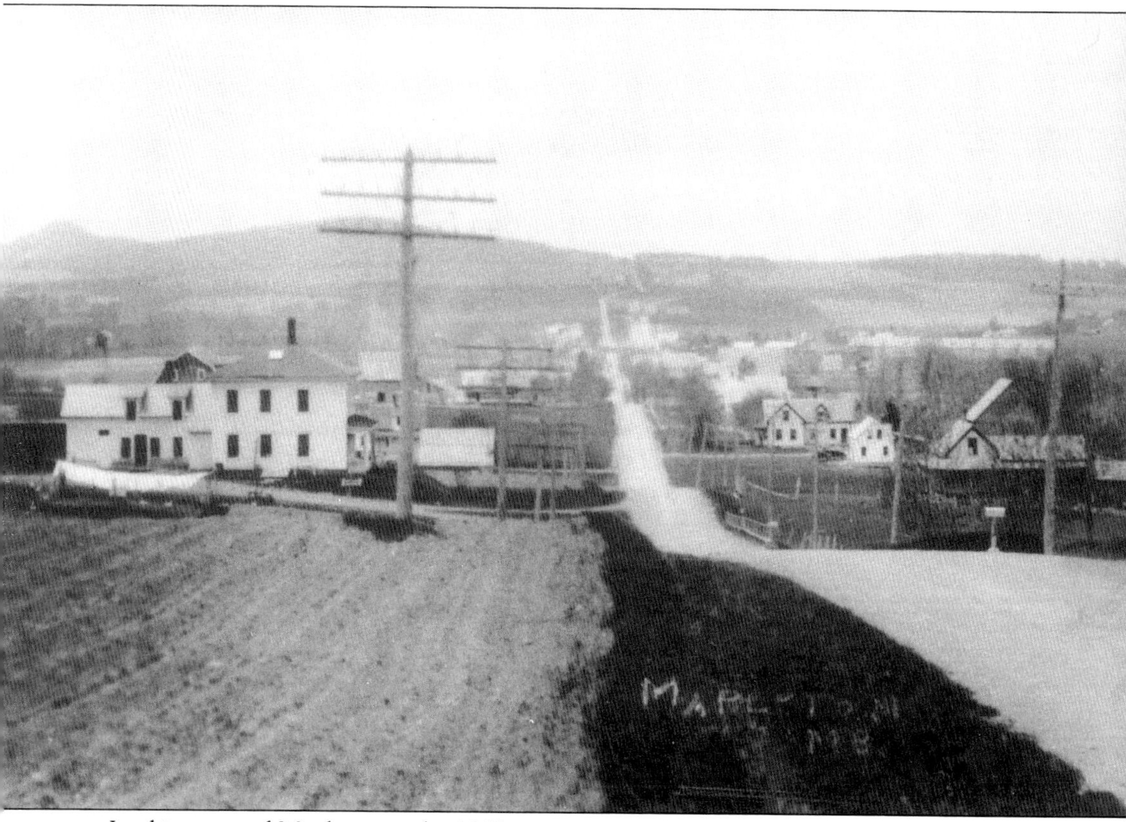

Looking toward Mapleton in the 1900s.

Two

The Hale and Hardy

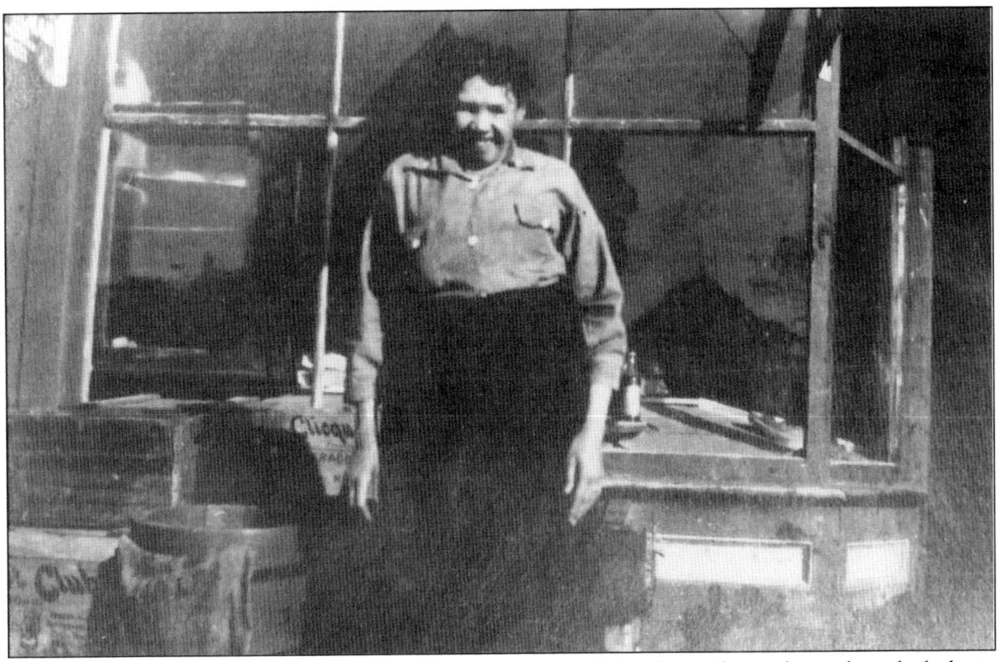

A 1920 photograph of Annie Marble. Known as one of the first, if not the only, saleslady in Aroostook County, Annie Marble rode the trains to sell her goods. Wherever it stopped, she would disembark with her two large black valises.

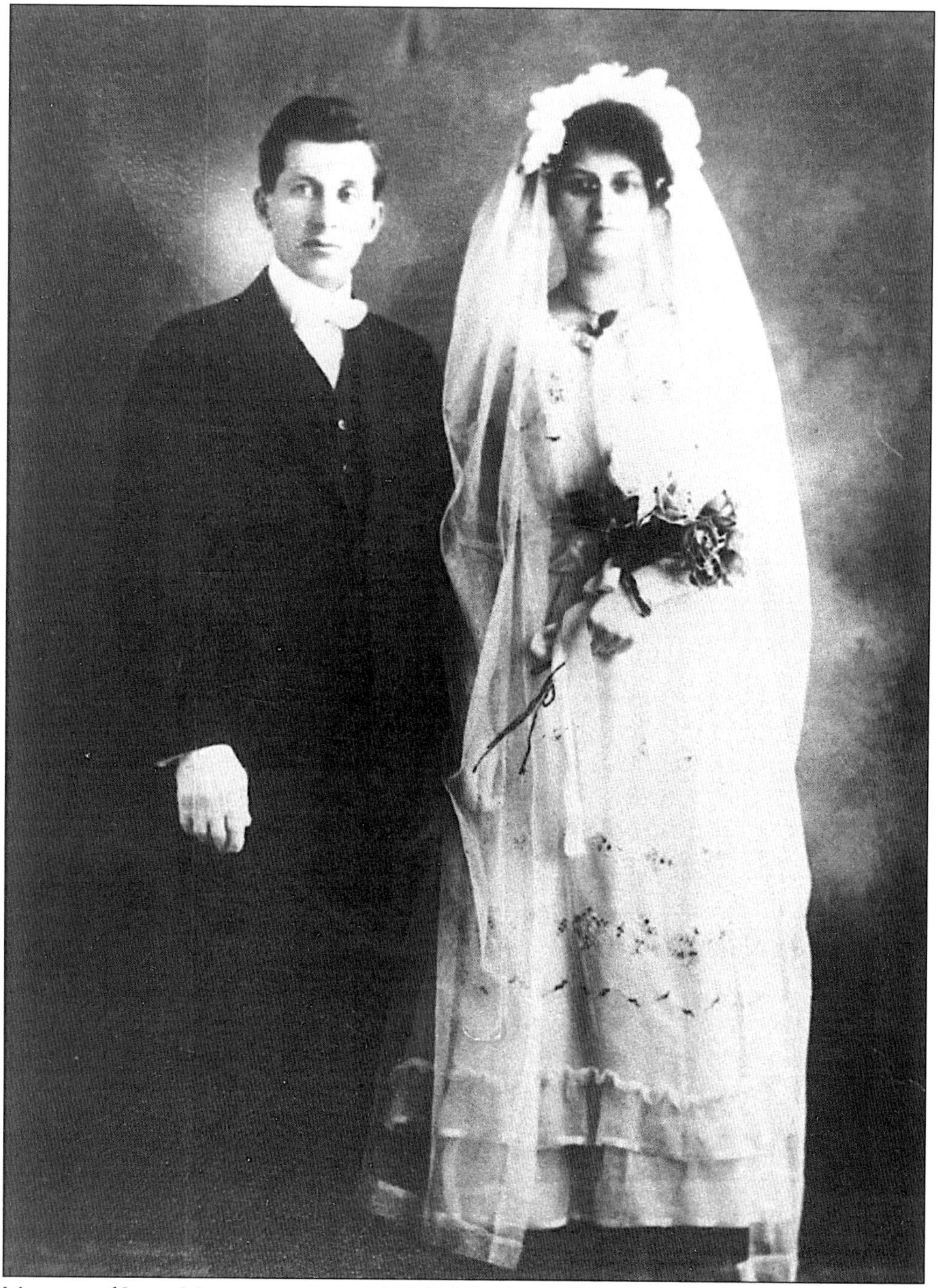

Mangus and Laura Monson were married at the New Sweden Lutheran Church on November 13, 1916. Mangus had immigrated from Sweden, worked in the Woodland sawmill, and eventually bought a farm on Thomas Road in Woodland. He lost a large portion of his foot while at the sawmill one day, but being of stalwart ancestry he finished out his shift! A doctor operated on it that night on the kitchen table. Laura, who was from Allagash, came to help keep house.

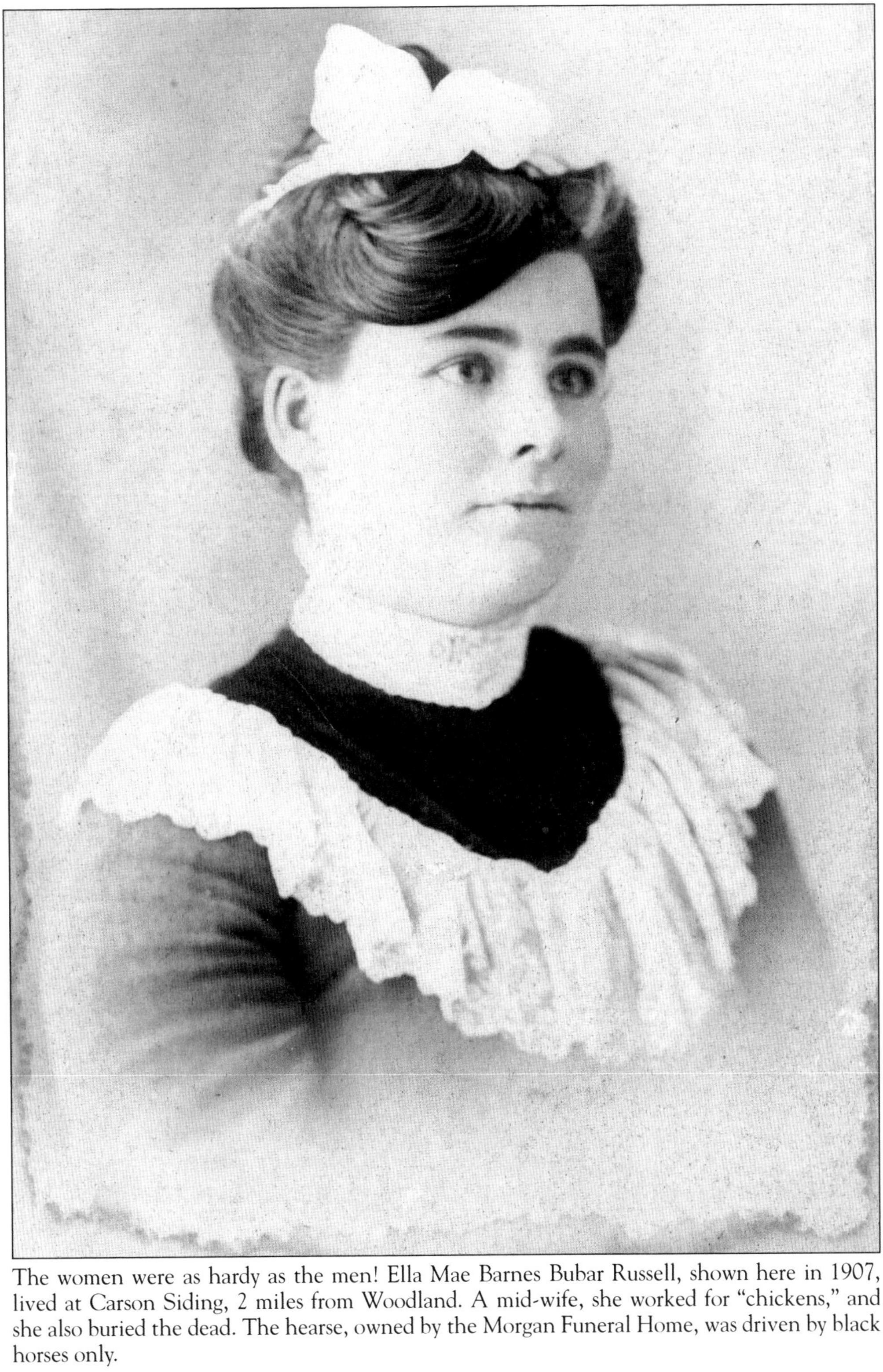

The women were as hardy as the men! Ella Mae Barnes Bubar Russell, shown here in 1907, lived at Carson Siding, 2 miles from Woodland. A mid-wife, she worked for "chickens," and she also buried the dead. The hearse, owned by the Morgan Funeral Home, was driven by black horses only.

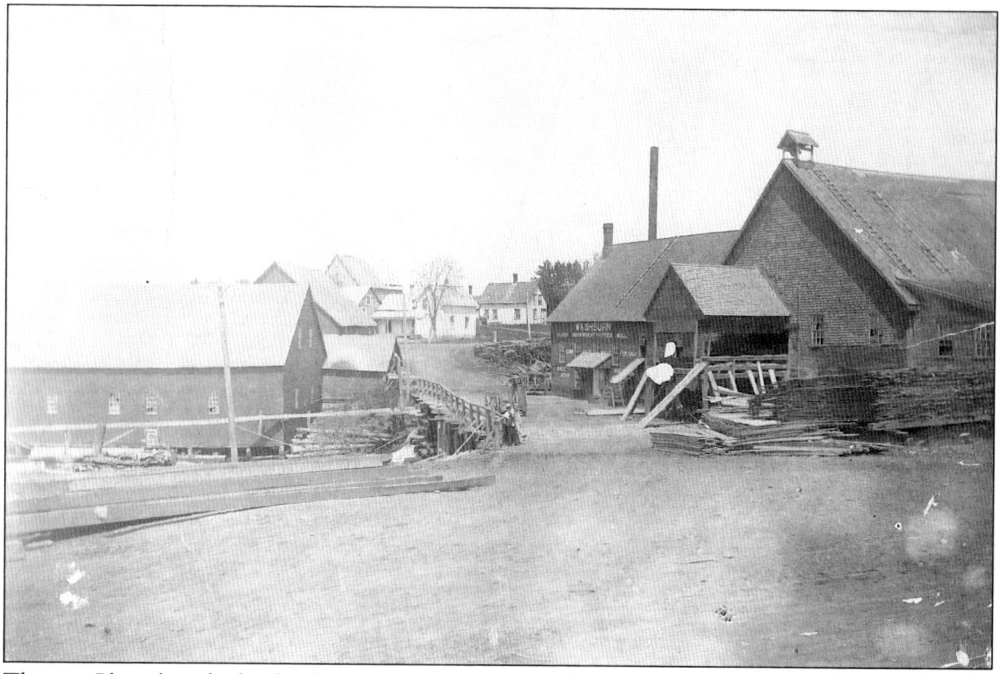

Thomas Phair bought his lumber, grist, and starch mill in 1879. By 1910 he was recognized as the "Starch King" of Aroostook. Later the building burned.

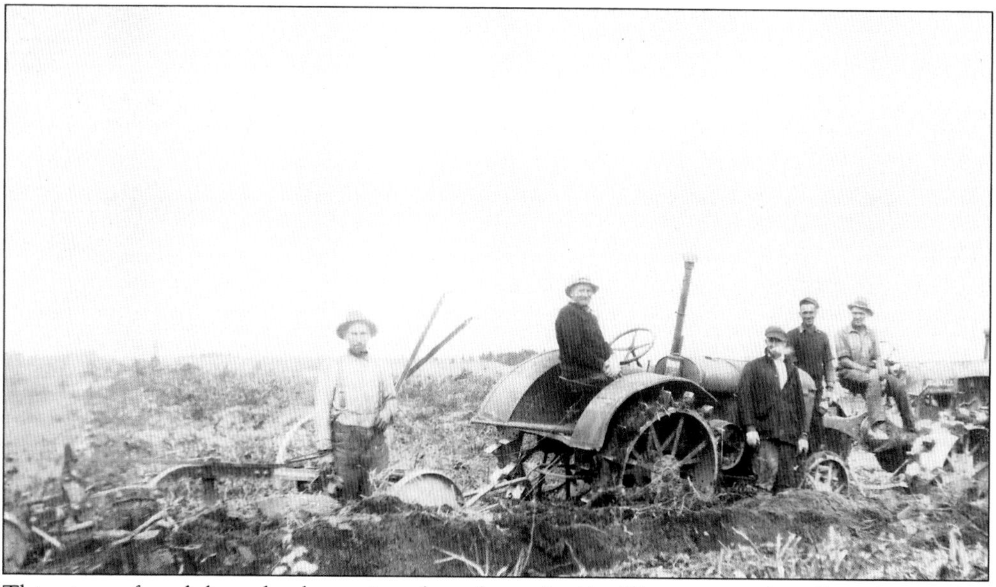

This piece of work brought the natives from far and wide. "I've got to take off my hat to that job. What if Harry and Charlie could see this outfit?" was written on the back of this picture. Plowing the fields in Ashland in 1920 was taking on a new look. Horses were beginning to be retired from their arduous pulling, and more planting could be accomplished. From left to right are Joe Martin, G.B. Smith, John Alieff, Burt Wilson, and Lyman Graham.

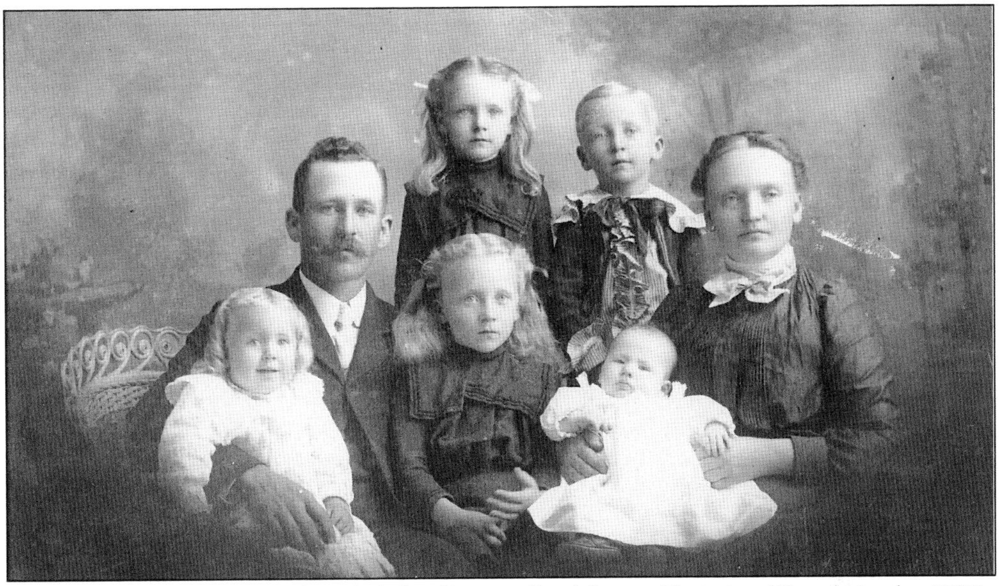

Wilmot Crouse's ancestors founded the Crouseville Advent Christian Church in the 1870s, and the town was named for them. Several descendants still live there. In 1900 this family photograph was taken in the home across from the current post office. From left to right are: (sitting) Avis, Wilmot (father), Bertha, baby Musa, and Avis (mother); (standing) Eunice and Willie.

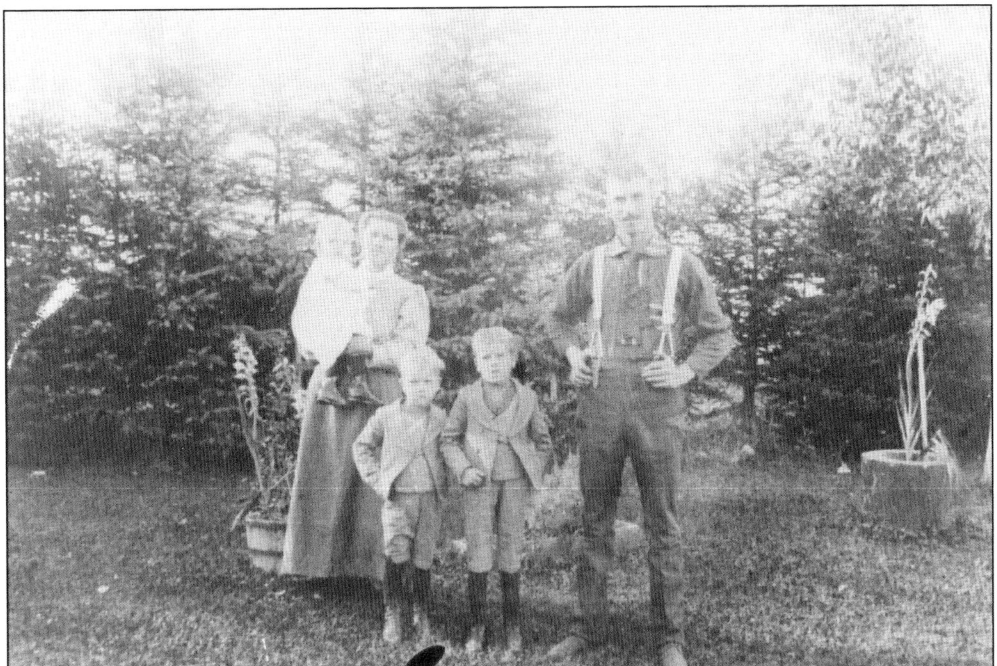

William Cochran's father was the first Cochran to come from Caribou in Woodland. William's first wife died when their son Walter was born. Her sister Isobel came to help with the new baby, stayed, and subsequently married William. In this 1907 photograph are, from left to right: (front) Gene and Walter; (back) Isobel (holding baby Dave) and William.

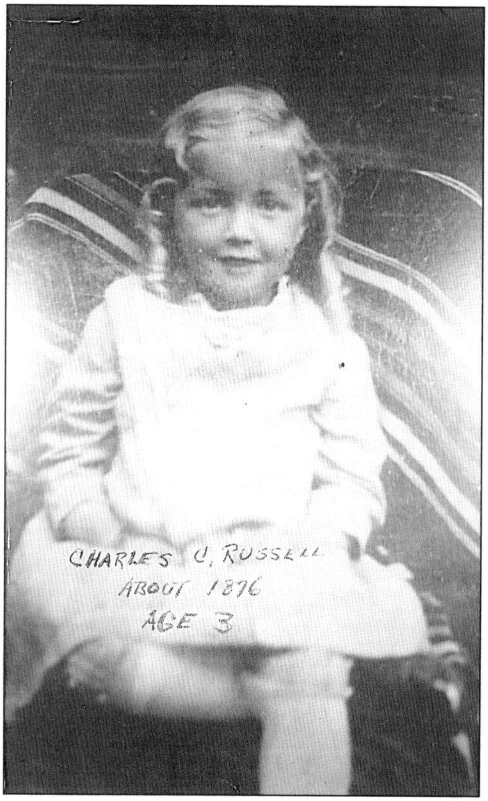

In this 1876 photograph, Charles C. Russell (at age three) could be the envy of any little girl, yesterday or today. His appearance would change radically in later years as he became a rugged potato farmer in Woodland. Immigrating with his family from Island Falls, he helped perpetrate the individual solidness of the community.

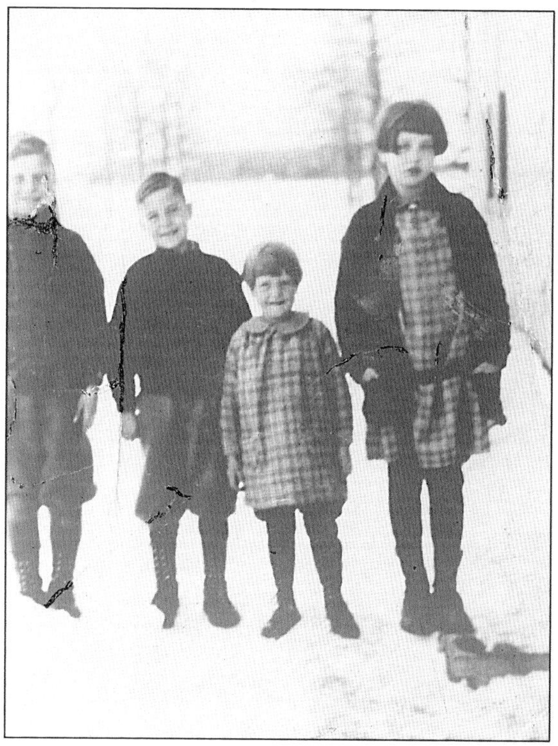

Mangus Monson arrived on a boat from Sweden when he was seventeen years old. From left to right are his four children, shown here braving the cold snow in 1938: Morris, Albert, Beulah, and Pauline.

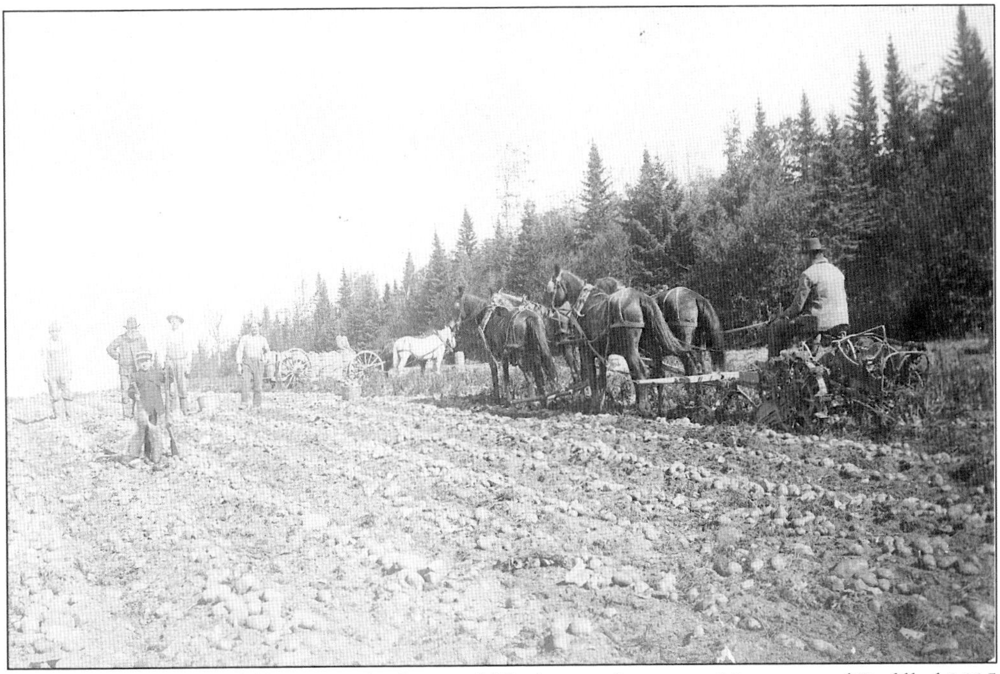

This "On the Line" field between the Roy and Blackstone farms was 10 acres, and "it filled 1415 barrels" of potato seed planted on May 10 and 11, and harvested September 20 and 21, 1902. From left to right are Bert Blackstone, Bowdoin Blackstone, Hartson Blackstone (the boy with the foxes and gun), Roy Peary, Linnius King, and Fayette Blackstone (on the digger).

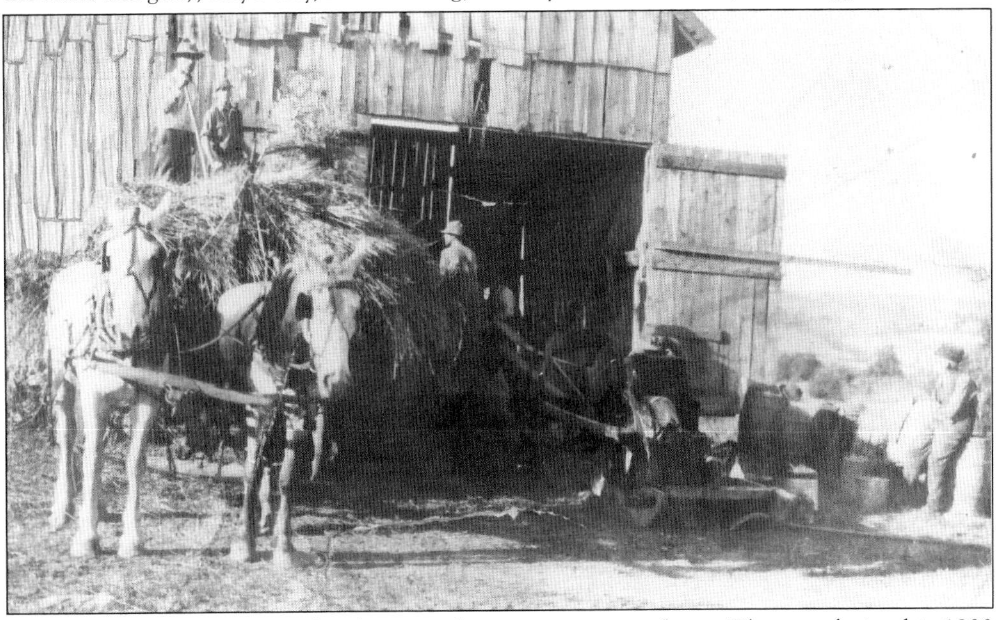

An old, #2 Keystone grain-thrashing machine is put to good use. The people in this 1920 photograph are: (standing on top of the load) Chester Turner and grandfather George (Walter) Alley; (on the thrasher) Braighton Alley; (barely visible to the far right) Oscar Alley and his grandson, George Alley. Chester Turner was a wrestler at the Northern Maine Fair for many years.

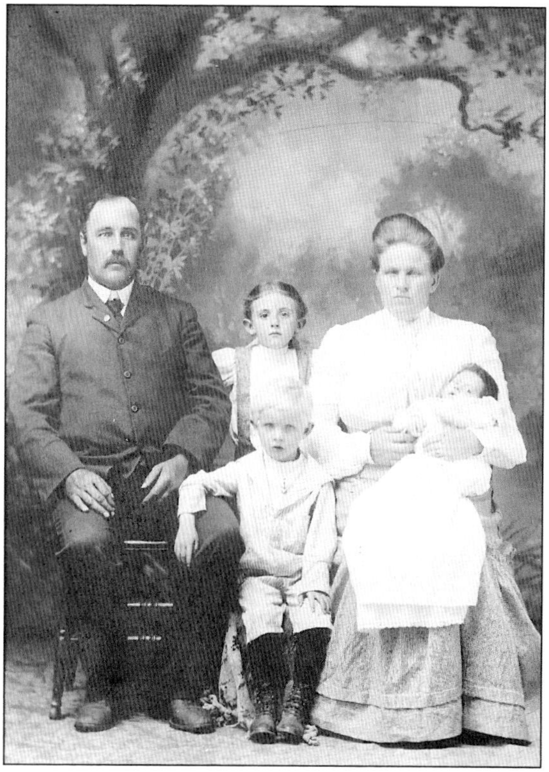

Calvin Ellis and his wife Carrie (Tilley) with their children, Herbert S., Beatrice, and baby June.

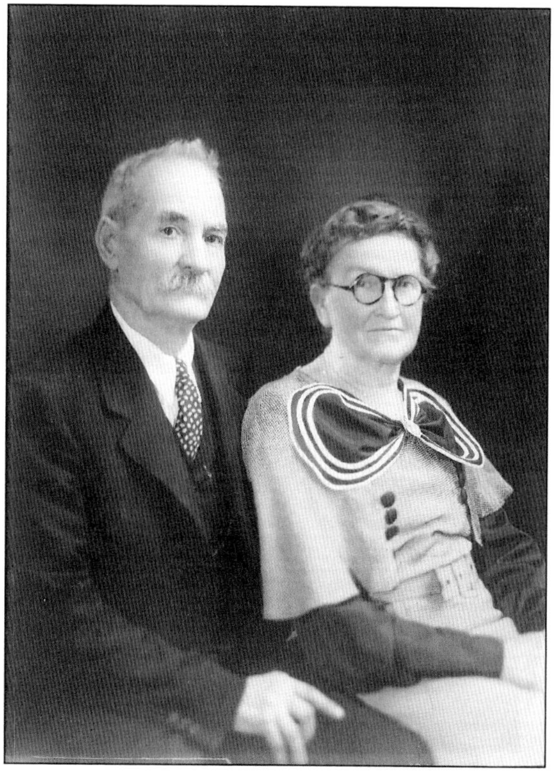

David Duncan and his wife both immigrated from Scotland. Catherine arrived in 1873 at the age of five. David managed the starch factory owned by Thomas Phair and served as Washburn's post master. His sister, Bessie Duncan, helped him in the post office for over thirteen years.

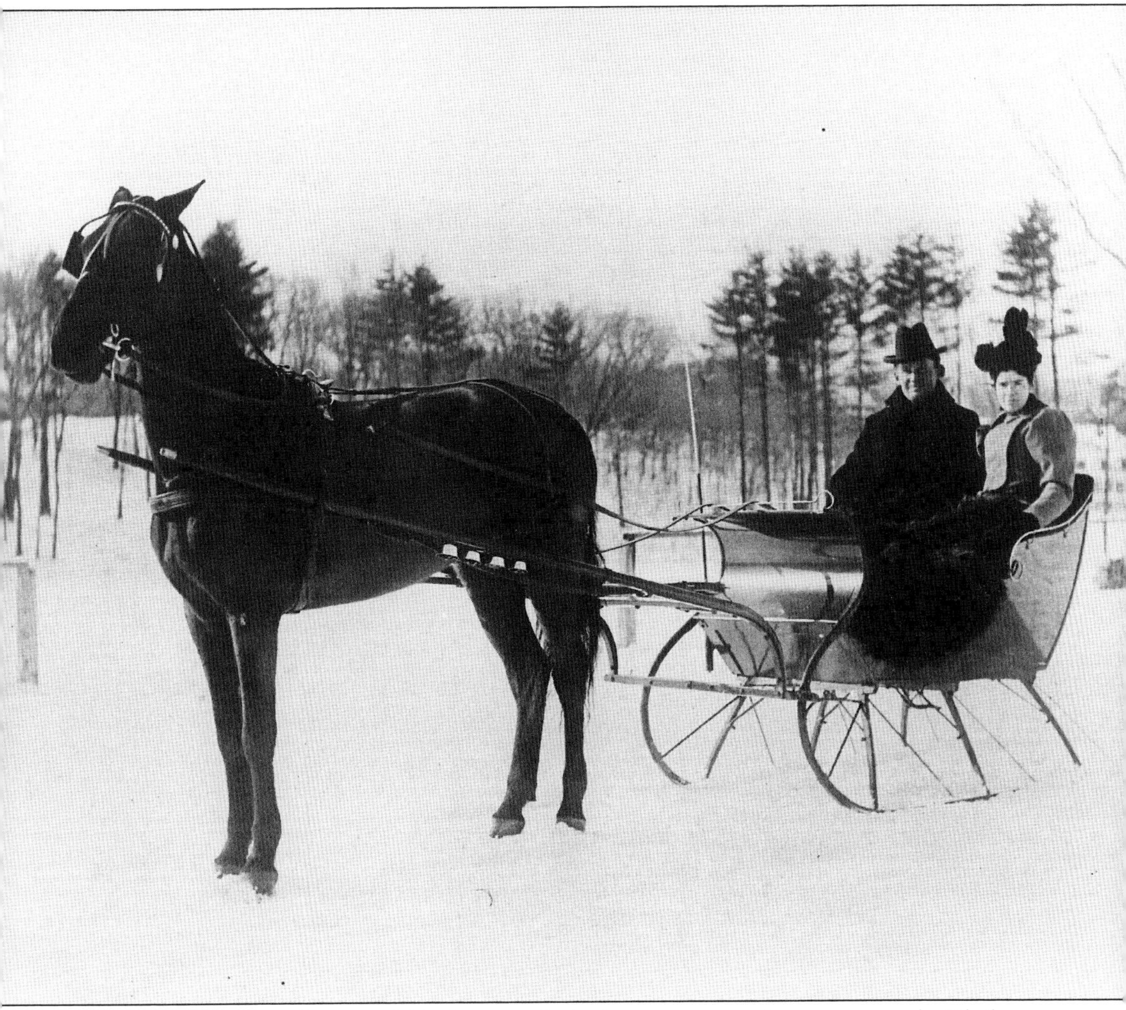

"Jingle Bells, Jingle Bells." In this 1910 photograph the horse can proudly prance to as he "dashes through the snow" in Washburn. Wisely, the occupants in the sleigh take along a buffalo robe.

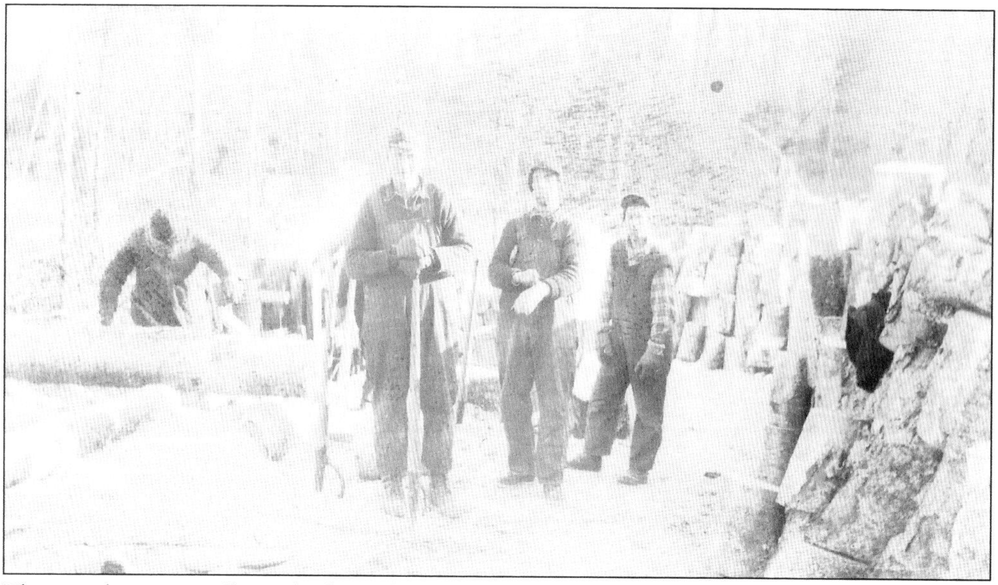

This woods crew usually worked together as a team. From left to right are Henry Drost (who was blind), Warren Drost, unknown, and Gerald Seward.

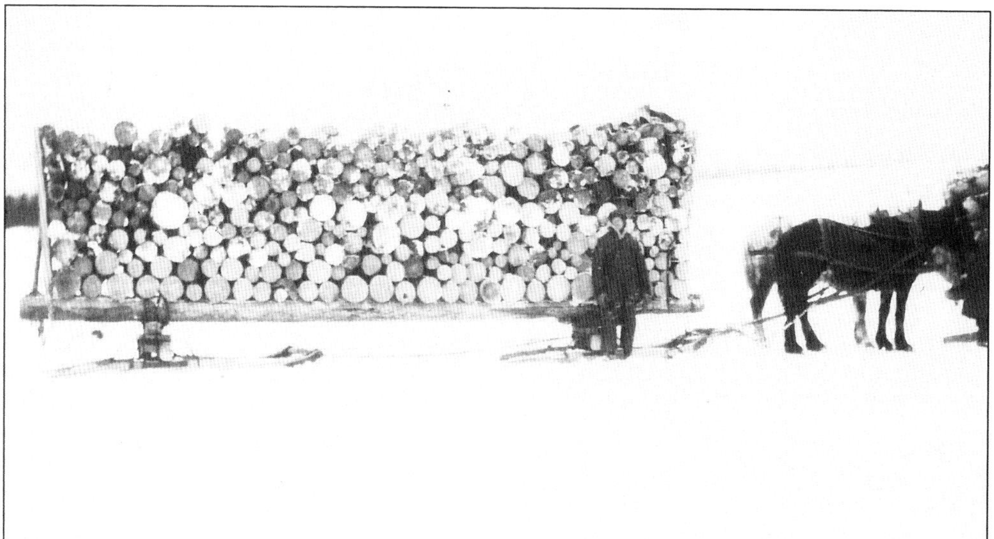

Cutting and hauling logs is a traditional heritage of the northern Maine woods. Many farmers found this a source of income during the winters. Hauled to waterways, the pulp was floated down in the spring. In 1927 Braighton Alley had the biggest load from Gardiner Creek to go down the Aroostook River that year. Bess and Colonel provided the "motor power."

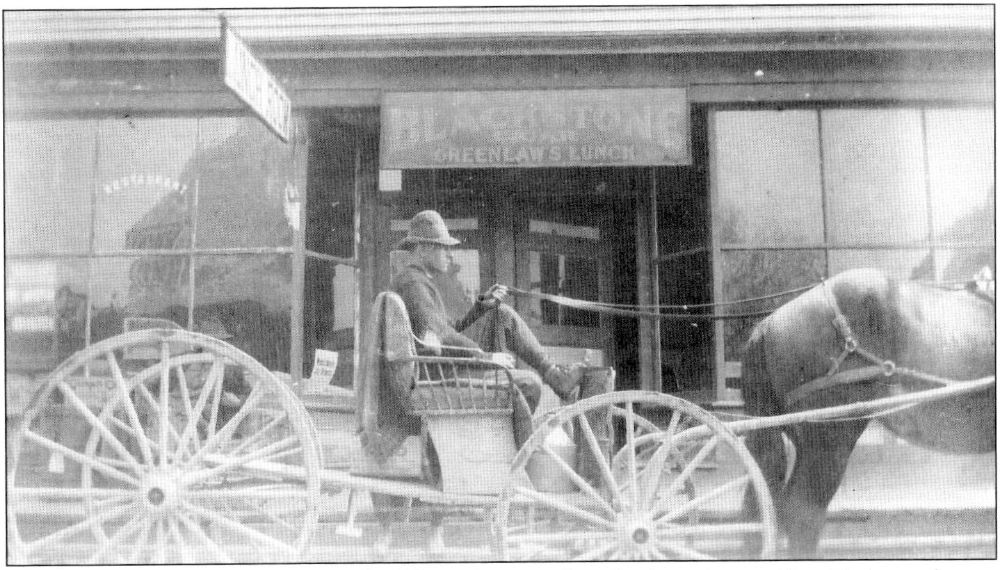

Life in the early 1900s consisted of long hours of work, but this unidentified gentleman with his feet up is relaxing a bit or waiting for a friend to come from lunch at the restaurant in Masardis.

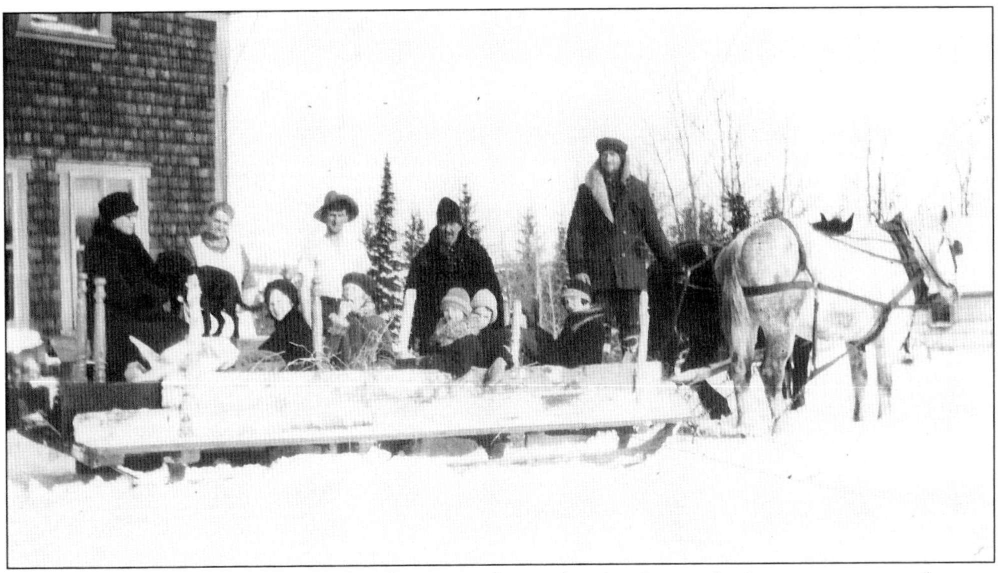

In 1927 or 1928, going to a family Christmas dinner by sleigh was the best way to travel, even if it took a half hour to go 2 miles. The horses, Bess and Colonel, wait patiently. From left to right are: (front row) Muriel Alley Farley, Vernon Alley, Garold Alley, Flora Alley Monson, and Edna Alley Sharpe; (back row) Carrie Alley, Barney (the dog), Mrs. Butler, Chester Turner, George Alley, and Braighton Alley.

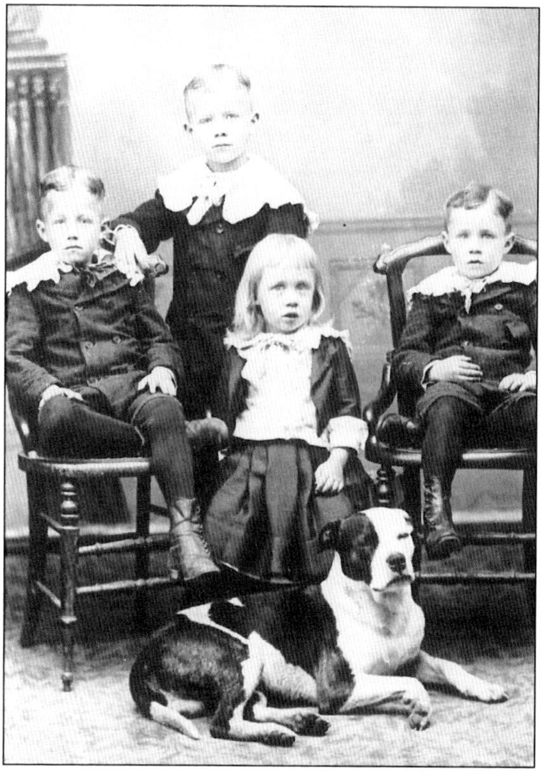

Starched white collars for the boys as well as girls made the task of laundering and ironing a much larger project than today. Posing for a family portrait, from left to right, are the three Sylvester boys: Woodford, Auburt, and Glen. Vera is surrounded by them, and Pat, the dog, "guards" them all.

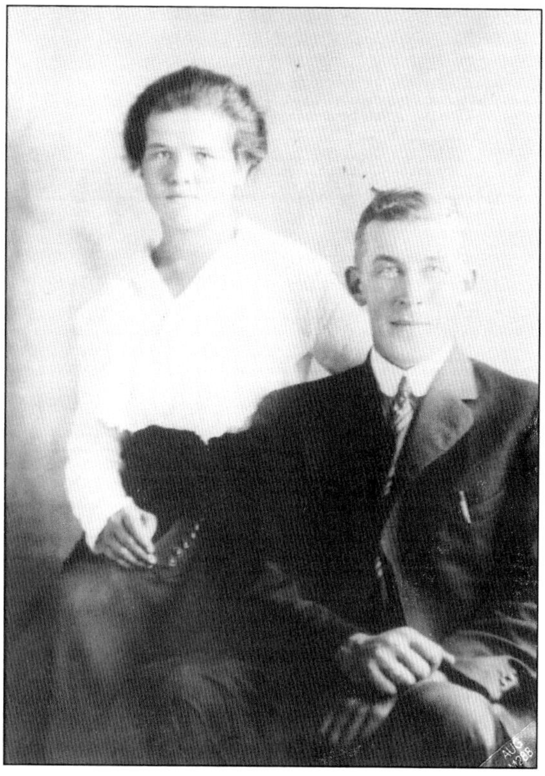

Clarence and Olive (Henry) Espling were married in New Sweden and moved to Woodland. They had eleven children.

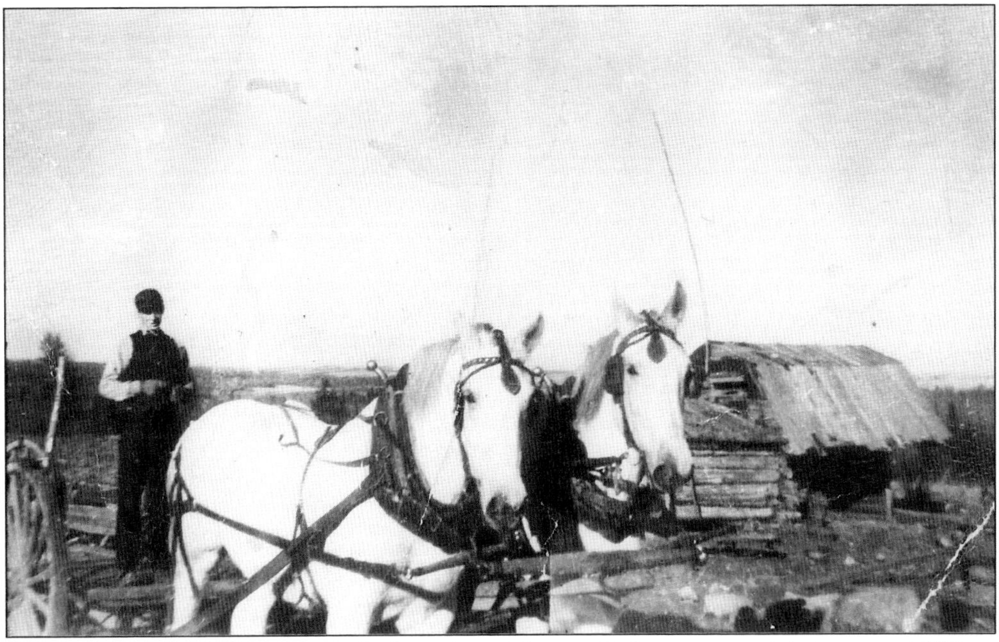

Patiently waiting, Ted and Queen look ready and fit to pull the wagon and their owner, William Baker, away from the barn in 1935.

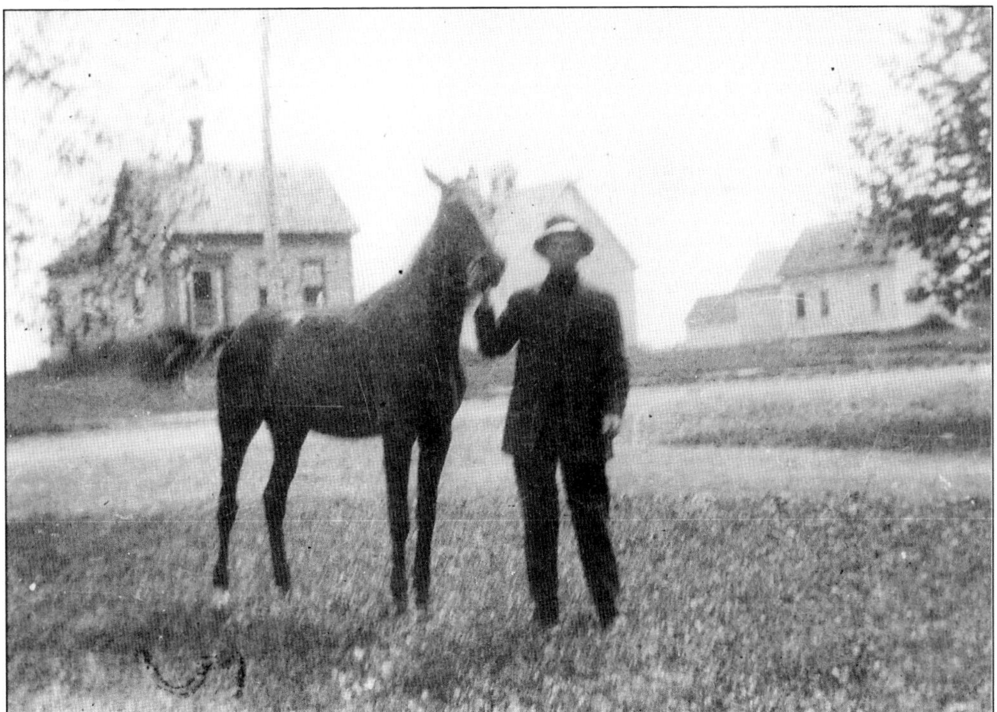

Houses were constructed to endure the severe winter weather. The house on the right was built in 1843 and in 1910 was moved on logs halfway up the street. The house on the left is still on its original foundation. Both structures are still being used. This photograph of Harold Umphrey and his horse was taken in 1906 or 1907.

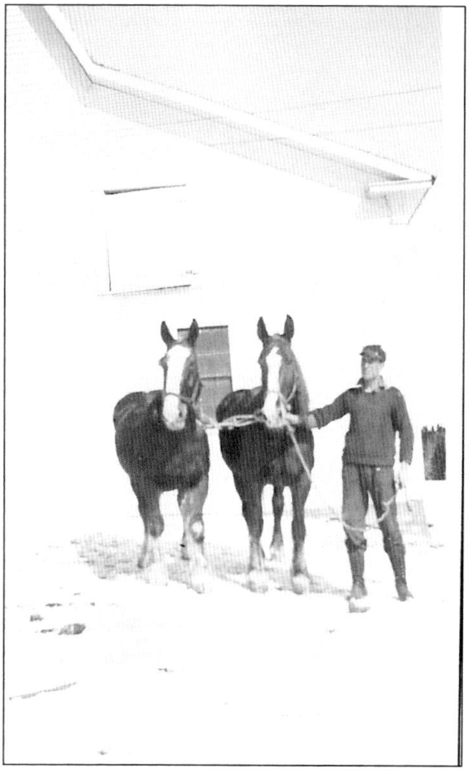

Hired hands were considered part of the family for most farmers and given the same respect. This gentleman, shown here in 1930 with horses Bob and Queen, was always called Mr. Hestings and never referred to by his first name.

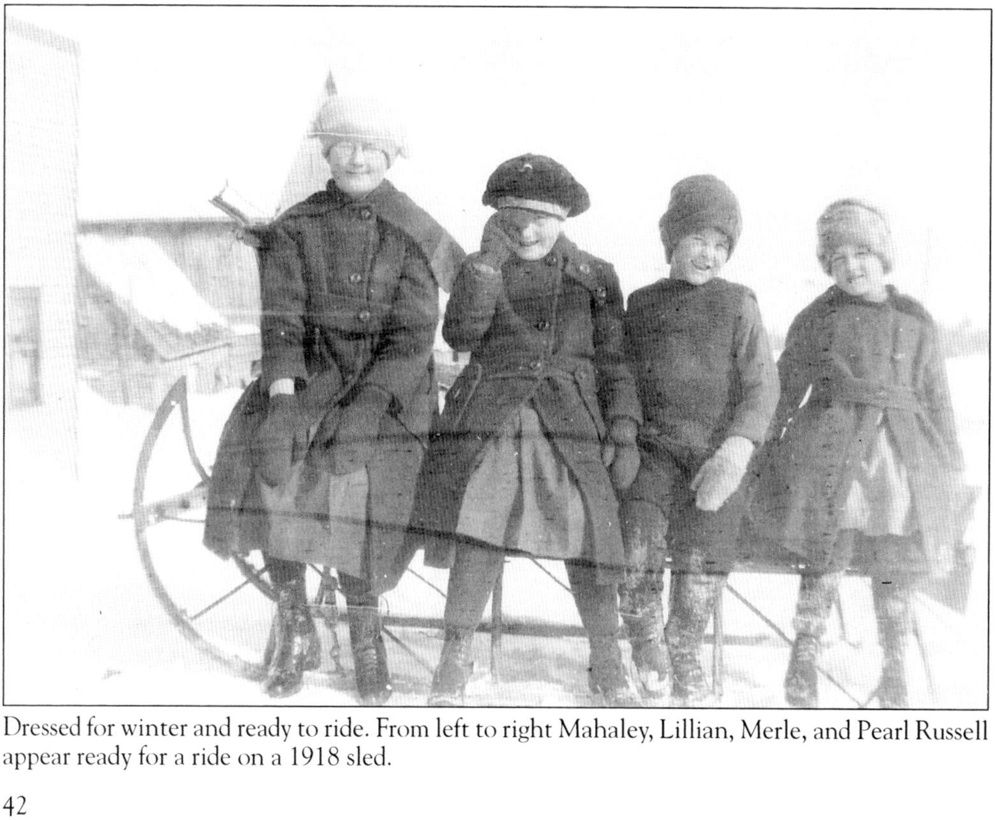

Dressed for winter and ready to ride. From left to right Mahaley, Lillian, Merle, and Pearl Russell appear ready for a ride on a 1918 sled.

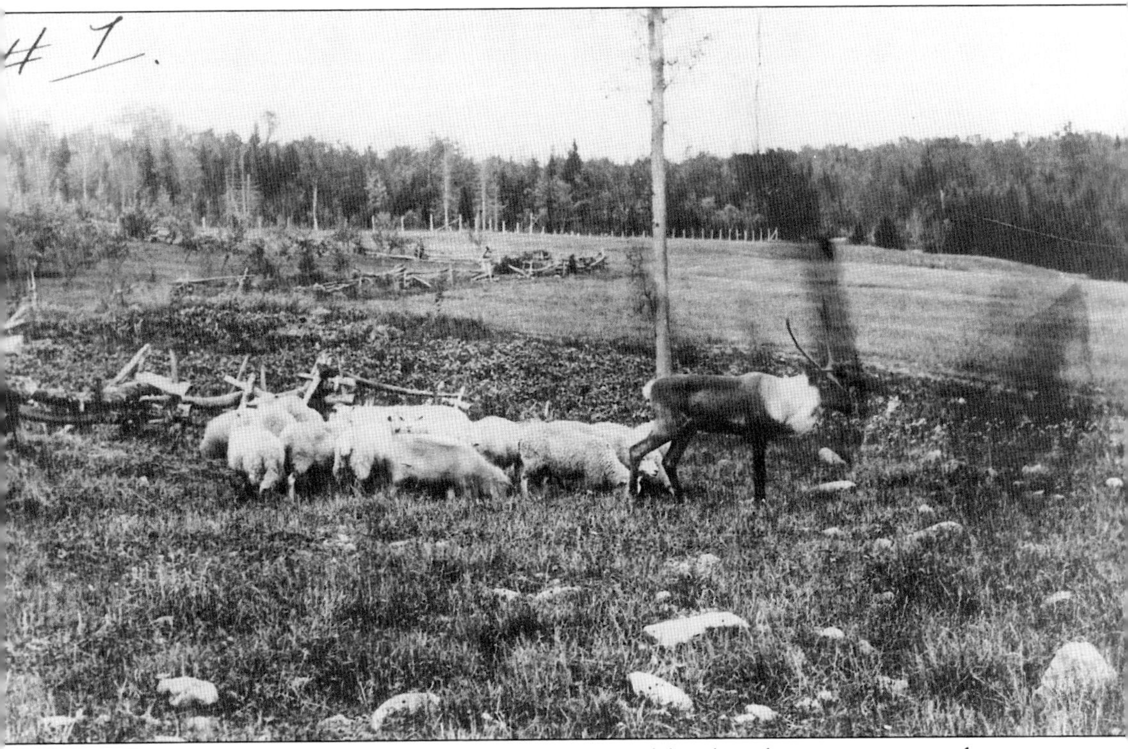

A 1915 photograph of a pasture in Ashland. Undaunted by their large visitor meandering through their pasture, this herd of sheep appear to say "share and share alike."

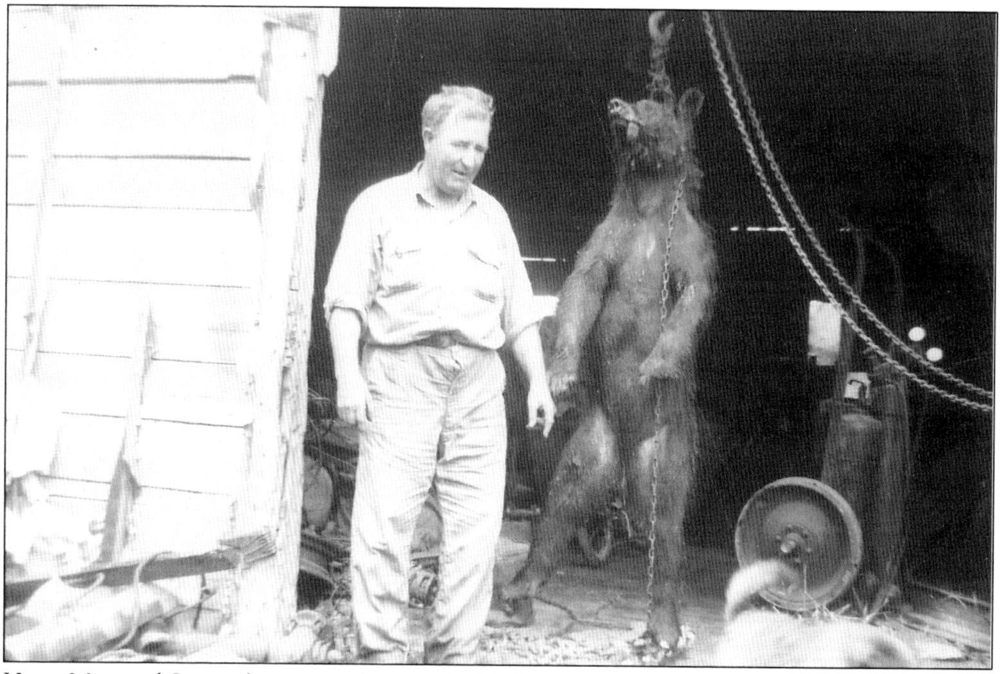

Harry Maynard Sr. was known in the area for his bear-trapping expertise.

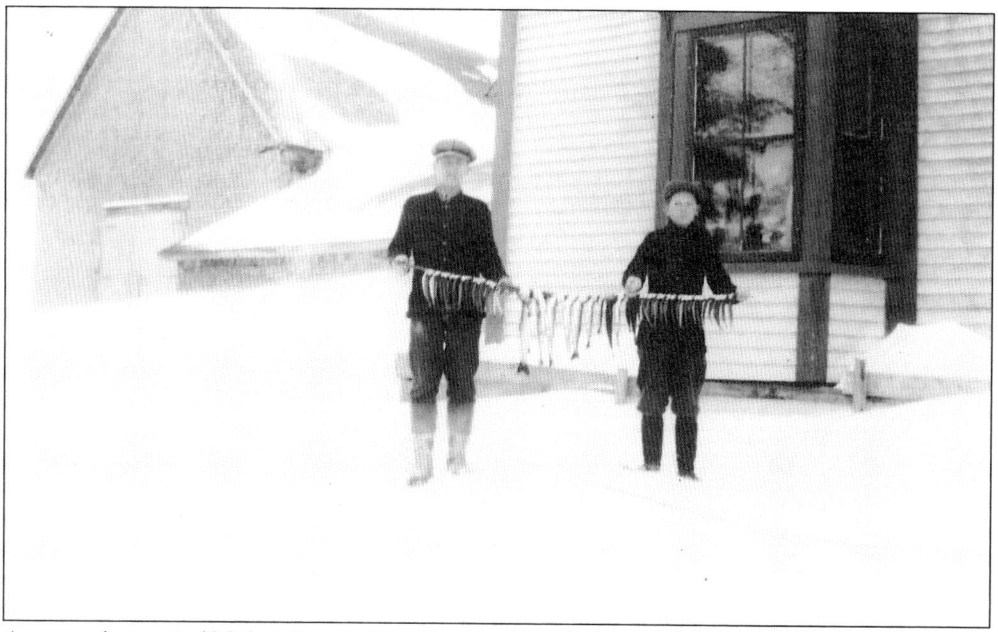

Apparently unmindful that there is snow on the ground, Abram (left) and Lloyd Crouse proudly display their catch after a day of ice fishing. They are in front of the Abraham Crouse farm on Cross Road in Crouseville, c. 1915.

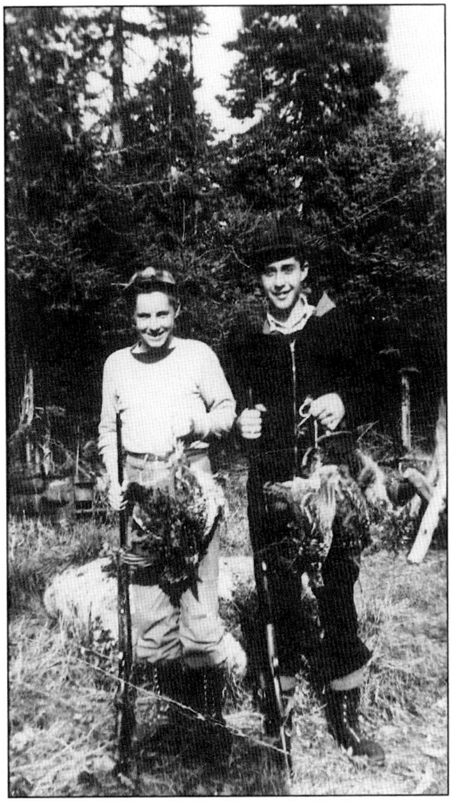

Jim Skinner and Dick Blanchard took advantage of the good hunting in and around Ashland. In the fall of 1943 they bagged their share of partridge. Many years later Jim was killed in Vietnam.

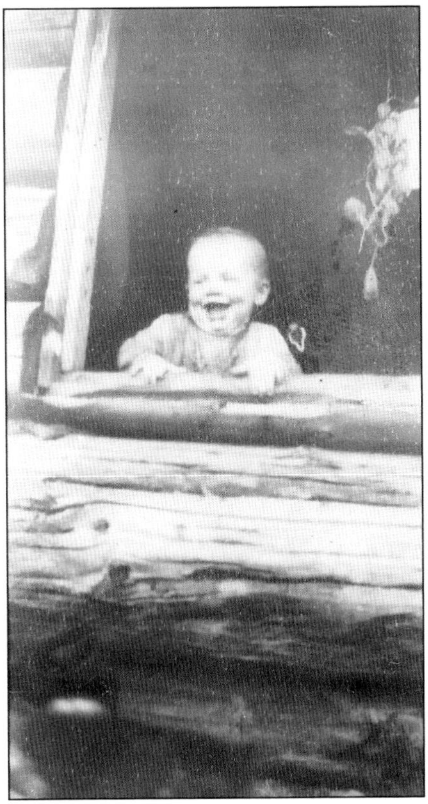

Caught looking out the "picture window," Patricia Baker appears extremely happy about her surroundings.

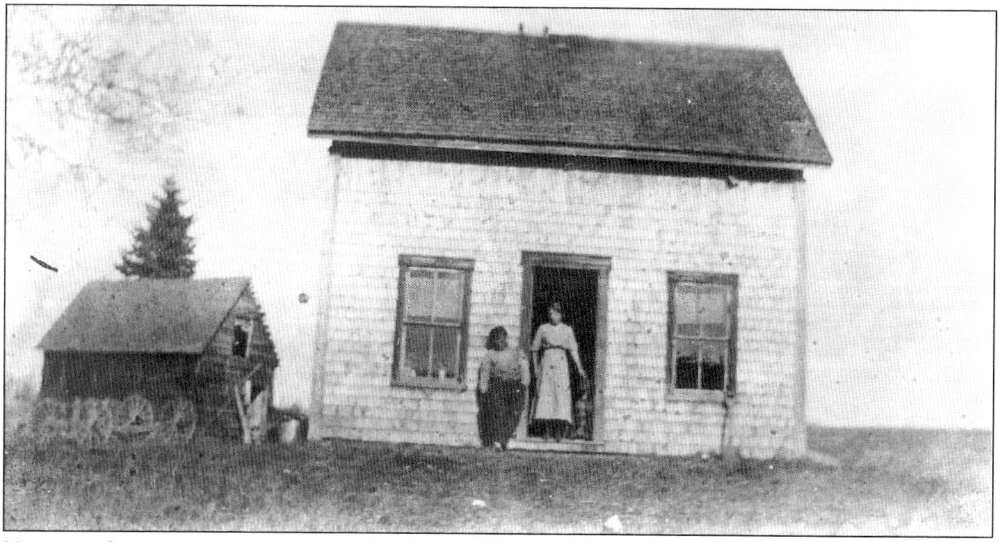

Harry and Maggie Maynard Sr. begin their married life in 1916 in their Gardiner Creek Road home.

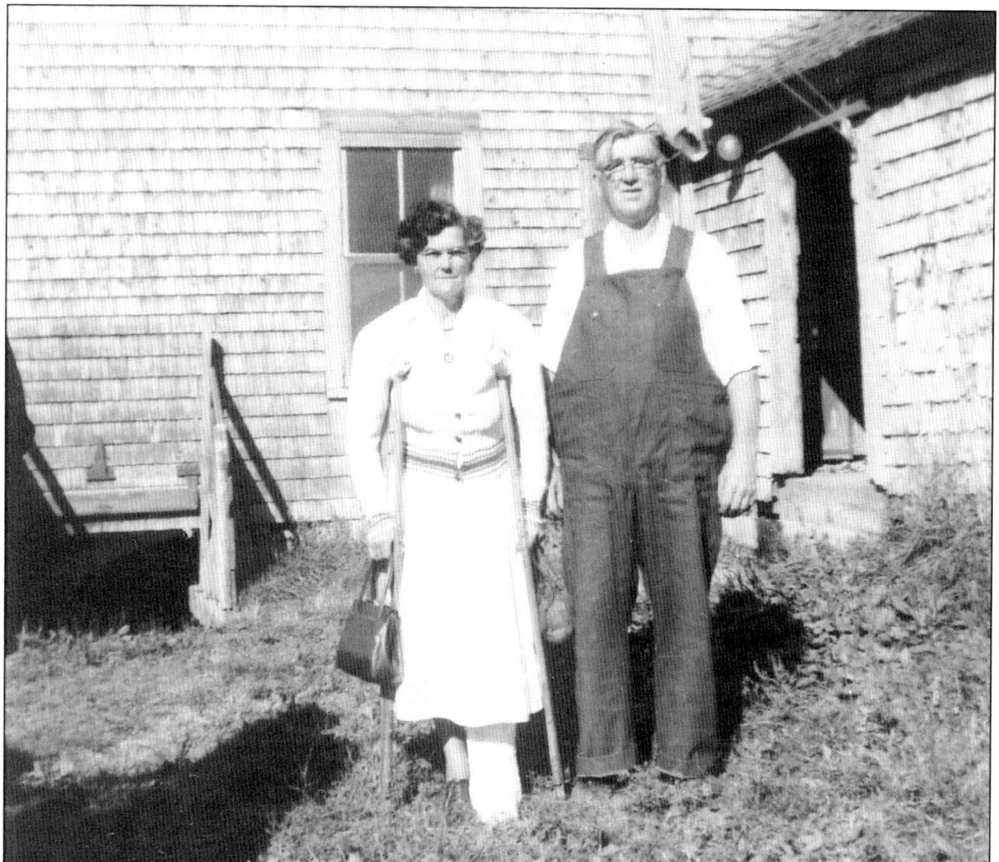

Families involved in pulp-driving and farming are stalwart people. Crystal Alley did not let a broken leg deter her, as Braighton could attest to.

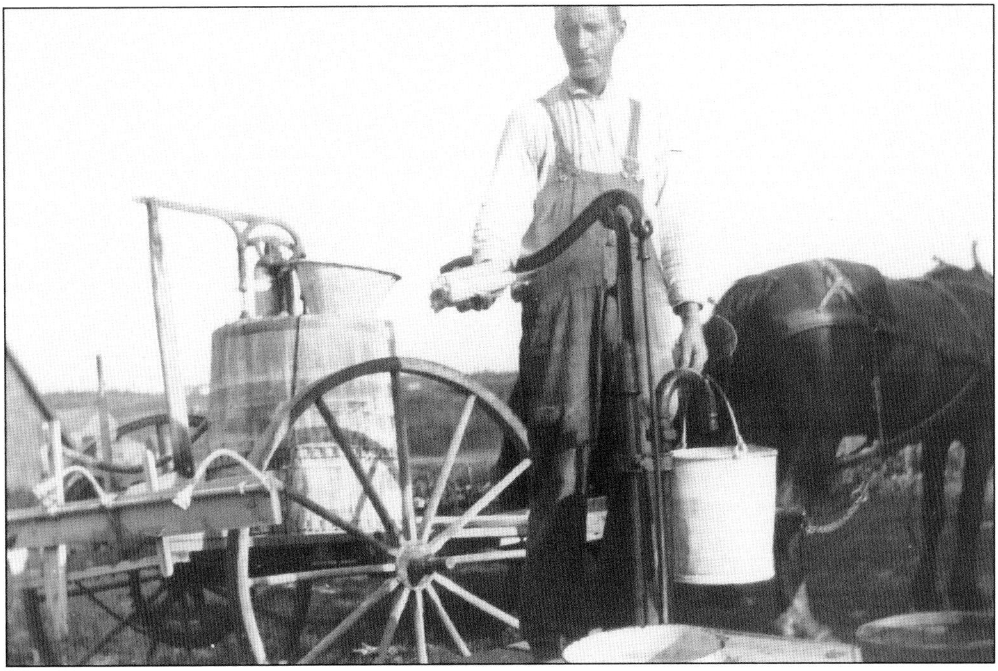

Charles Collamore Russell readies his 1910 sprayer.

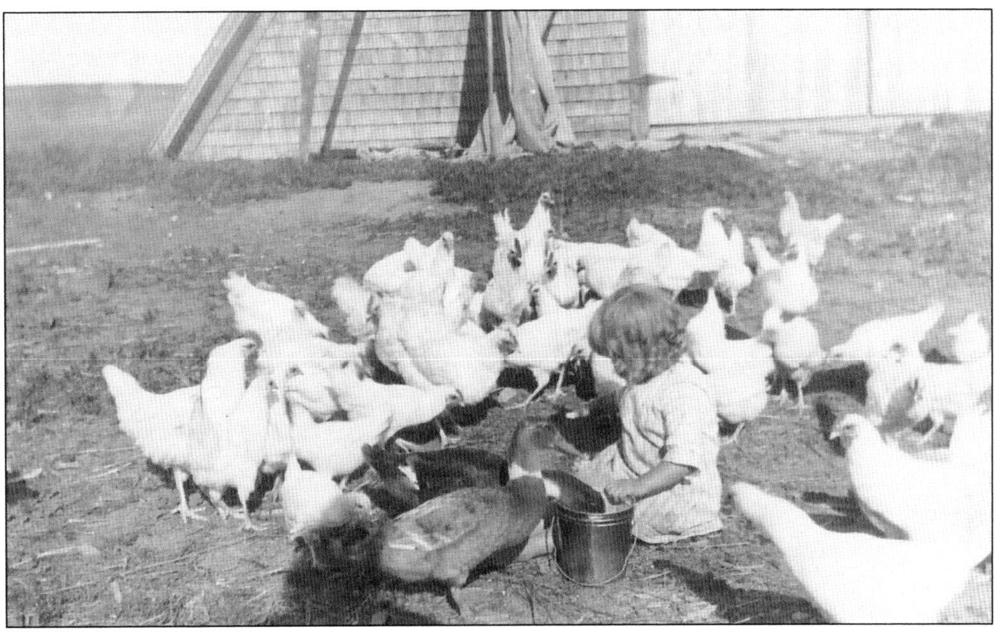

Everybody on the farm works! Ella Mae Russell's chores in 1919 included feeding the chickens, pigs, and calves.

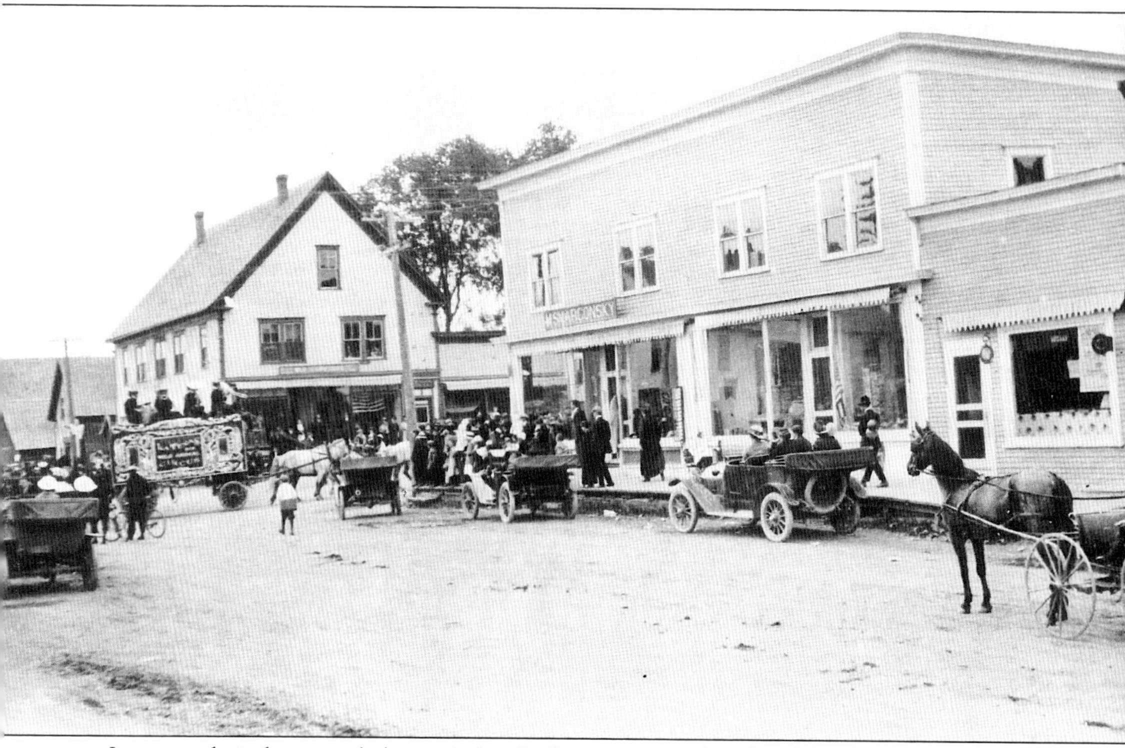

Leaving their long work hours behind, the townspeople of Ashland enjoy a circus parade in 1920.

Three

The Innovators and Innovations

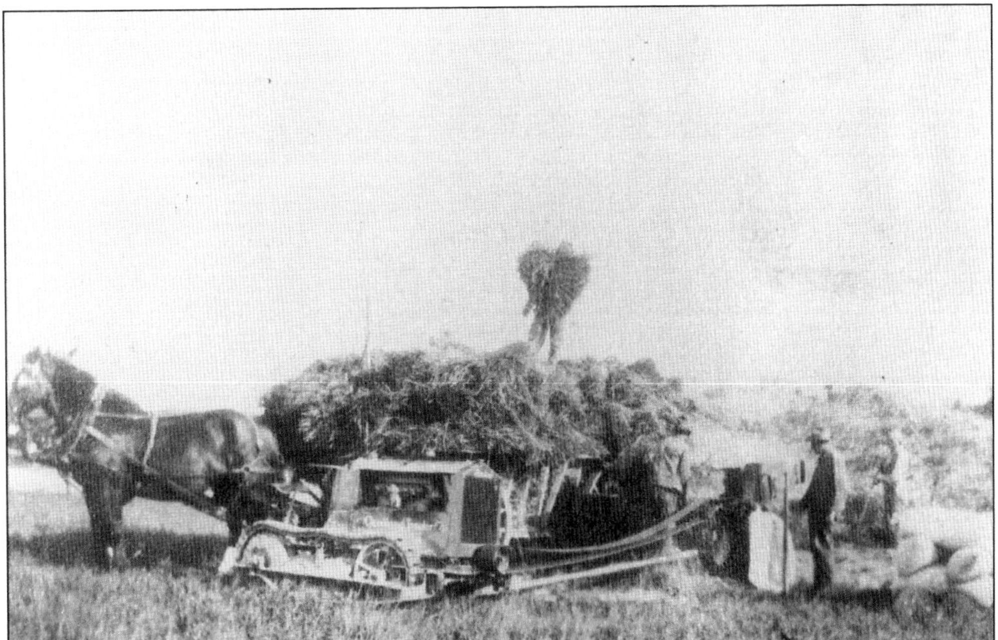

"Little Giant," a thrashing machine in 1919, was powered by a Cleveland Tractor. Feeding the mechanical device is Abram Crouse with Arthur and Lloyd Crouse helping.

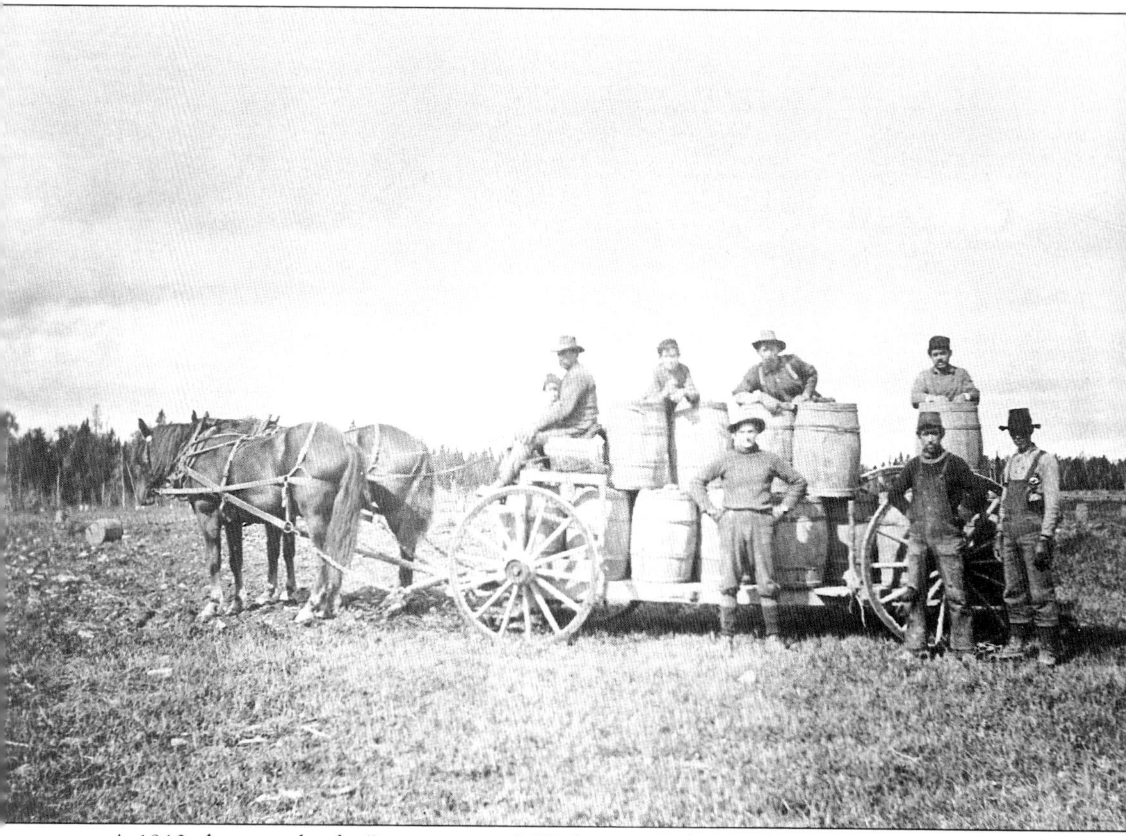

A 1910 photograph of a "jigger wagon." With more and more land being cleared, the need for advanced equipment was in demand. Built close to the ground, the "jigger wagon" was designed to save the backs of workers who had to lift the heavy barrels of potatoes.

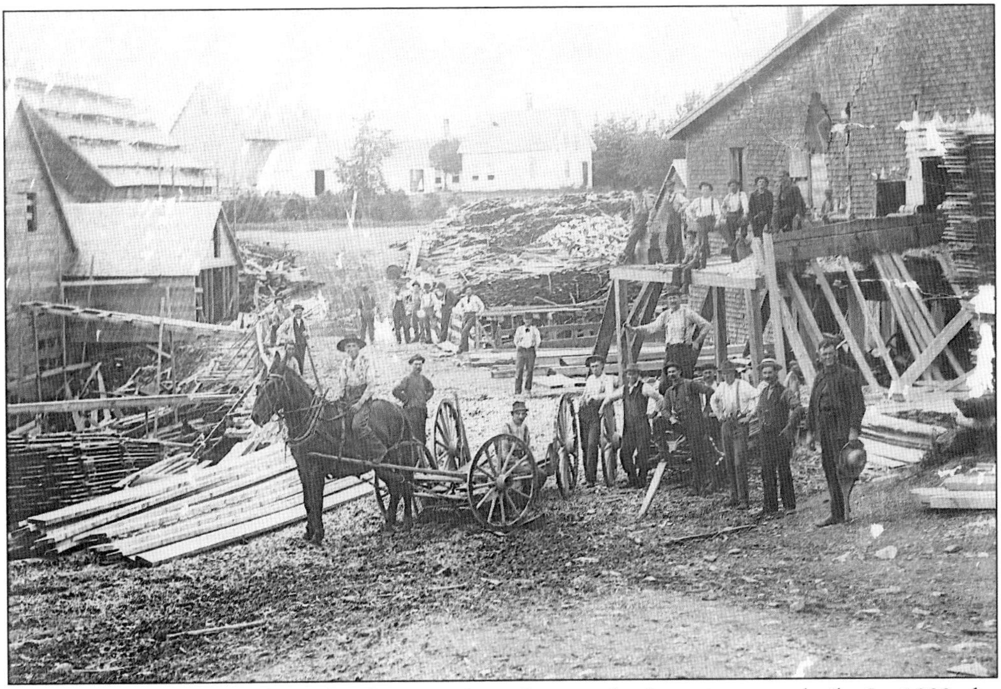

As production increased on the farms and in the woods, factories were built. In 1922 the old mill and starch factory was under construction in Washburn at the Mill Pond site, N. Main Street.

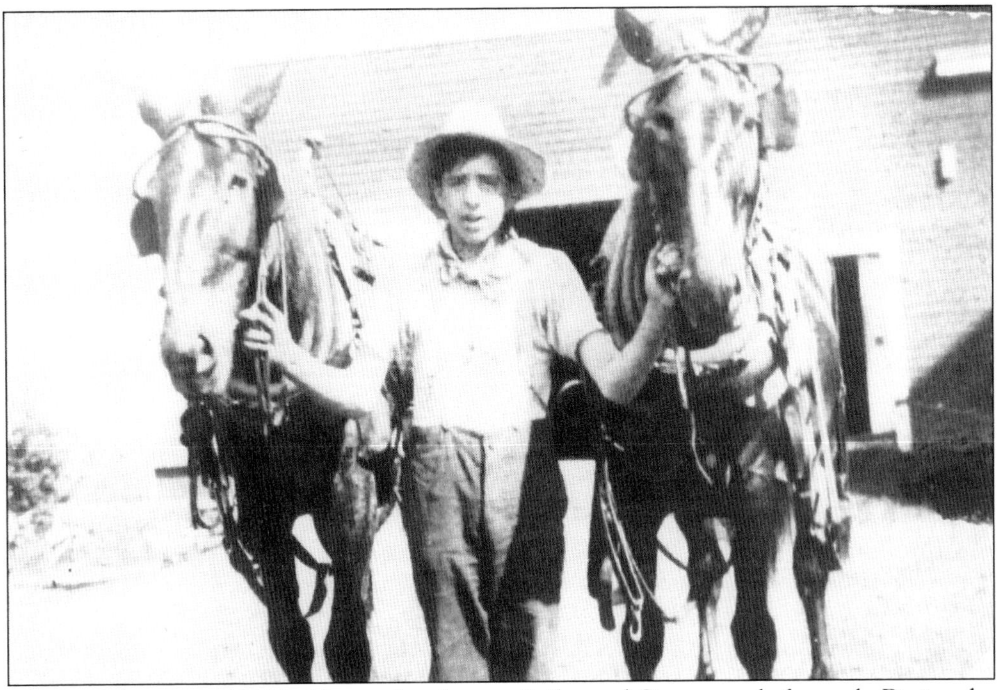

Charles Sylvester in 1918 holds two farm horses, Sailor and Queen, ready for work. During the summers one pastime for young people was to climb to the top of the barn and jump from the hay lofts.

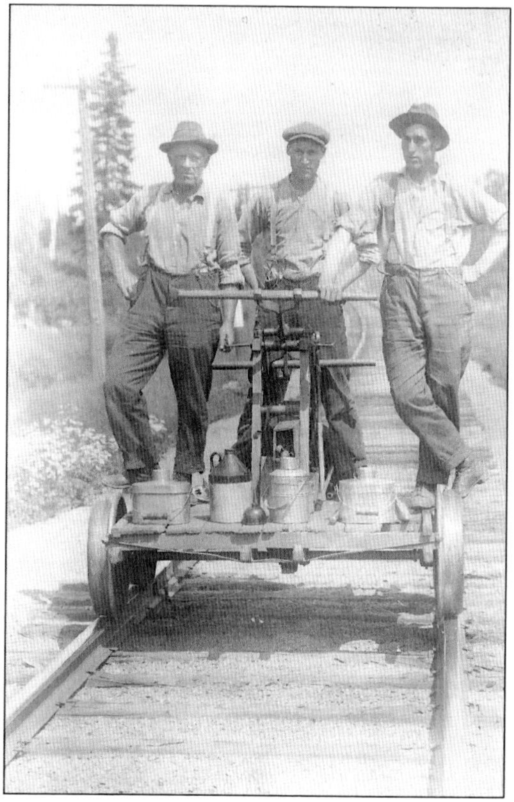

Work crews for the Bangor and Aroostook Railroad traveled from site to site on what were called hand cars. Designed to place men in remote areas, this mode of transportation required from one to four men to pump the handle bars. In 1915, from left to right, Billy Kirkpatrick, Lance Hathaway, and Arthur Madore were working between Ashland and Portage for the Bangor and Aroostook Railroad.

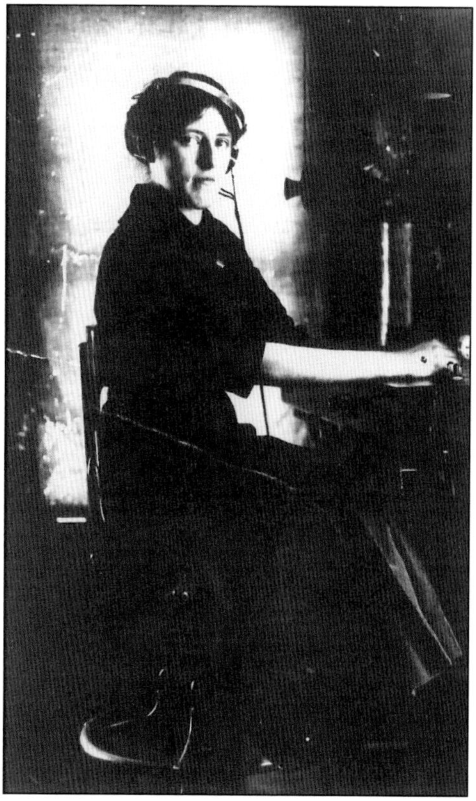

The advent of the telephone brought many changes to the widely-scattered farms and villages in Aroostook County. Here Pearl Estey, one of the Washburn Telephone Company's first operators, is ready to place calls in 1912.

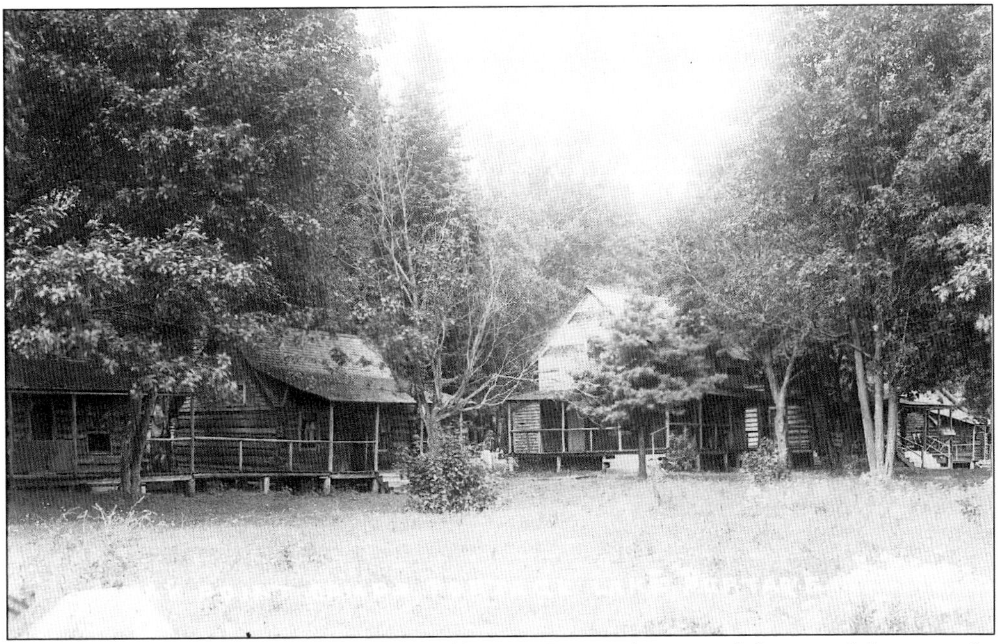

Known as the Oak Point Camps, these buildings in Portage have a rich history of their own. In 1905 they were built by Moses McNally and Mr. Iverson for local hunting and fishing. Between the 1920s and '30s they were used as a camp by the Congregational church. During the 1940s, they became a recreation and rest camp for the U.S. Army, which installed a power plant and water. Huge rock fireplaces were considered state-of-the-art for the times.

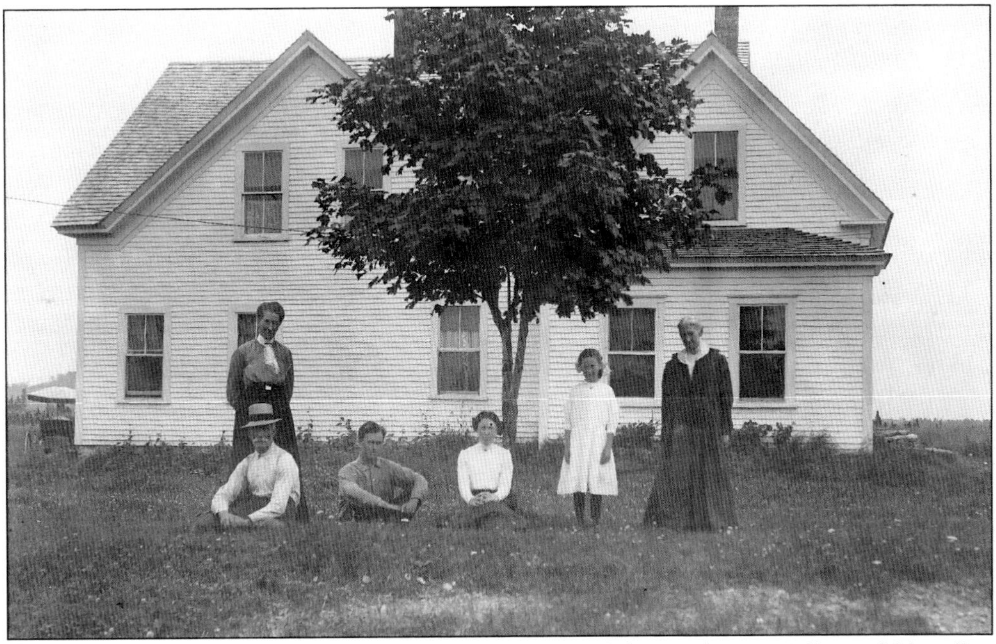

Enjoying a pleasant summer day in 1912 or 1913. From left to right are Nellie and Llewellyn Foss, Halsted Foss, Hazel (Foss) Higgins, Mariam Foss, and Mariam (Mazie) McGlauflin of Mapleton.

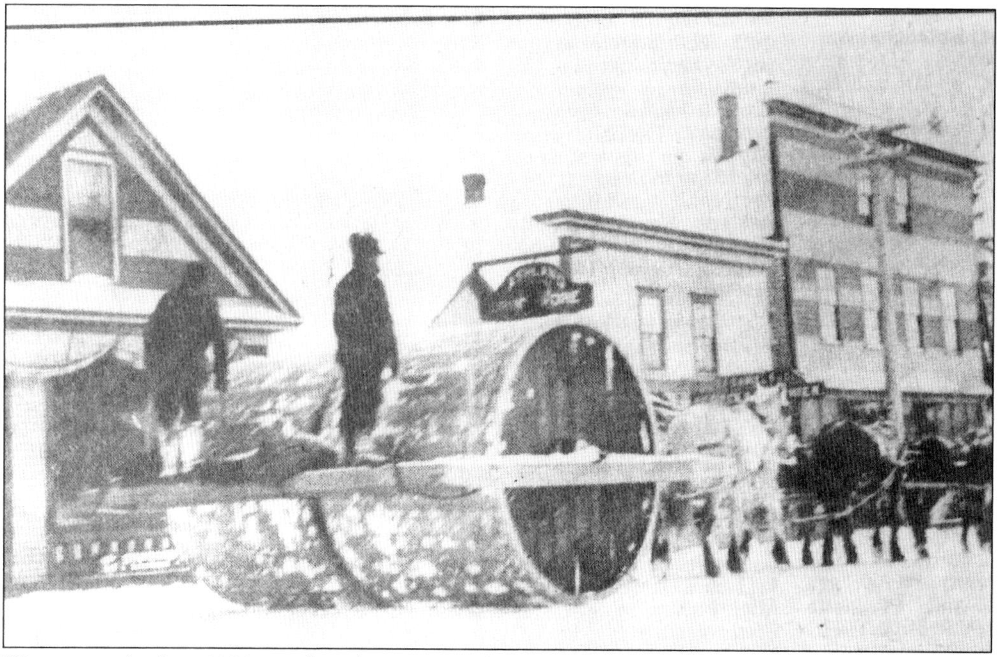

Winters in the late 1890s produced just as much snow as the winters today do. Using Aroostook ingenuity, Ashland utilized its only known "horsepower" to pack the white flakes into a solid mass.

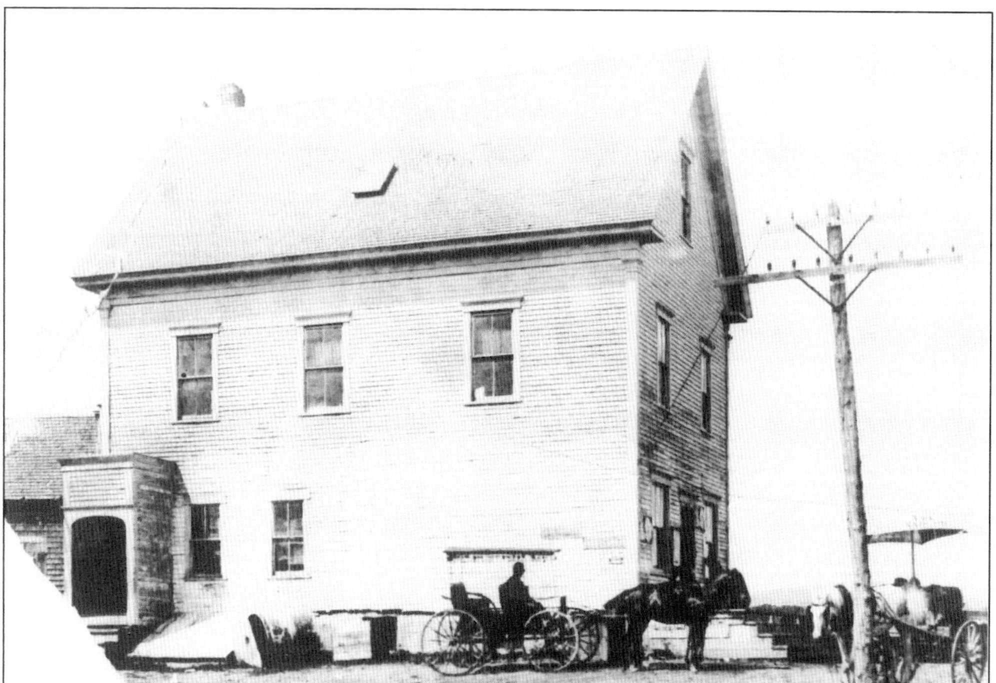

Grange halls played a large part in the business and social life of farming communities. The Mapleton Grange burned in 1923.

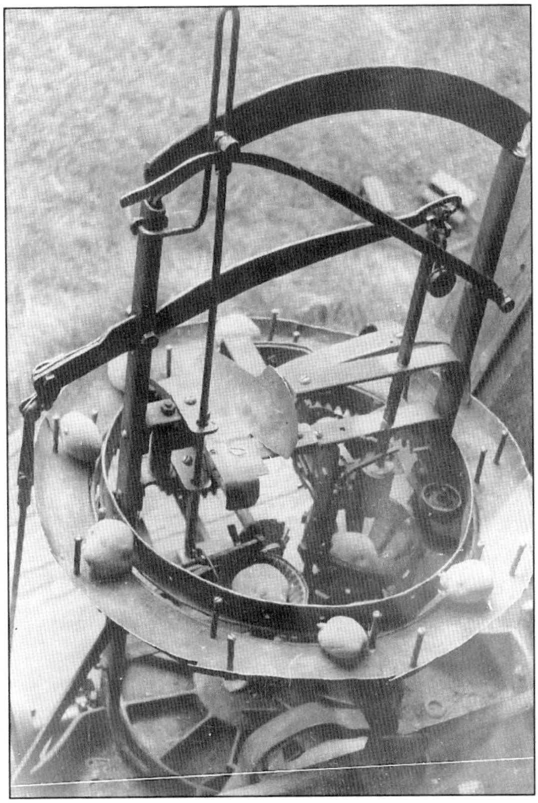

Attempting to find an easier and quicker manner to seed potatoes, Albion Thompson's father, sometime between 1920 and 1925, invented the first tuber-unit seed-cutter attachment for a planter.

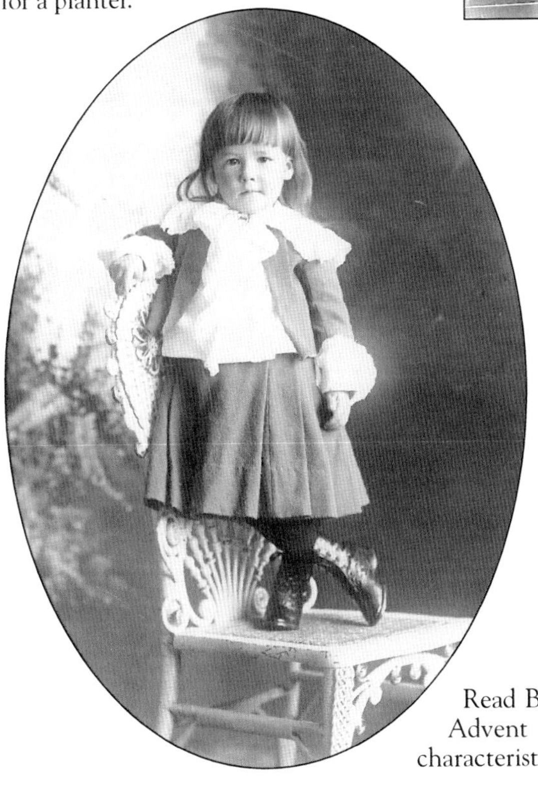

Read Blackstone, the future minister of the Wade Advent Christian Church, practices his spiritual characteristics and compassionate attitude in 1903.

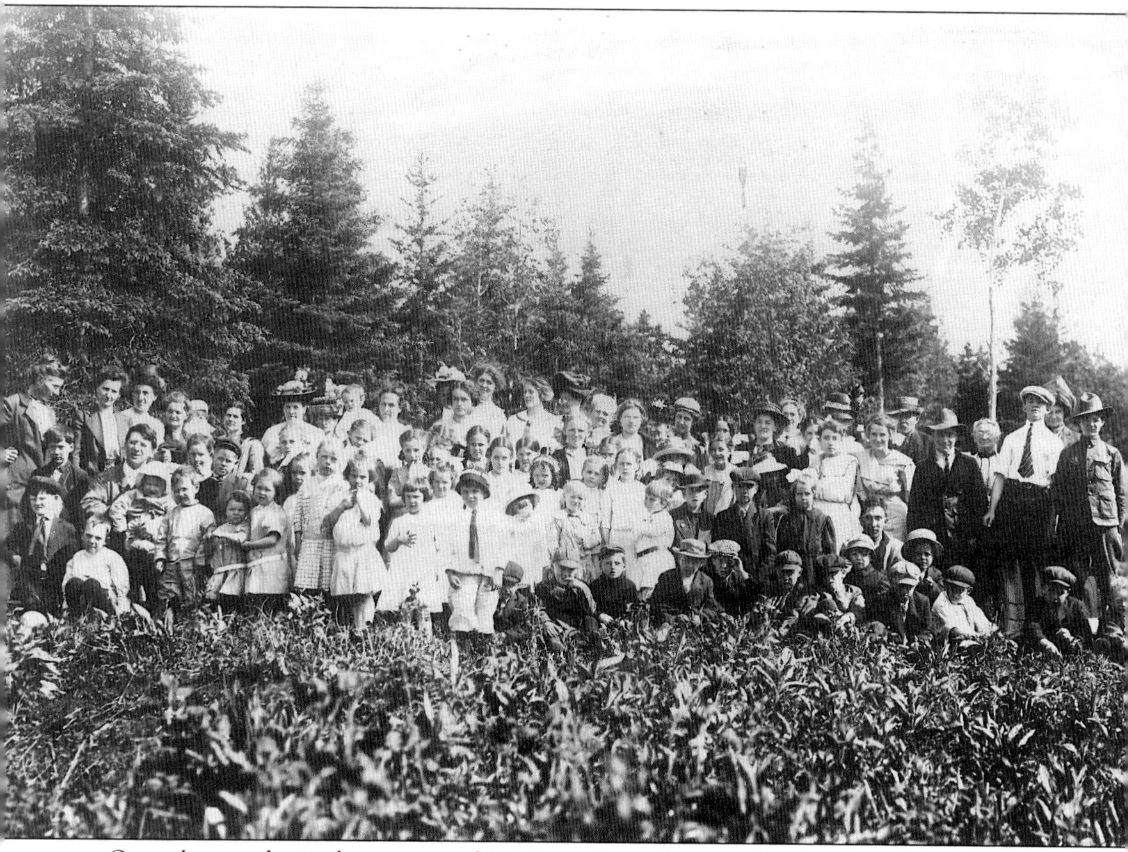

On a pleasant day in the summer of 1912 members of the Washburn Baptist Church journeyed to Haystack Mountain in Mapleton for a picnic.

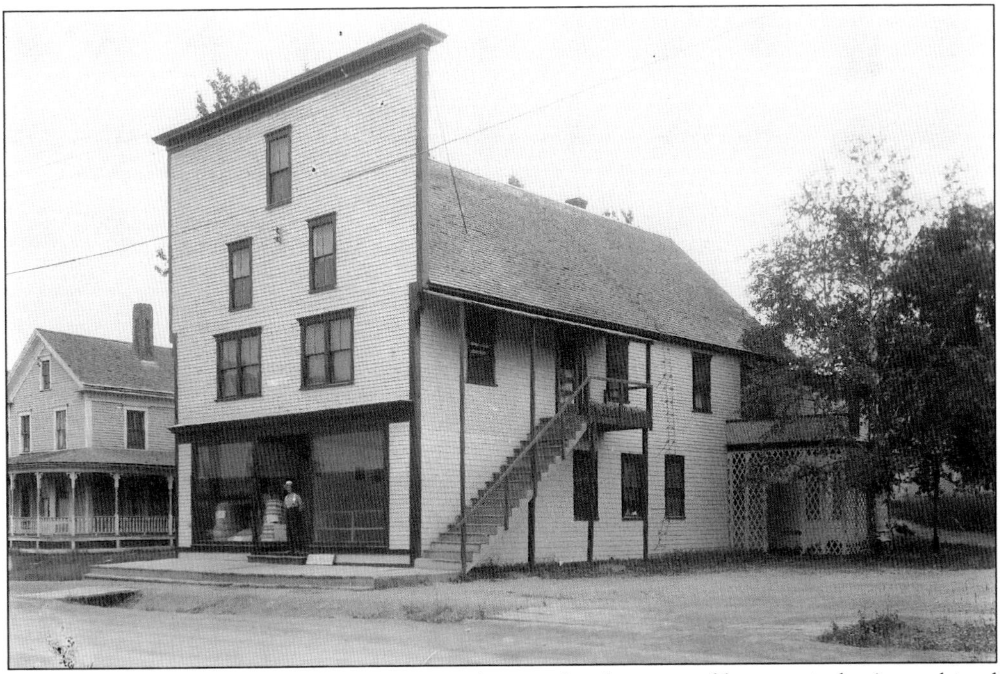

A 1920s photograph of David Duncan standing in the doorway of his son-in-law's combined furniture store and funeral home in Washburn.

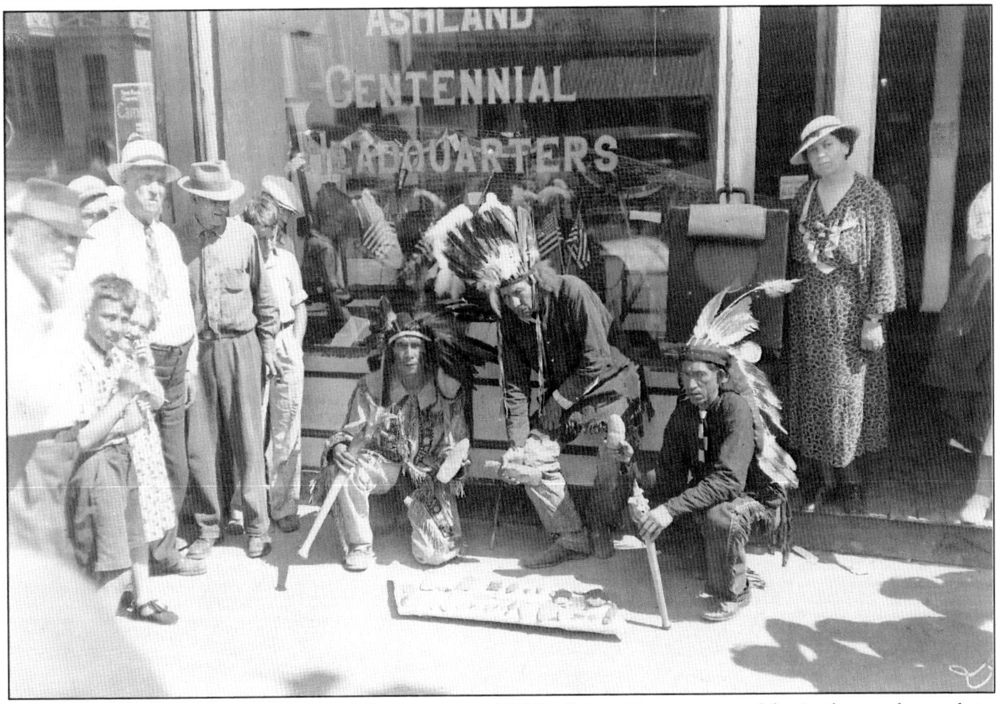

During Ashland's centennial celebration in 1937, three Passamaquoddy Indians dressed in their native attire and exhibited Indian relics. Chief Sabbatis Tomah (center) holds a perfect flint tomahawk. Watching, from left to right, are Joe Collier, Phillip Noyes, Anita Lovely, Asa Rafford, Sam Bass, Phillip Cheney, and Mrs. Clarence (Lizzie) Gallop (on the far right).

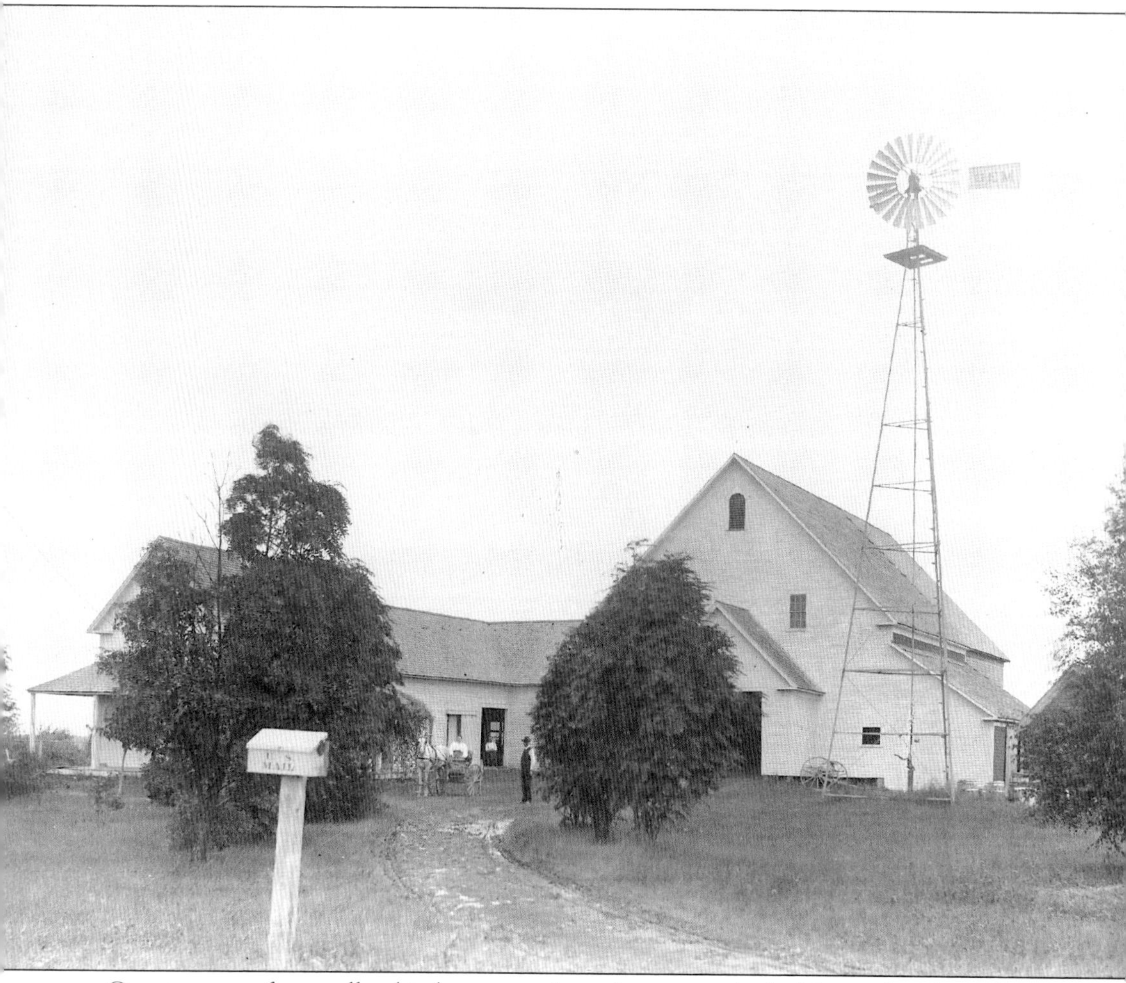

Carrying water from well to kitchen was a chore that no one looked forward to doing, but James K. Blackstone found the answer to "running water." By 1906 his farm boasted a windmill.

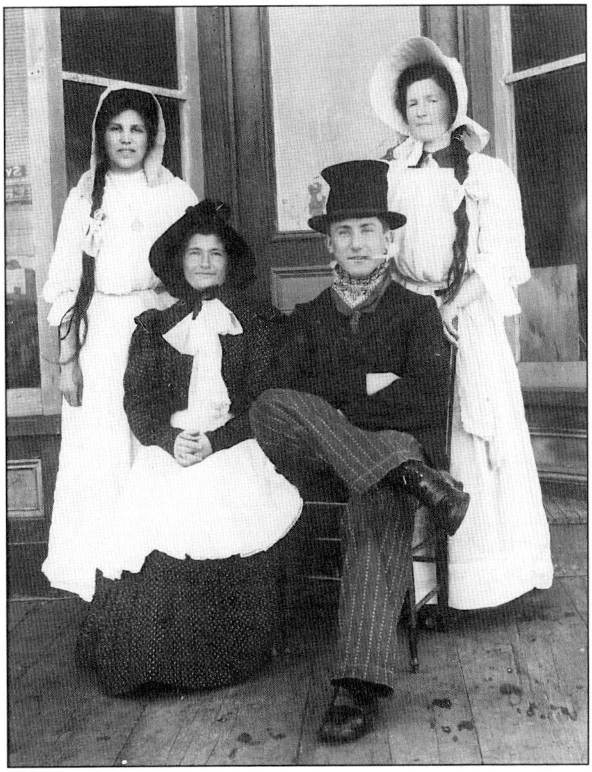

Making believe they live in the "olden days," these Washburn artisans dress in the attire of their predecessors, *c.* 1912. From left to right are: (front) Daisy Story and Bill Ballard; (back) Hazel and Abbie Ballard.

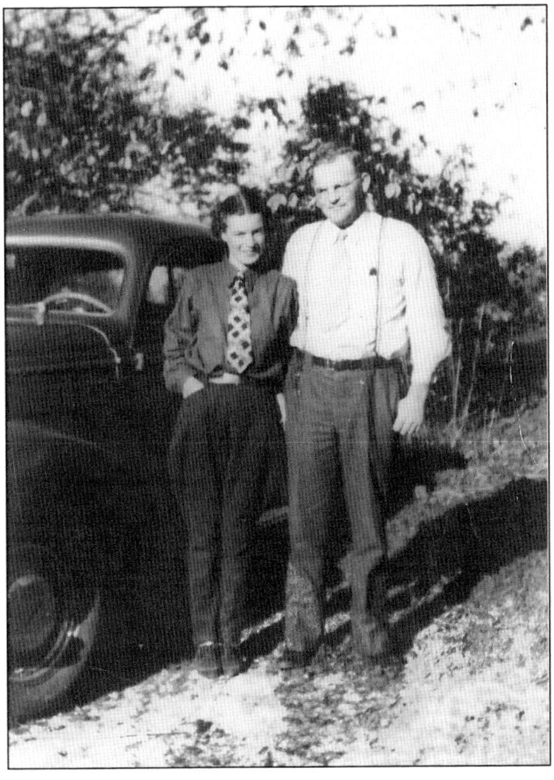

In October 1938, Arvard and Janice (Sherwood) Crouse were married. Arvard, born 1/11/'11, still lives on the original homestead and cuts his own wood from log lengths.

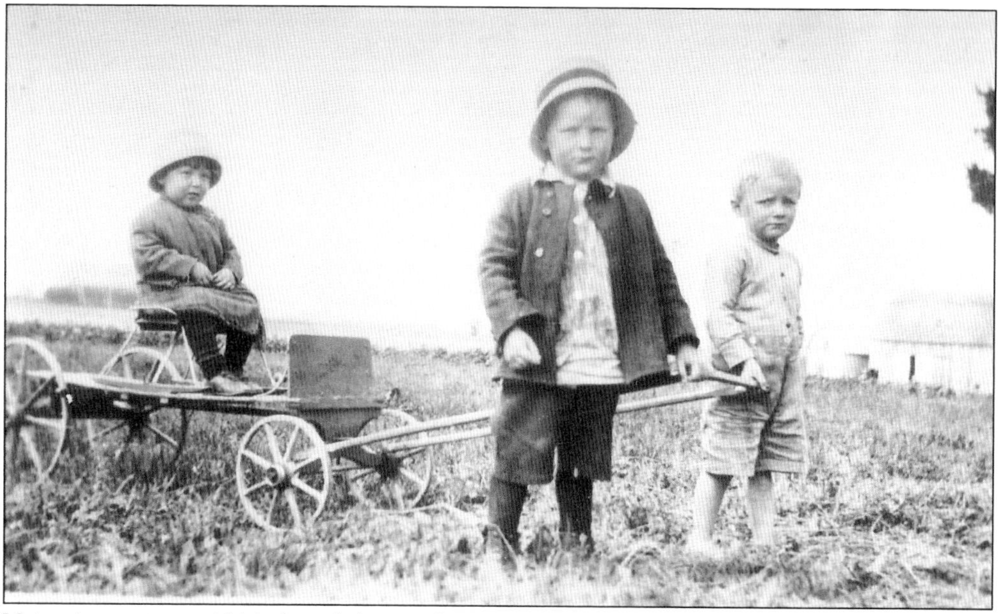

Using ingenuity in 1916, from left to right, Moses Crouse, Arnold Crouse, and their cousin, Ralph Crouse, improvise a mode transportation to see the sights of the farmland on Cross Road, Crouseville.

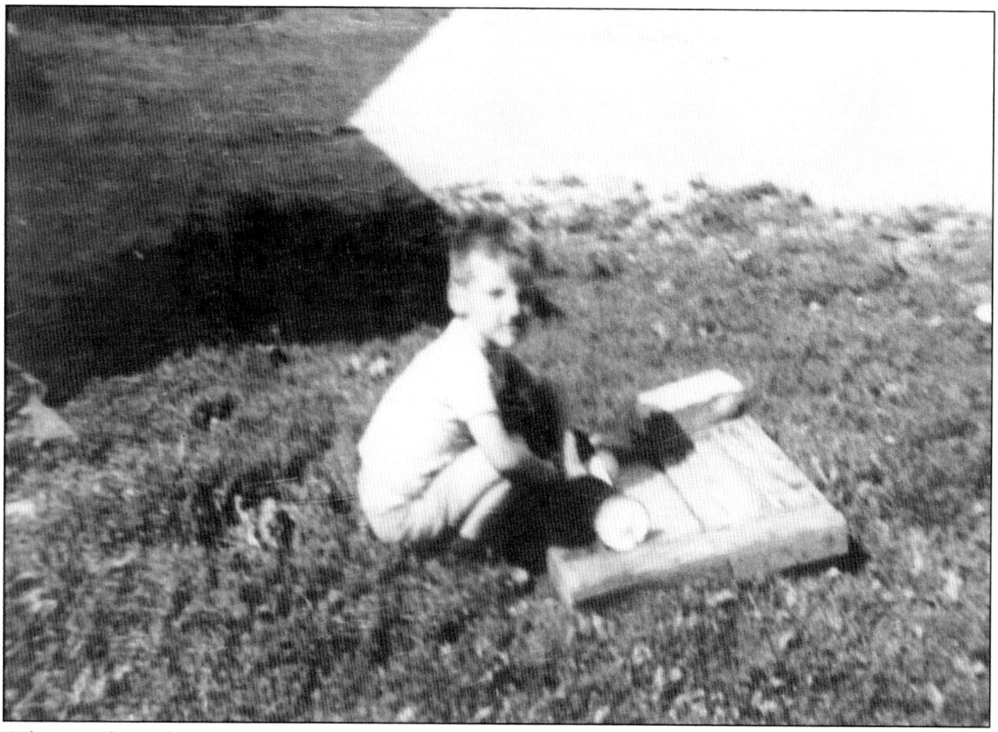

Who needs sophisticated toys? Michael Cochran from Woodland discovered that by picking up small pieces of wood he found in his grandfather's barn, he could build a car and ramp that worked just fine.

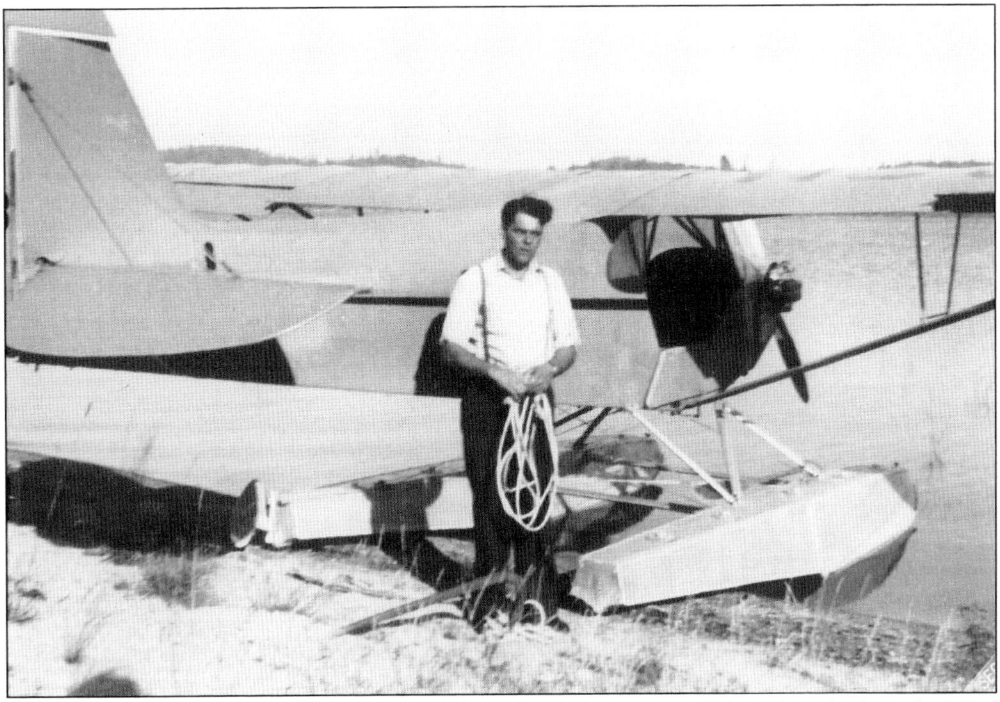

With the influx of sportsmen from "down state" and "out of state," and with the advent of improved technology, sea planes were implemented to ferry goods, hunters, and fishermen in and out of the remote camps and lakes to the west of the county. "Fod" Currier is shown standing beside one such plane in 1939.

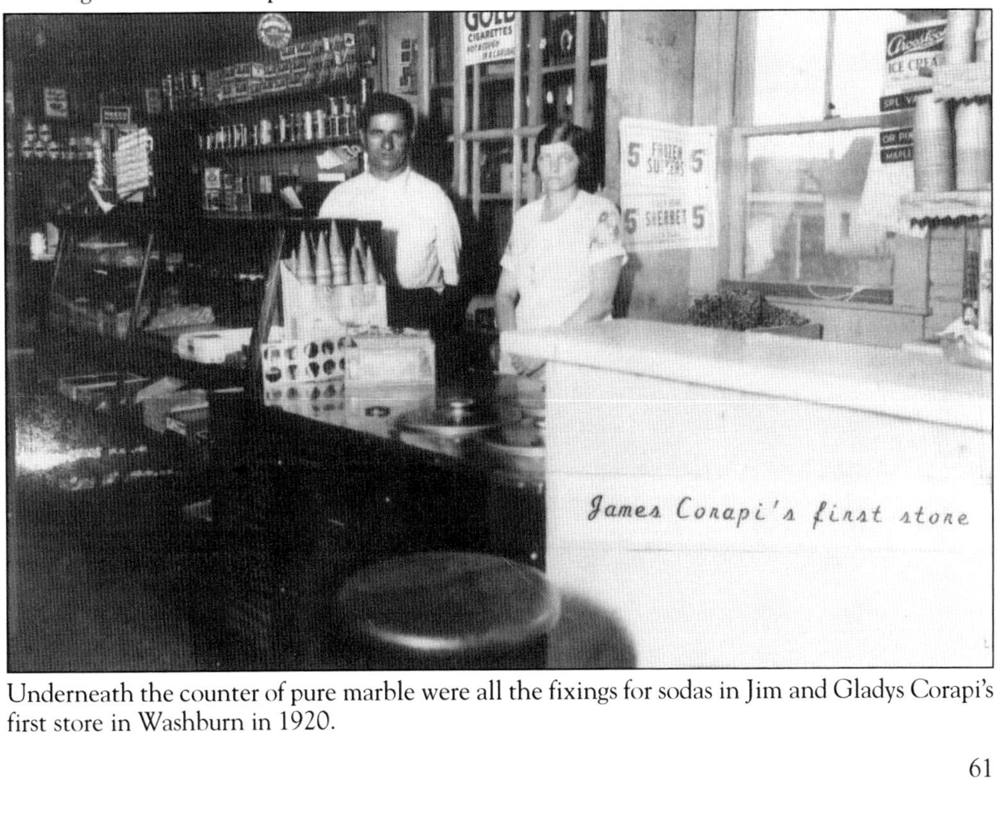

Underneath the counter of pure marble were all the fixings for sodas in Jim and Gladys Corapi's first store in Washburn in 1920.

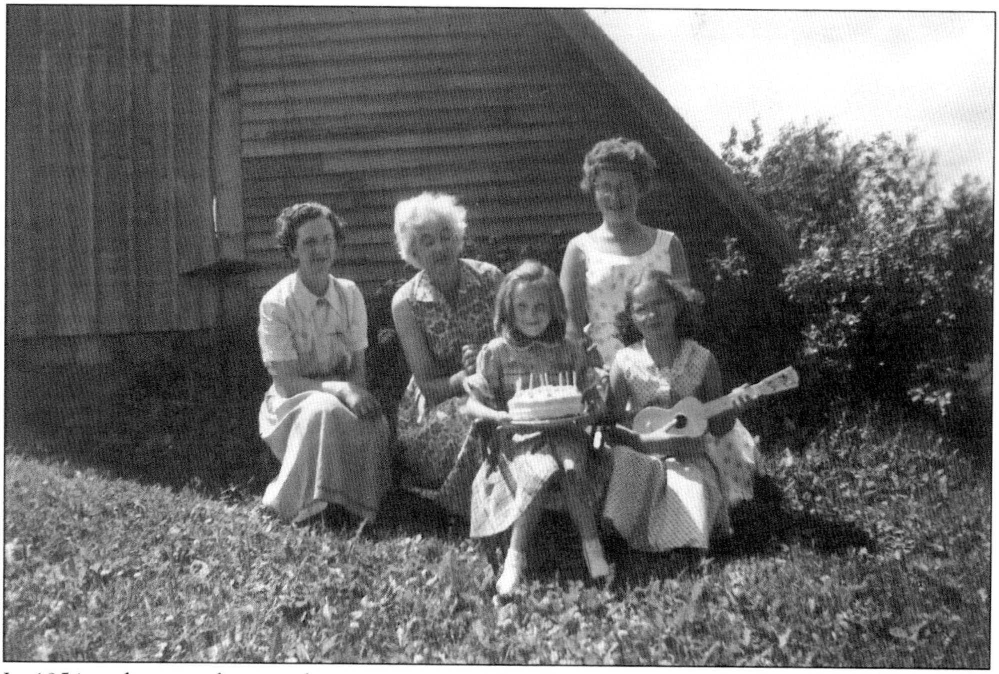

In 1954 underground potato houses were considered proper storage for the staple tubers. With only its roof showing, this building became a backdrop for a birthday picture. From left to right are: (front) Arlene Harmon and Danna Kelley; (back) Hazel Harmon, Mildred Kierstead, and Anneke Kierstead.

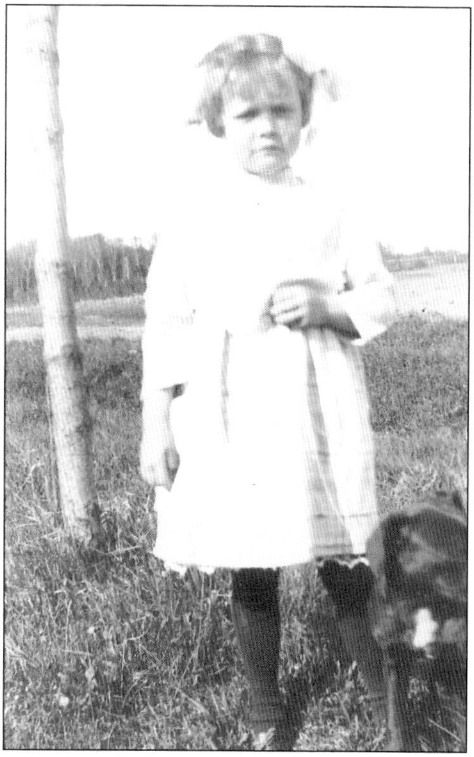

Even on a hot day when chores were done, girls were expected to "dress up" with long, dark cotton stockings and long sleeves, as Ella Mae Russell models 1922. Teddy does not appear to be impressed by his string leash.

By 1936, a more advanced way of spraying crops came to the area. This Ford tri-motor, owned by Wallace Woodman and the Woodman Potato Company, aided many farmers.

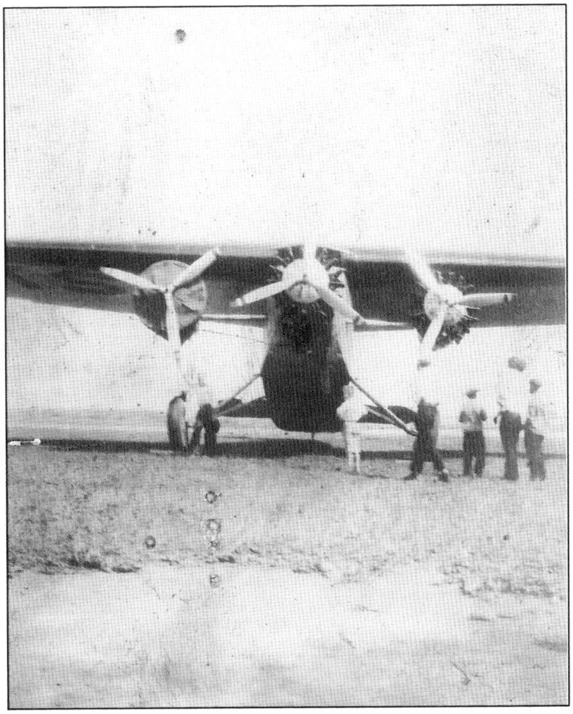

During the World War II years when worries were abundant and amusement scarce, Ashland's Rafford Band helped to lighten the tension by visiting many communities in the area. Burns McGowan played the drums; Leo Michaud, the banjo; Dana Rafford, the fiddle; and Helen Michaud, the piano.

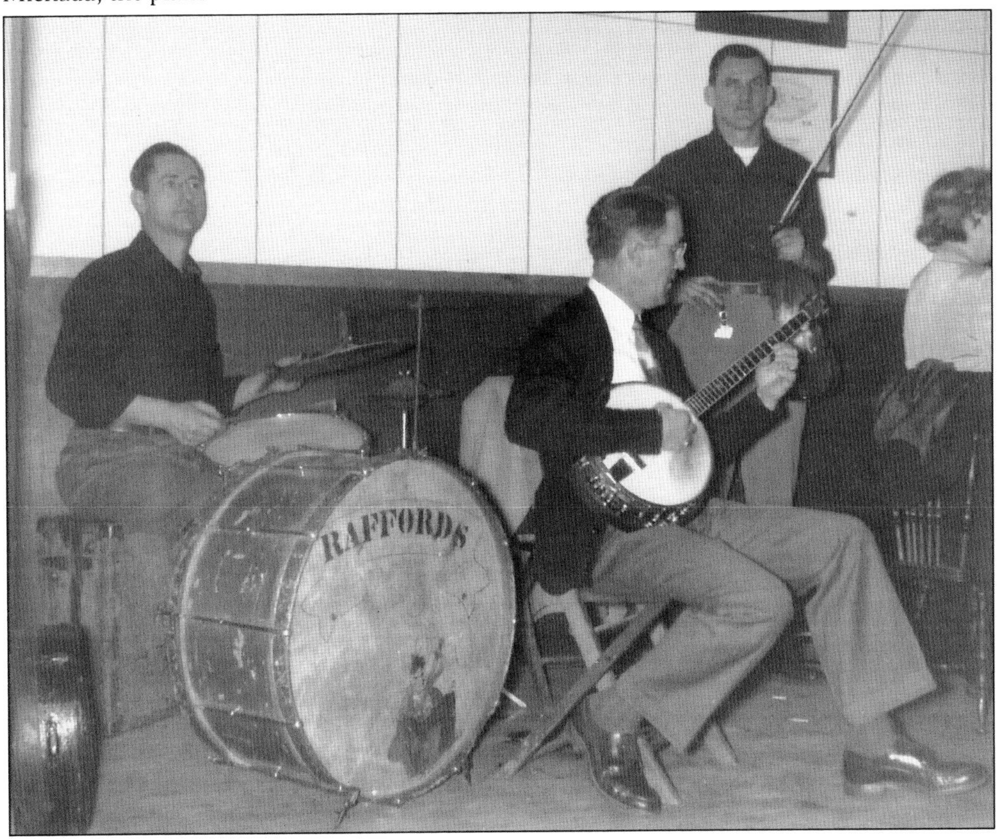

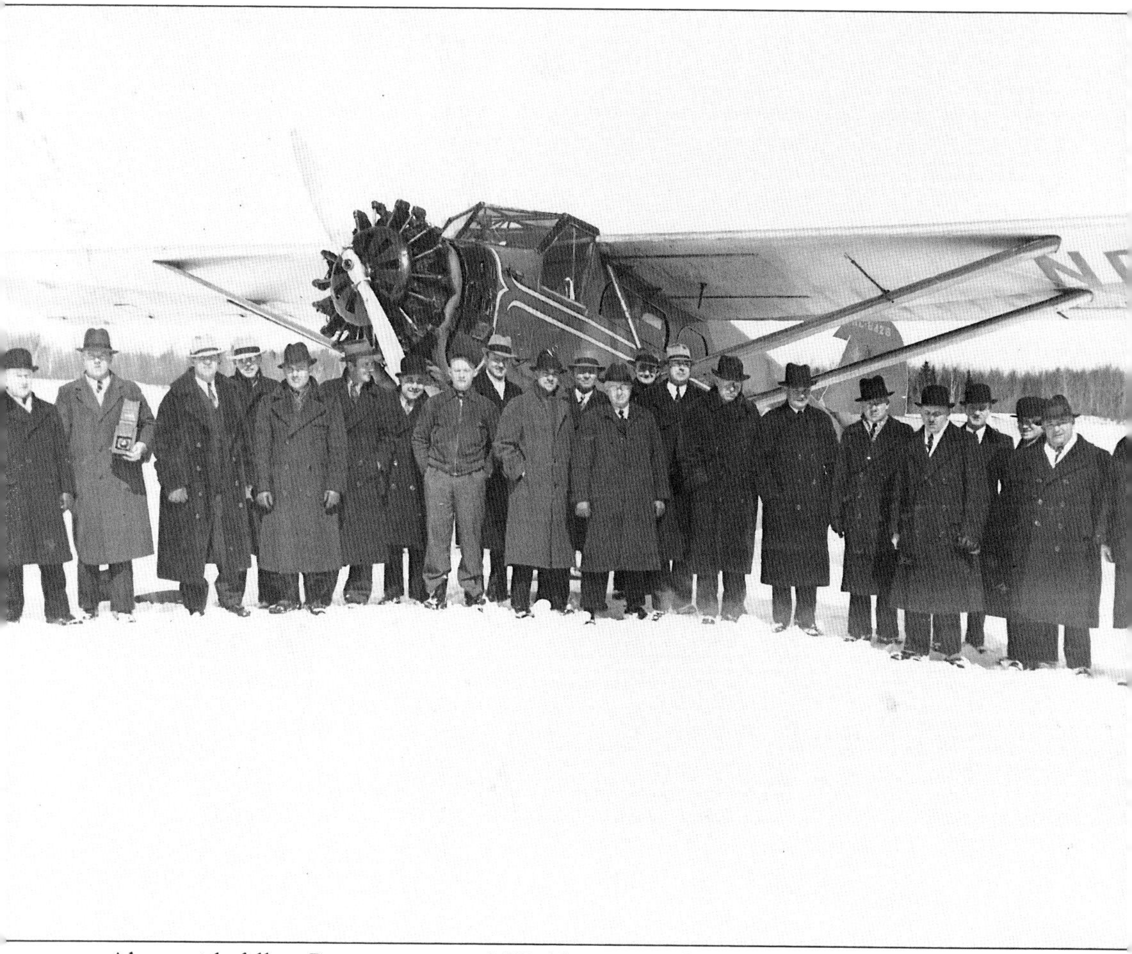

Along with fellow Rotarians, several Washburn men flew to Quebec City for a rotary supper in 1939. Lewellyn Woodman, sixteen years old, flew the Stinson airplane on the return trip. The cost of the flight and supper was $20. Among the delegation were: Harry Umphrey, Carroll Wilder, Alden Woodworth, Seth Urington, Laurel Thompson, Ernie Protge, Lewellyn Woodman, Abram Crouse, Wallace E. Woodman, and Robert Woodworth.

Four

The Builders and Business

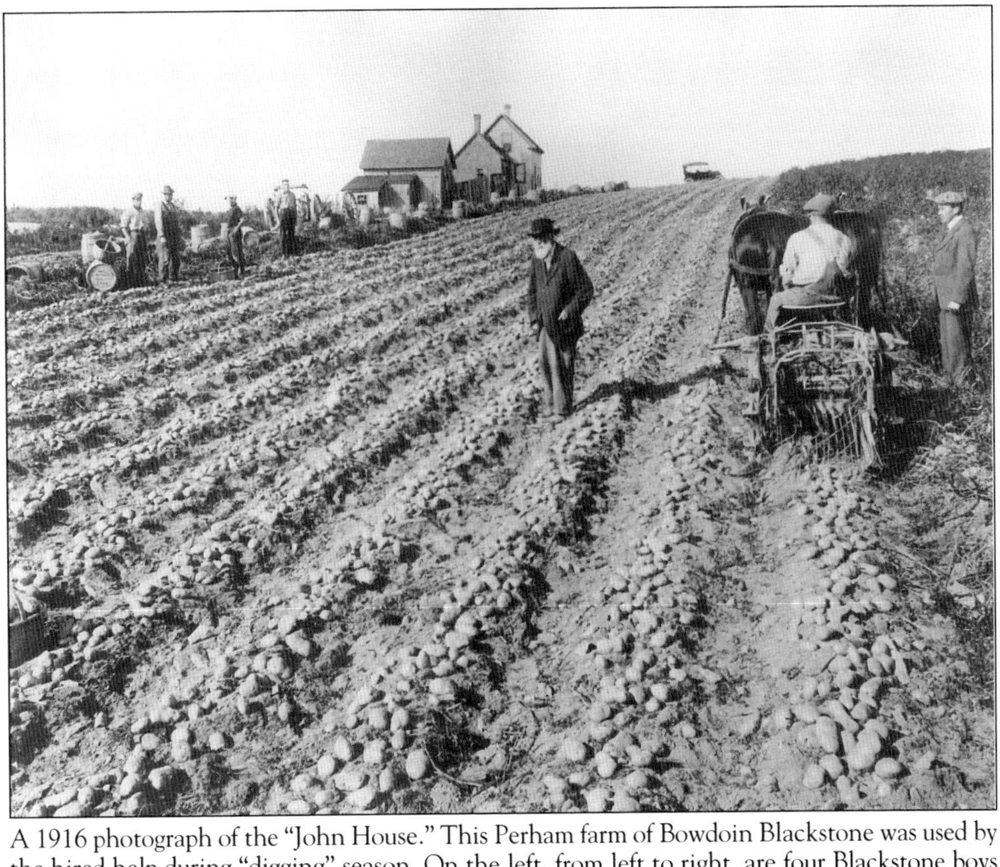

A 1916 photograph of the "John House." This Perham farm of Bowdoin Blackstone was used by the hired help during "digging" season. On the left, from left to right, are four Blackstone boys ready for work: Read, Fayette, Carroll, and Milford. Bowdoin Blackstone is in the center, and Hartson Blackstone is on the digger with a fertilizer salesman standing beside him.

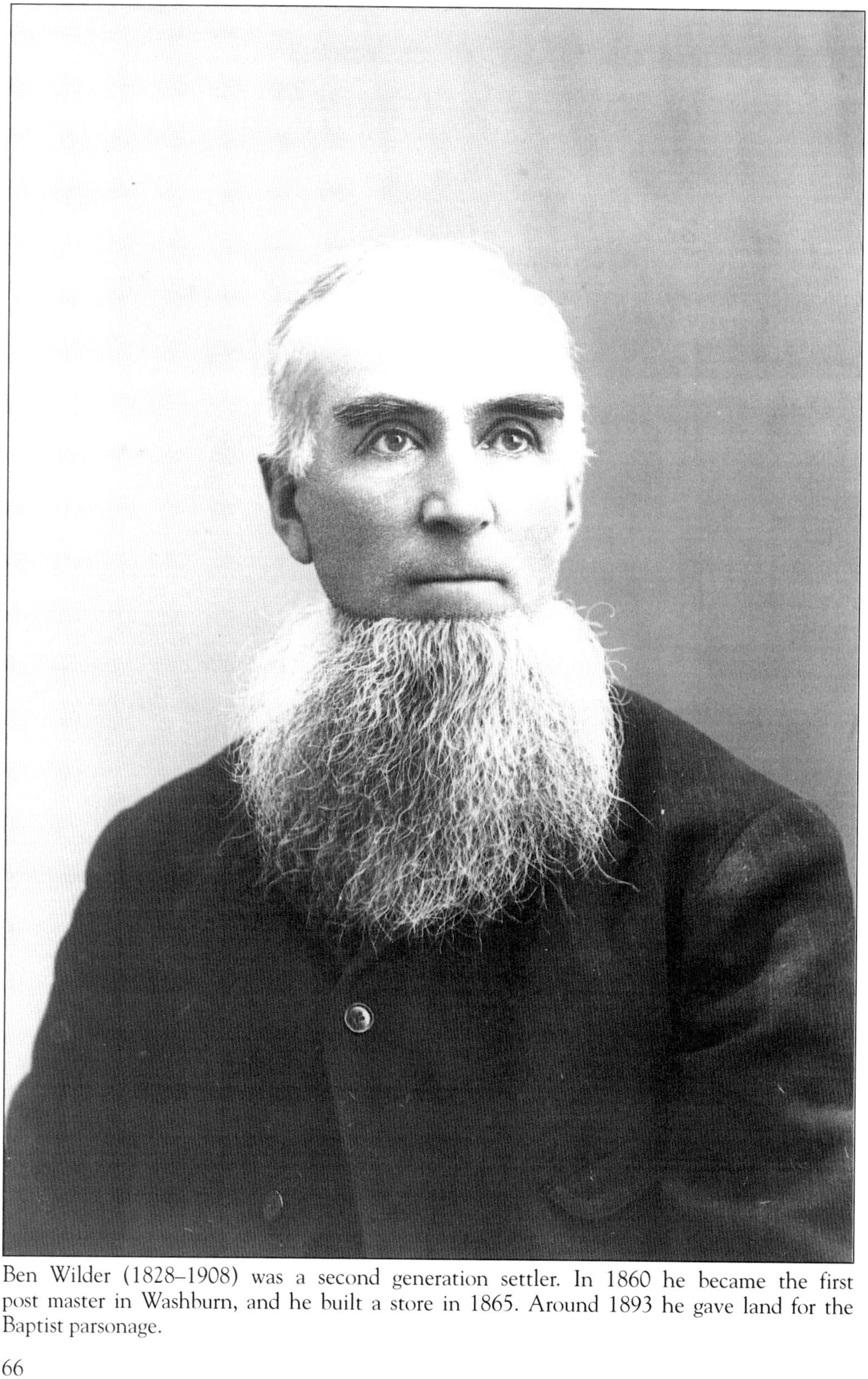

Ben Wilder (1828–1908) was a second generation settler. In 1860 he became the first post master in Washburn, and he built a store in 1865. Around 1893 he gave land for the Baptist parsonage.

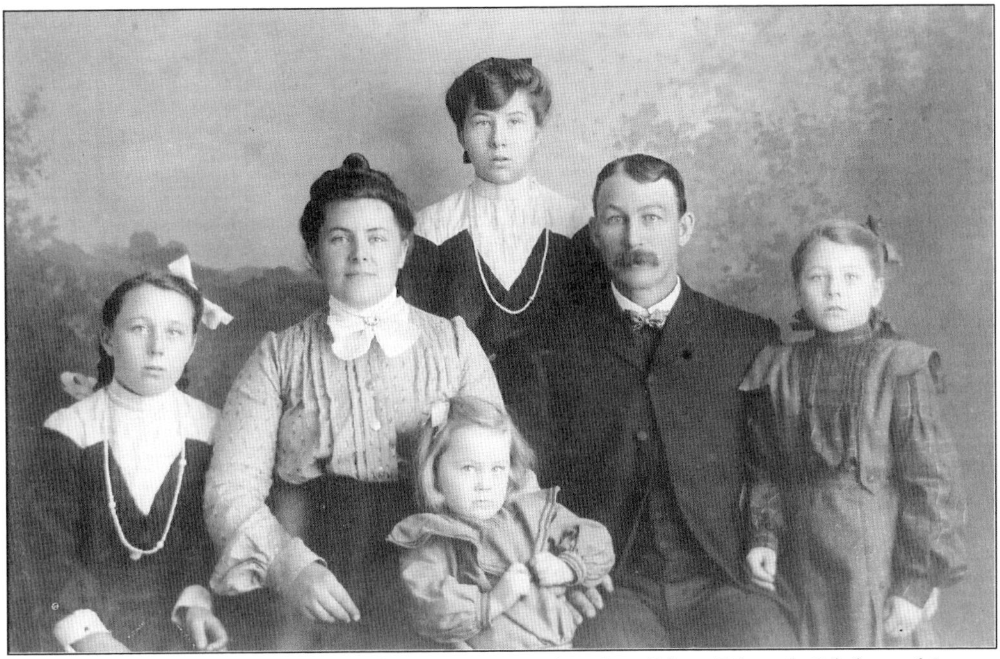

All in the family! From left to right are Loretta, Angelia, Edna, Edward, Edith, and Leona Roy (between Mom and Dad) in 1904. The three daughters married three Dickinson brothers, Harry, Berley, and Al. There was a fourth Dickinson brother, and shortly after her husband's death, Angela had a fourth girl. Years later, after their first spouses died, they met again and did marry!

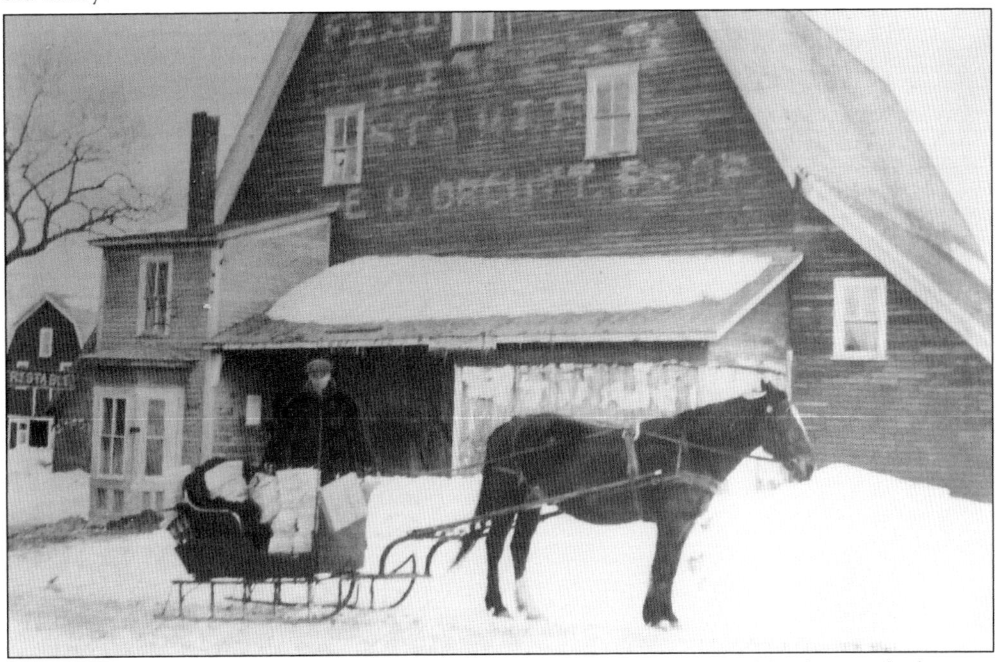

In the 1920s, Phineus Ellis began serving the public as a mailman in Ashland. Later he became a town manager of Mapleton and Castle Hill. He also served on the administrative board of the Presque Isle Hospital.

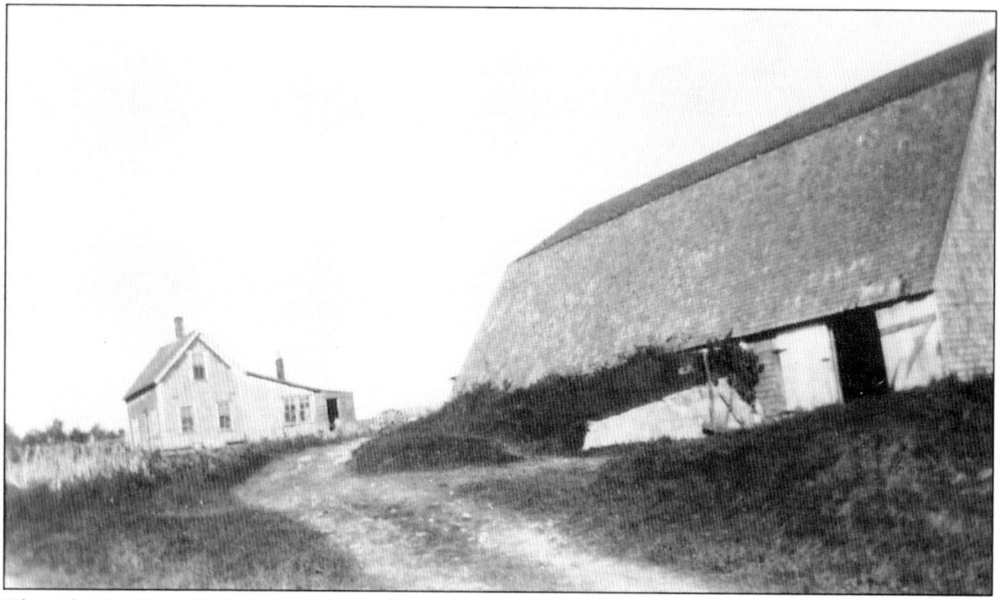
The Charles Russell farm and potato house at Carson's Siding in 1918.

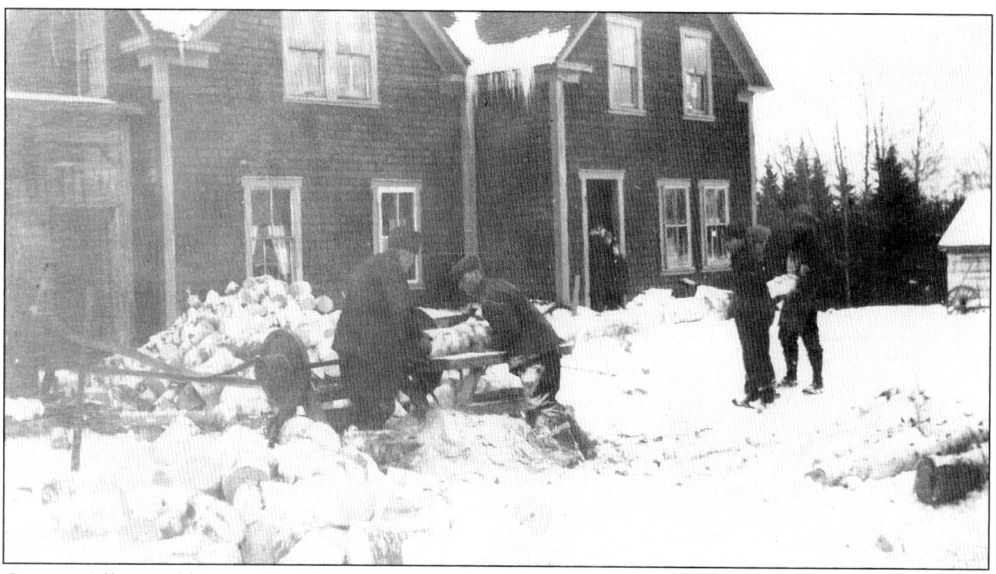
George Alley and his son Braighton saw wood in 1915 as the hired help bring them another log.

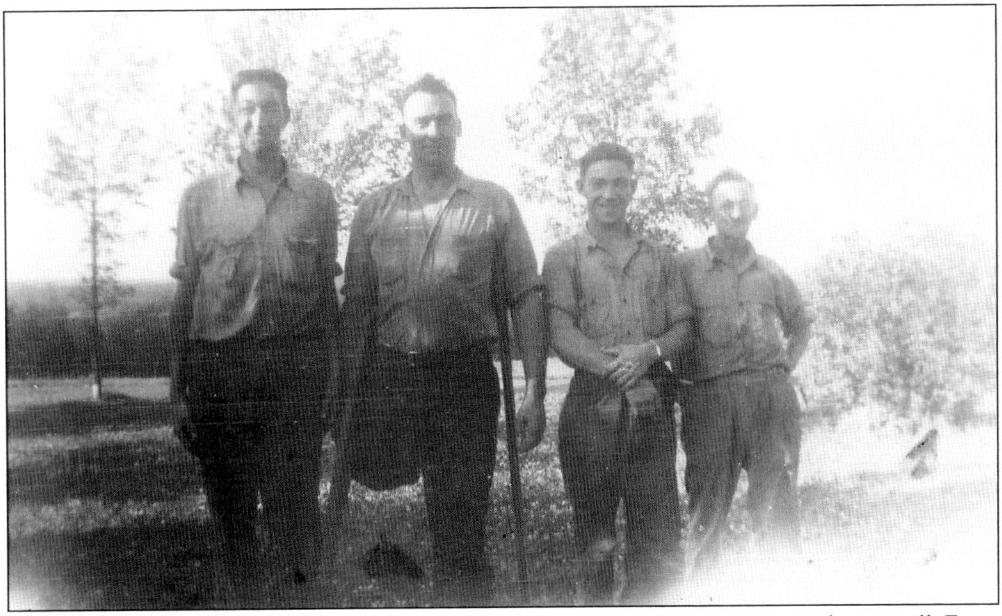

Farm work is hard enough with two arms and two legs, but Herb Drost managed very well. From left to right are Perley Drost, Herb, Liston Boyce, and Basil Ward.

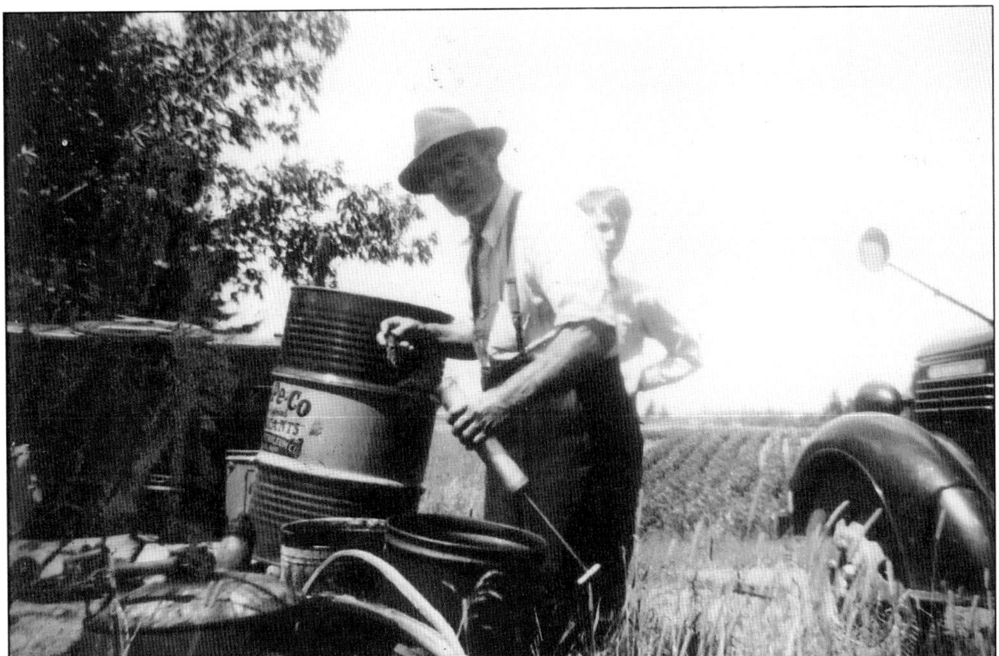

Ira Clayton, working on the old Randall farm on Gardner Creek Road, fills a grease gun "the old fashioned way" in 1945.

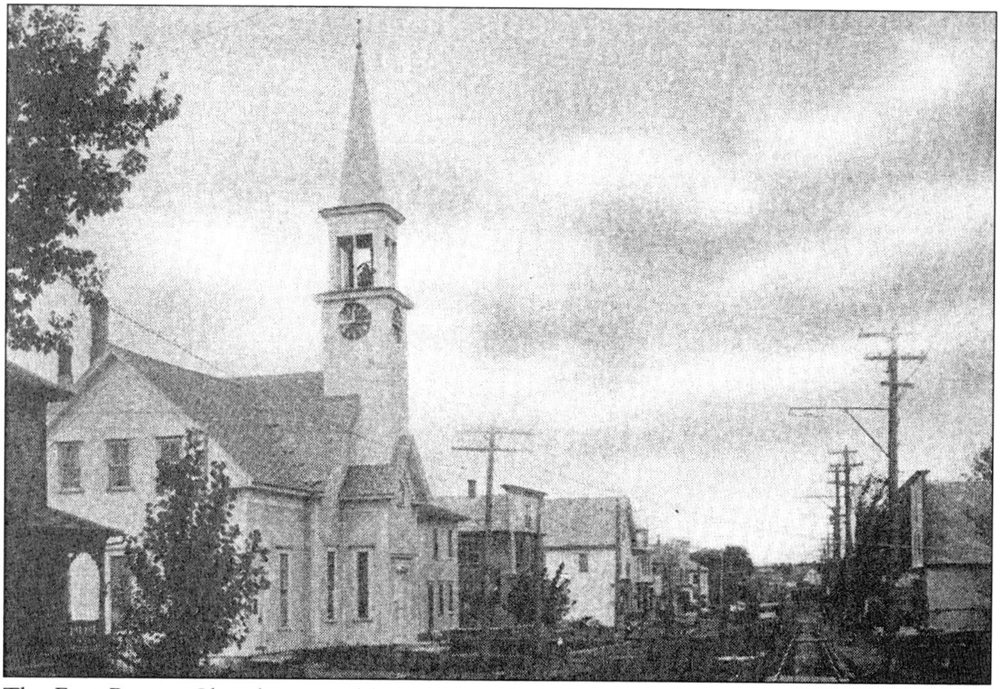

The First Baptist Church in Washburn was built in 1860 or 1862. Its first deacon was O.K. Story, who owned several businesses in town. The clock, which is now being restored to working condition, was donated by A.R. Gould in appreciation for the help of the townspeople when he put the Aroostook Valley Railroad through the town.

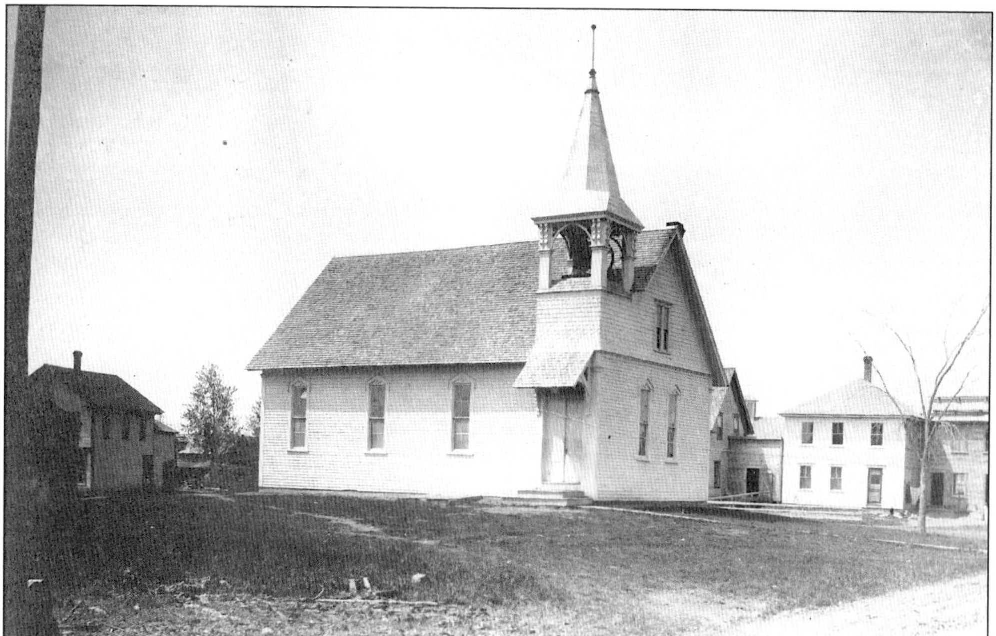

In 1907 the Washburn Methodist Church was built. It was later moved in a semi-circle so an addition could be added on. This is the only known photograph of the church in its original position.

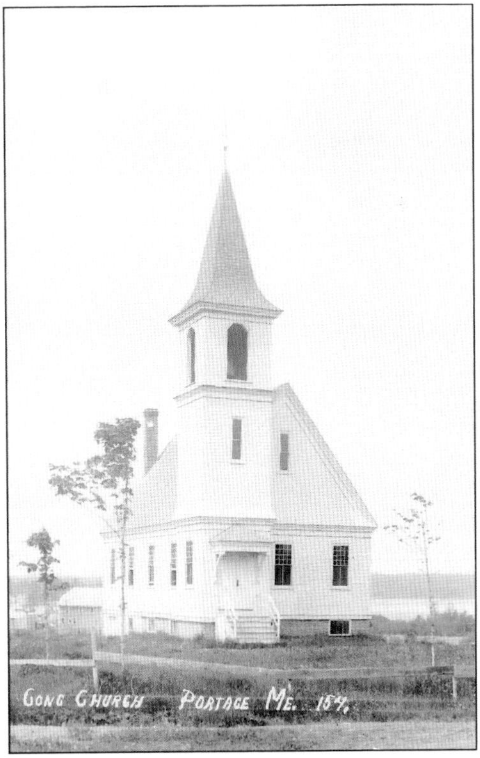

The Congregational church in Portage Lake sponsored church camps at Oak Point for both boys and girls from the 1920s to the 1930s.

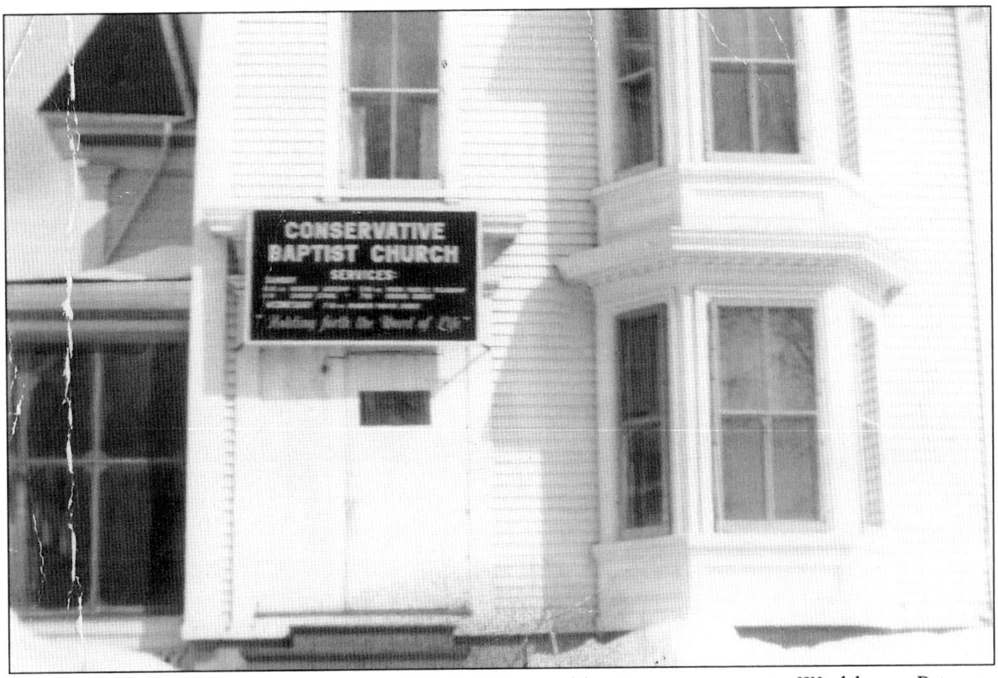

Built in 1890, this building was one of the earliest and busiest structures in Washburn. Prior to becoming the Conservative Baptist Church in 1951, it served as a maternity hospital; then it became the home of J.L. Woodman. After it housed the church, it became a home again.

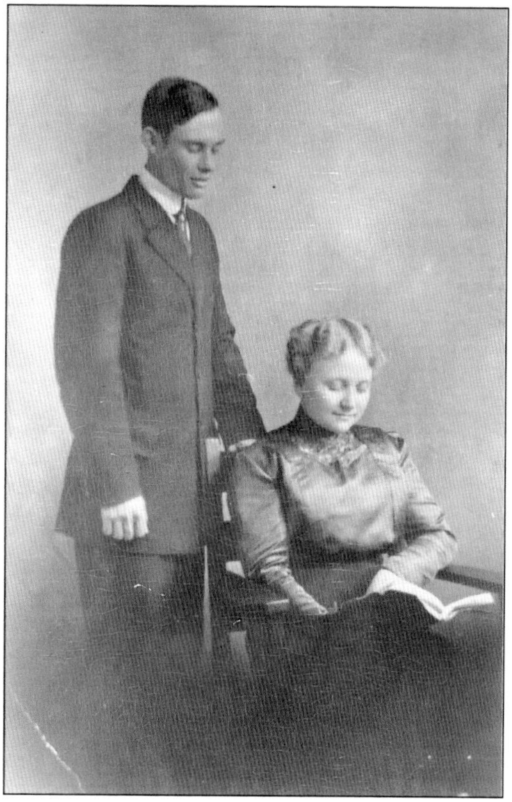

Potatoes, of course, have long been an important economic crop in Aroostook County. Contributing to that effort were Wallace and Bertha Woodman, who were married in Crouseville on October 18, 1913. Wallace started Sunny Brook Seed Farms and became one of the largest potato brokerages in the area at that time.

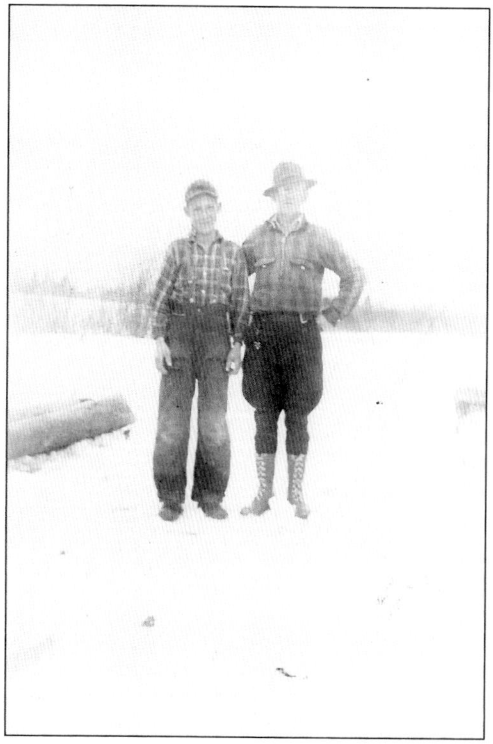

Basil Ward (left) and Liston Boyce put in long, hard days at the Wade Woods Camp.

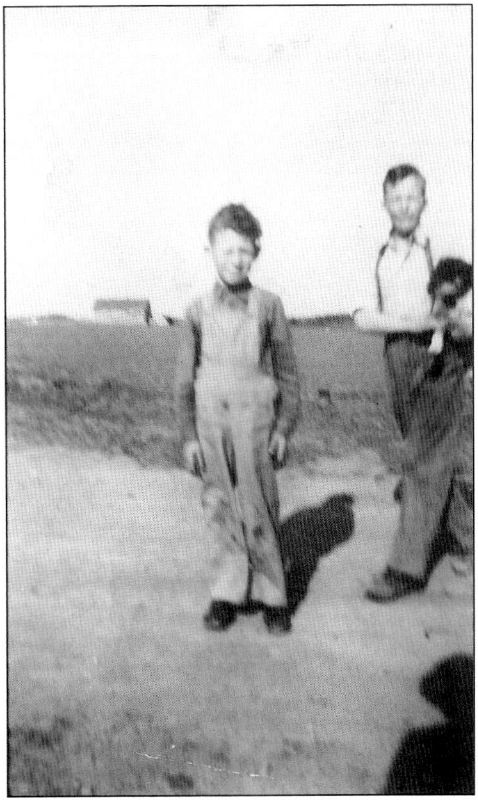

Clayton (left) and Danny Corey. Clayton grew up working in his father's garage. After serving in the military, he and his brother Rodney opened their own establishment. Danny is carrying Tippy, the dog.

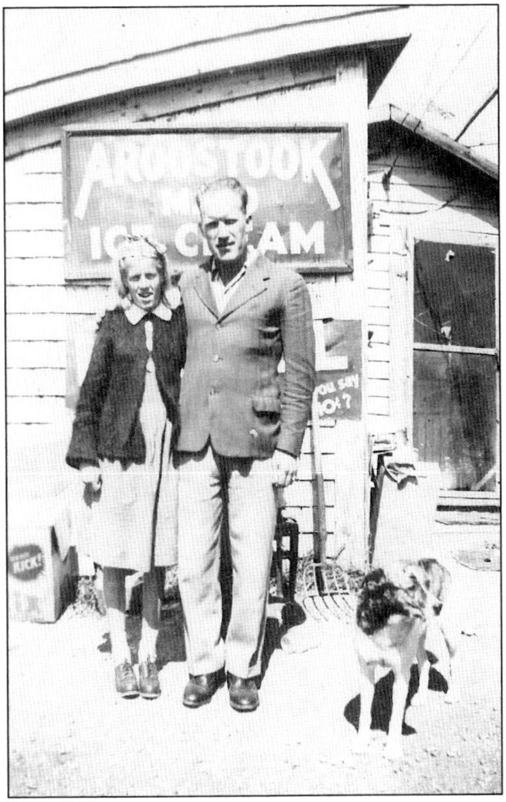

Percy Barnes and his daughter are ready for ice cream.

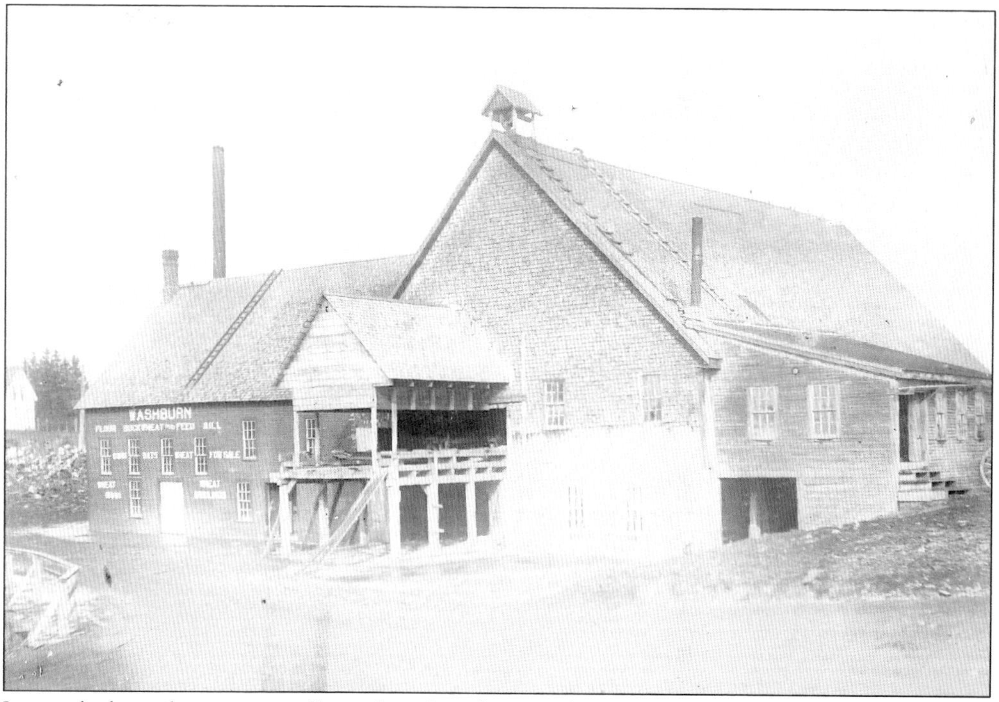

Located where the current mill pond is, the Thomas Phair Starch Factory flourished in 1922.

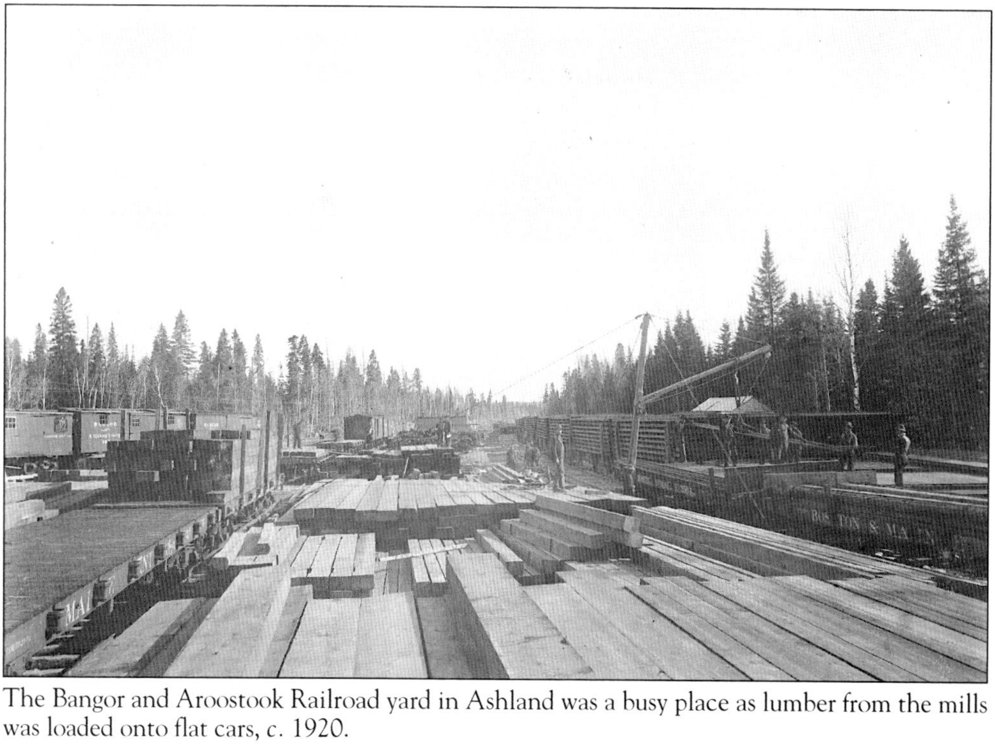

The Bangor and Aroostook Railroad yard in Ashland was a busy place as lumber from the mills was loaded onto flat cars, c. 1920.

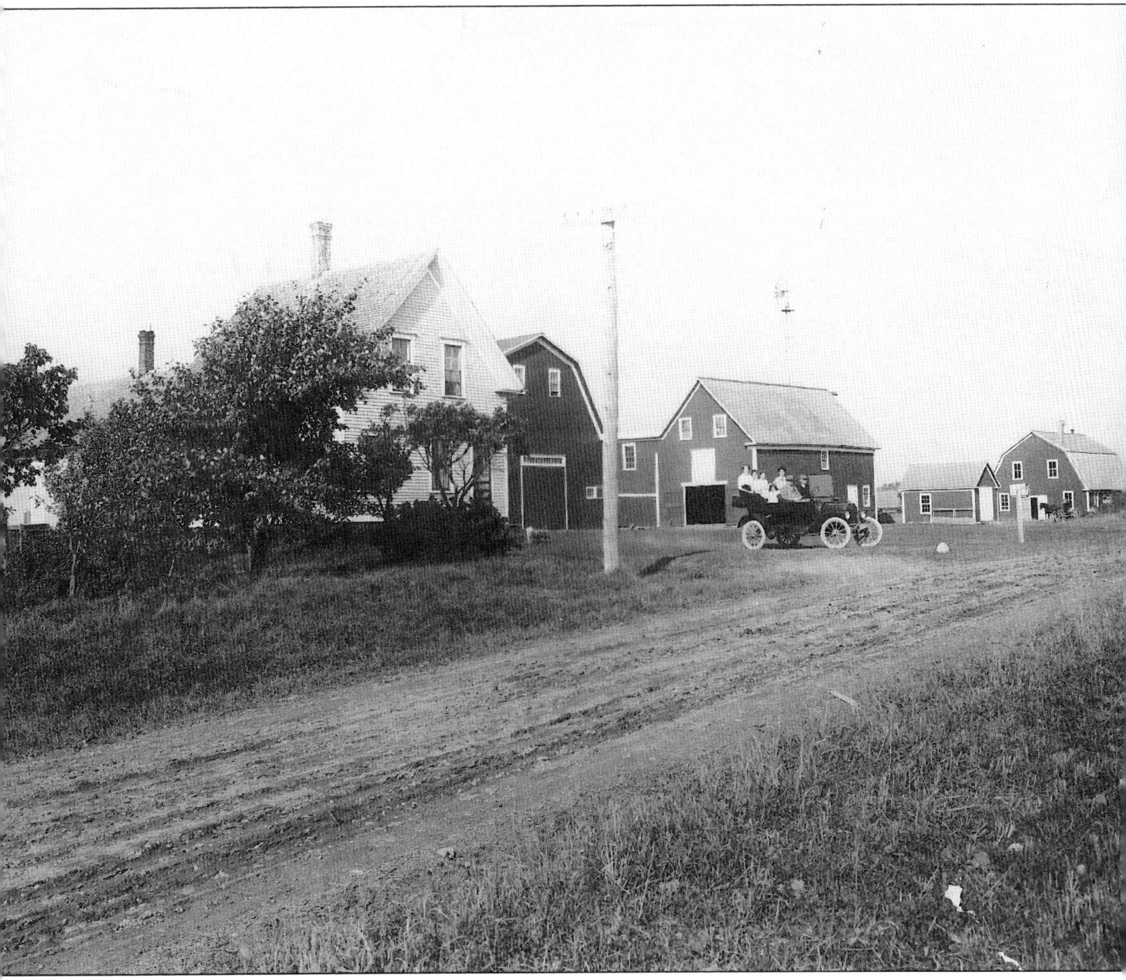

The same barn and house that belonged to Milton Smith in 1916 remain and are owned by his descendants today.

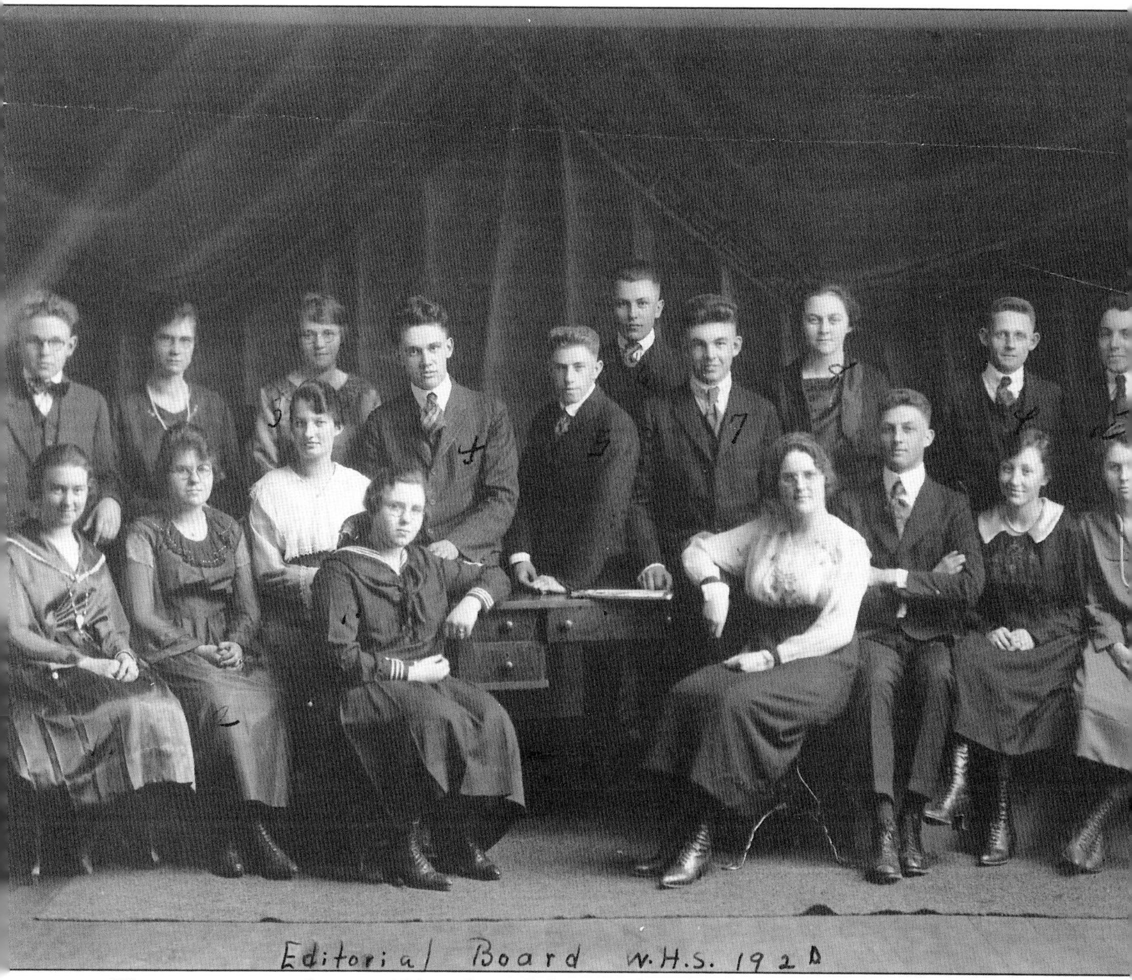

Writing memories that would last through history, the editorial board at Washburn High School in 1920 were, from left to right: (seated in front) Evelyn McIntire, Louisa Beardsley, Murry Churchill, Zoa Haines, and Ruth Turner; (front row) Mildred Duncan, Constance Brewer, Arlene Crouse, Job Churchill, Ray Carter, Ernest Grant, Howard Peary, Mary Churchill, Arnold Higgins, and Vaughn Kilpatrick; (back row, to the left) Harry Brewer, Lucia Stoddard, and unknown.

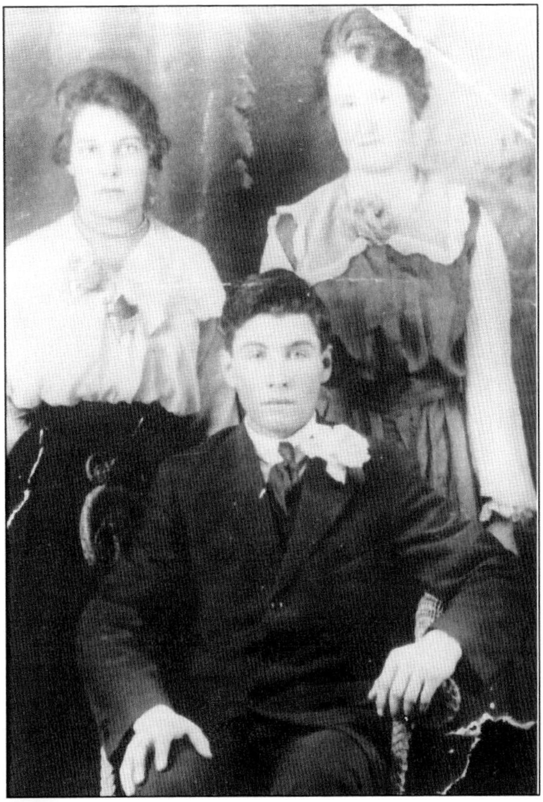

Henry Myshrall and Marguerite Myshrall were married in 1916 or 1917. Henry farmed and was in the Civil Service, working at military installations. Marguerite hired out as a housekeeper. And they had thirteen children! To the right is Henry's aunt, Ethel Embleton.

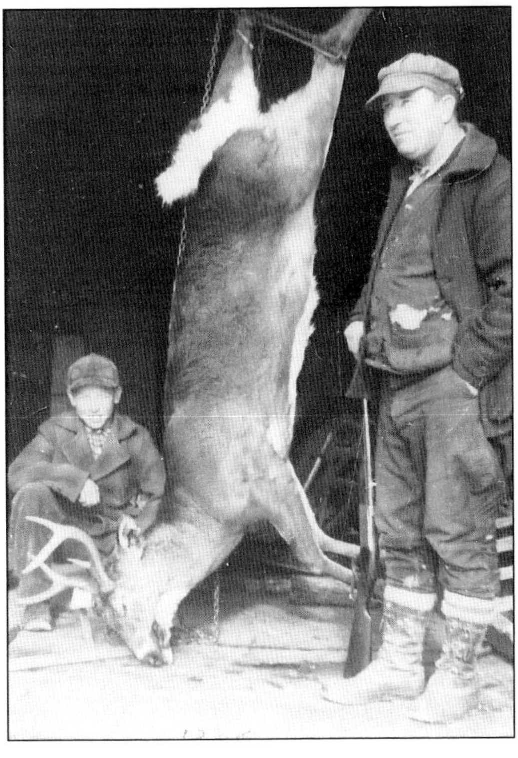

Harry Jr. (left) and Harry Maynard Sr. Harry Sr. was noted for his guiding, hunting, and fishing skills.

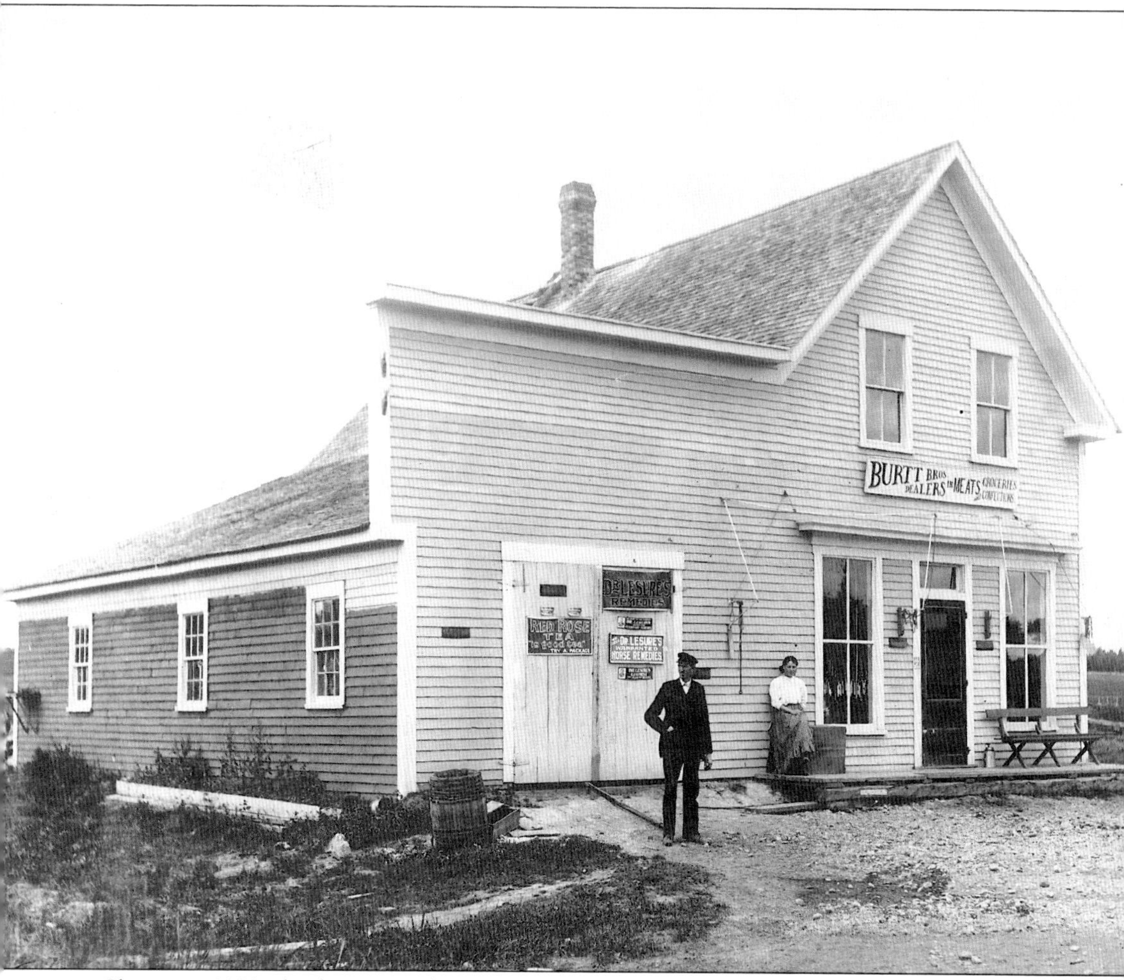

Shown in 1890, the first general store in East Washburn (what is known now as Crouseville) is now the post office.

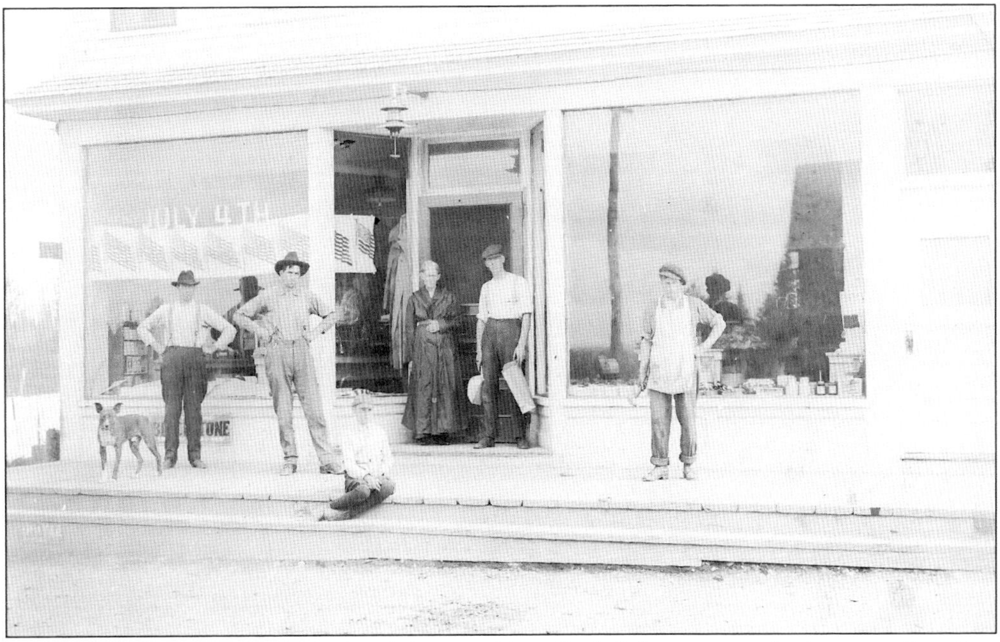

Fourth of July or not, the State Road Store at Chandler's Siding is open for business. Standing in the doorway are "Grammie" McGlauflin and Fred McGlauflin.

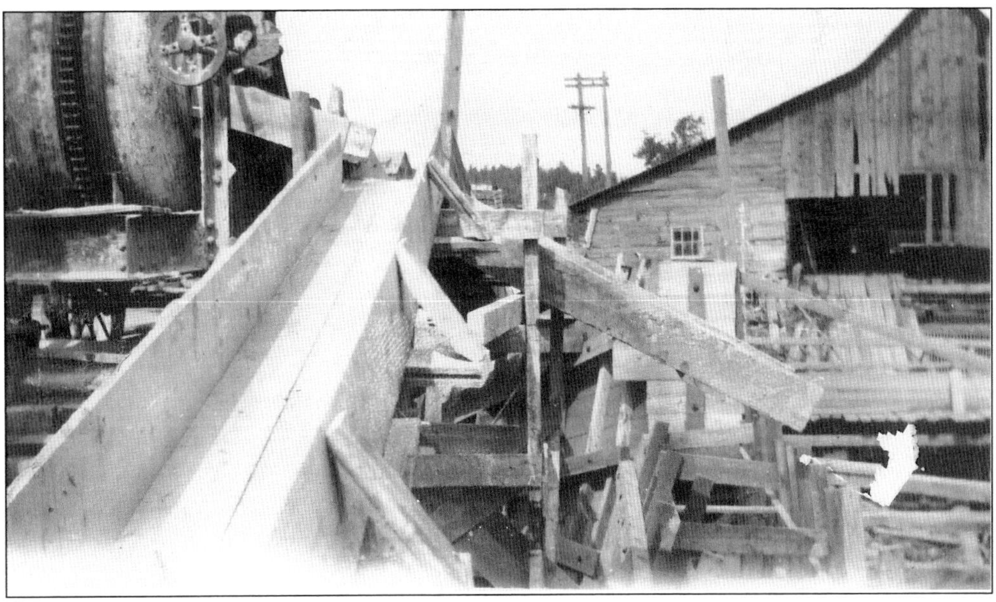
The Mapleton Saw Mill in the early 1920s later had a starch factory built behind it.

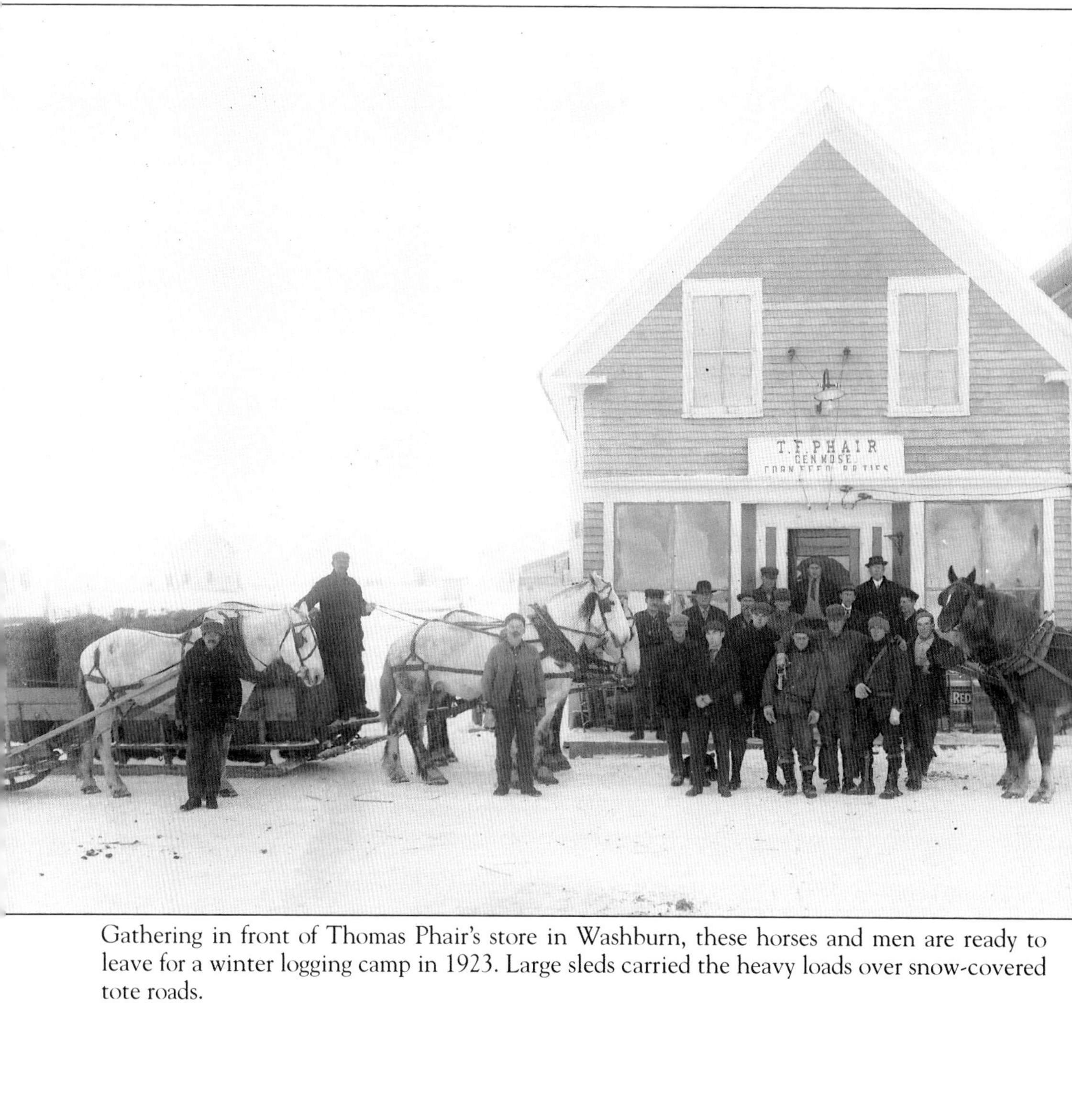

Gathering in front of Thomas Phair's store in Washburn, these horses and men are ready to leave for a winter logging camp in 1923. Large sleds carried the heavy loads over snow-covered tote roads.

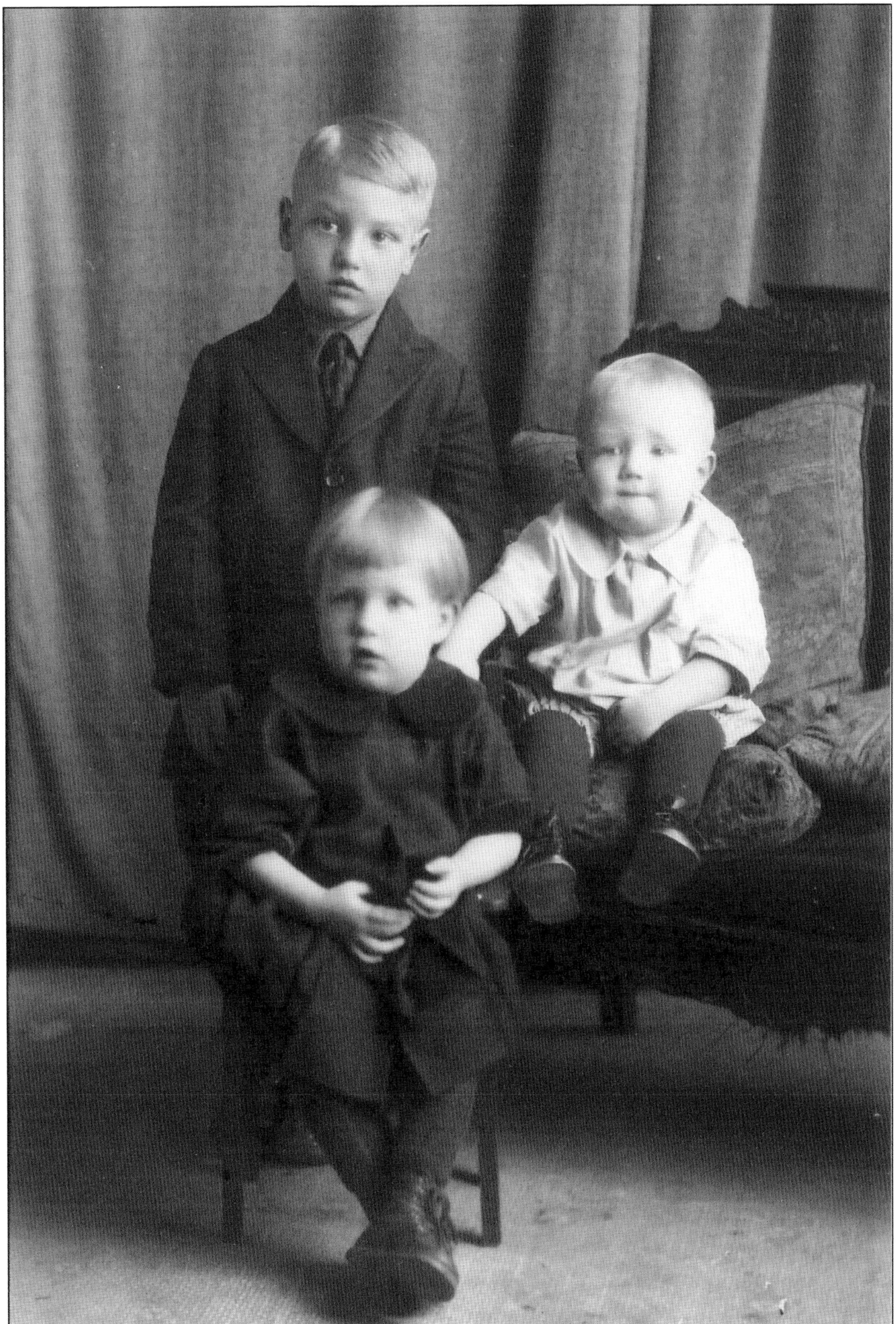

The third generation descendants from the owners of the Sperrey Hotel, Atwood Sperrey (standing), Millard Sperrey (seated), and Everett Sperrey entered into business and industry.

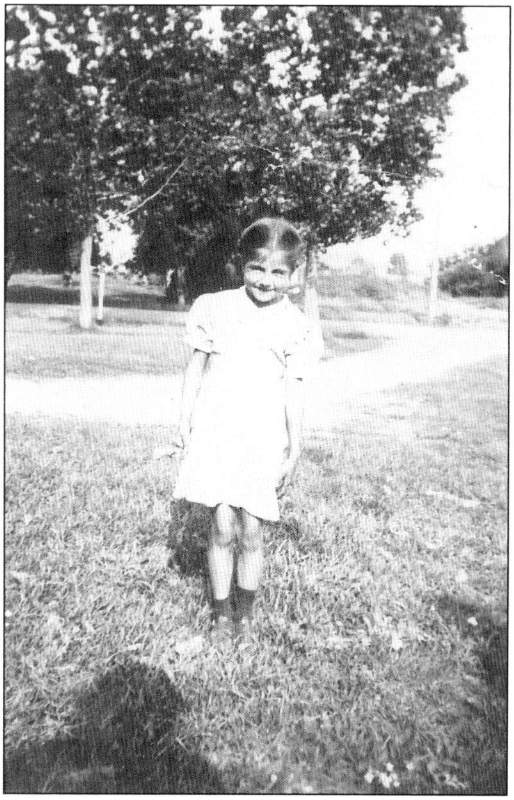

Norma Corapi worked in her father's store as a child and ran the Corapi General Store until 1982.

Housing Portage Lake's first post office, and originally owned by William Ross, this building was later sold to Ray Stevens and is still being used.

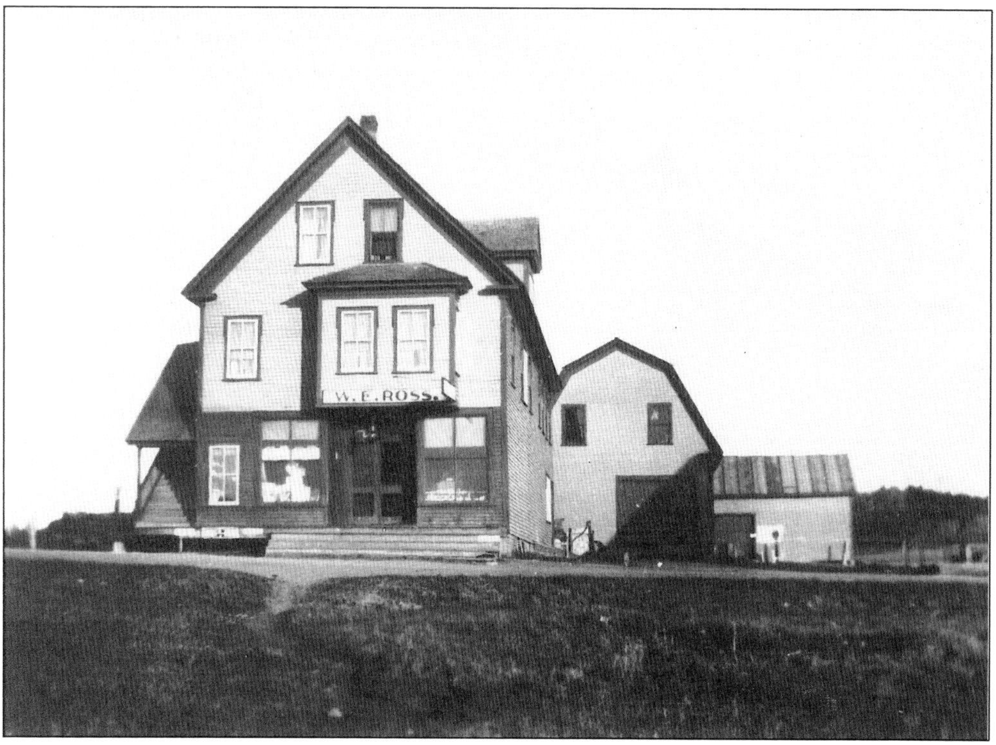

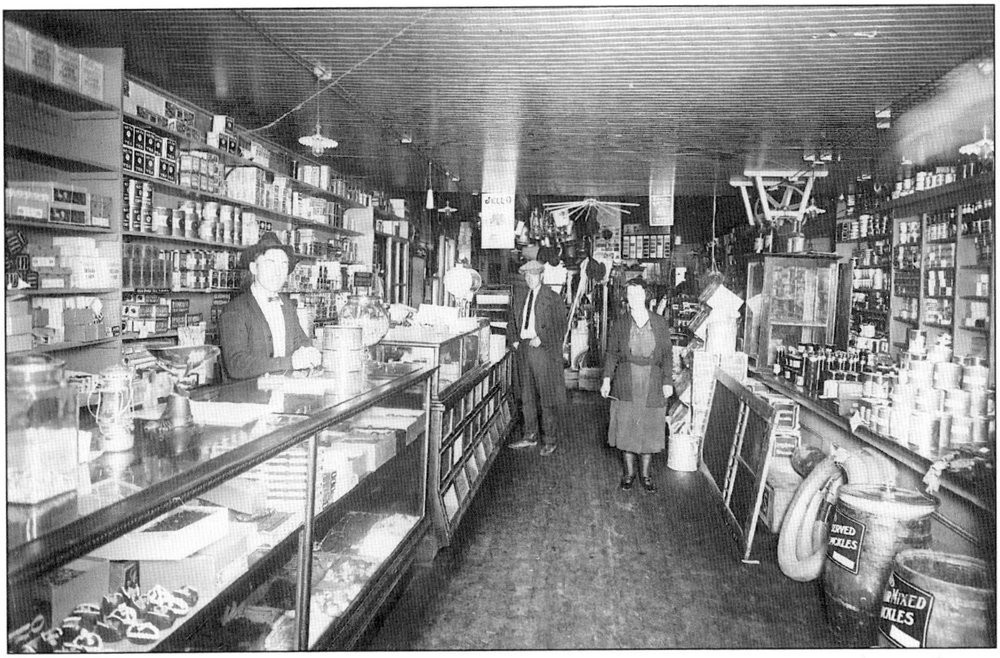

It is often quoted that "two heads are better than one." In this case, two stores together are better than one. Eva and Edna Crawford operated their area of business on one side of Lancaster's Store. In later years, Jesse Lancaster left Washburn, but he never forgot it. After he died, the First Baptist Church inherited a small legacy.

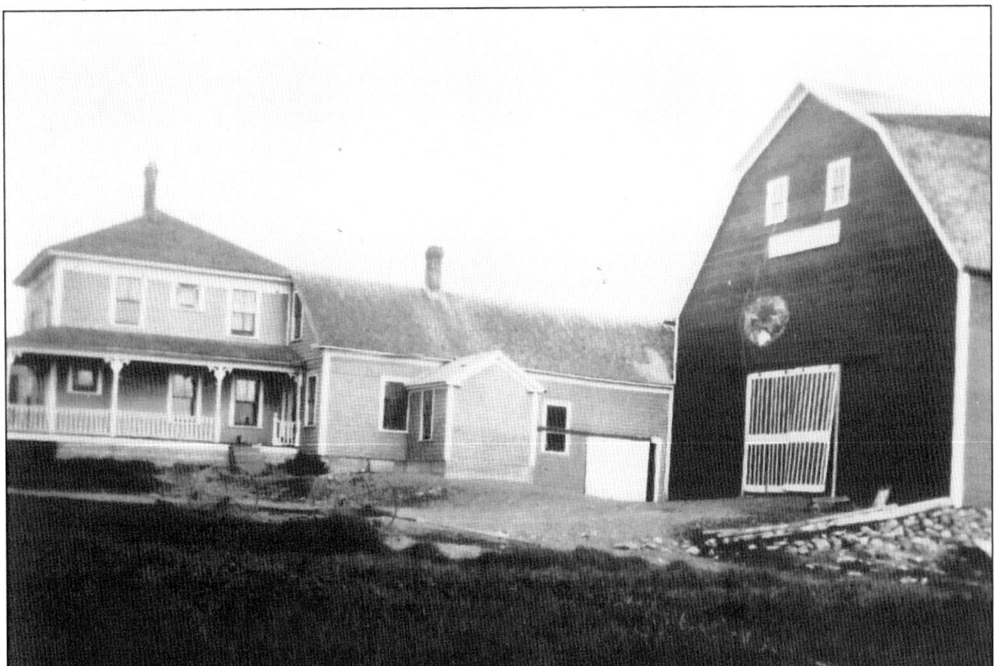

The sign on the barn says "Pleasant Hill Seed Farm." Belonging to Roy R. Higgins, the buildings burned in 1949, but they left a legacy of eight children, seven of whom went to college. The eighth continued the tradition of farming.

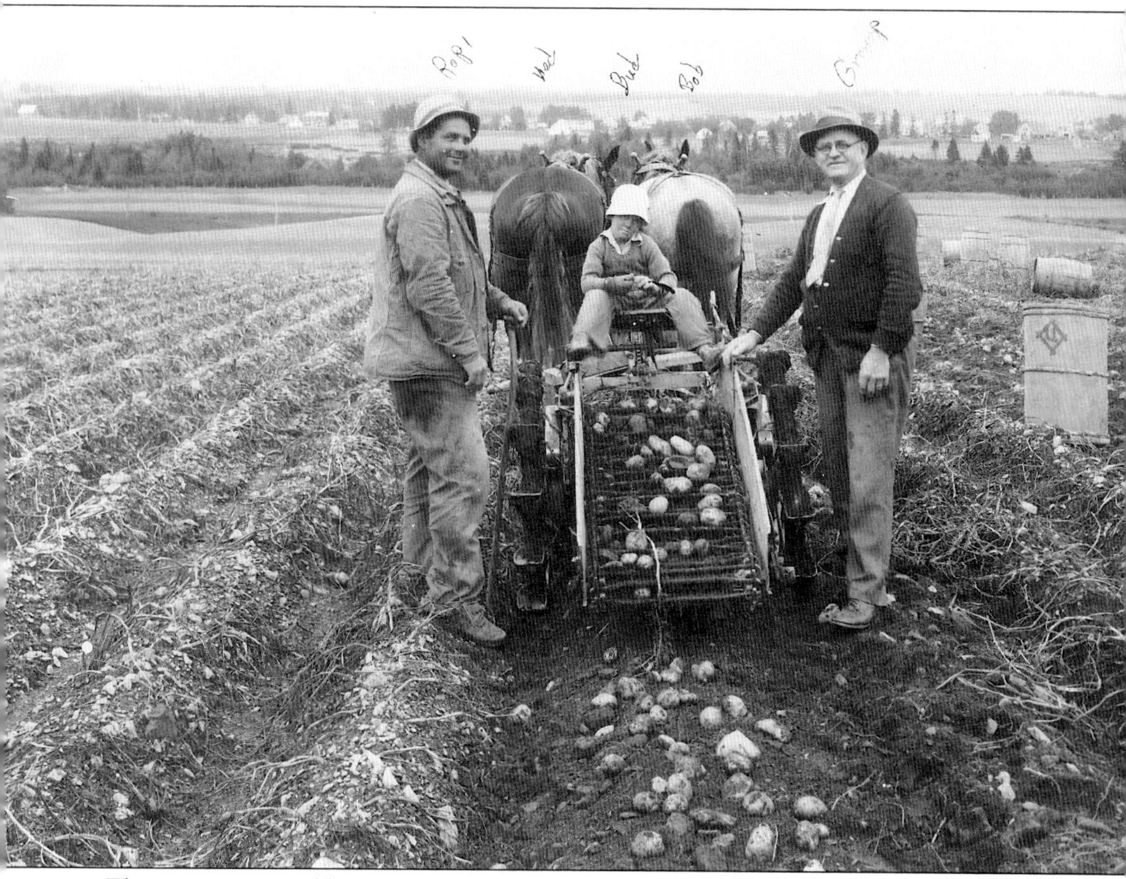

Three generations of farmers. From left to right Mac Umphrey, Bud Umphrey, and Ike Umphrey, assisted by horses Ned and Bob, work the homestead of Ike Umphrey in 1931.

Five

The Trials and Triumphs

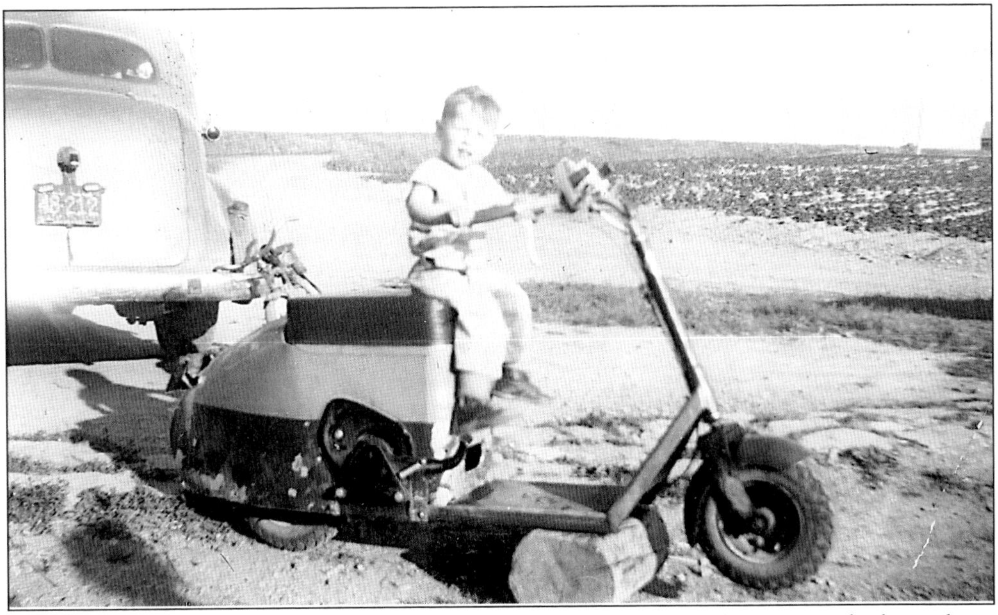

An "A" for effort! In 1948, Rodney Corey tries a motorized scooter that is just a little too large for him.

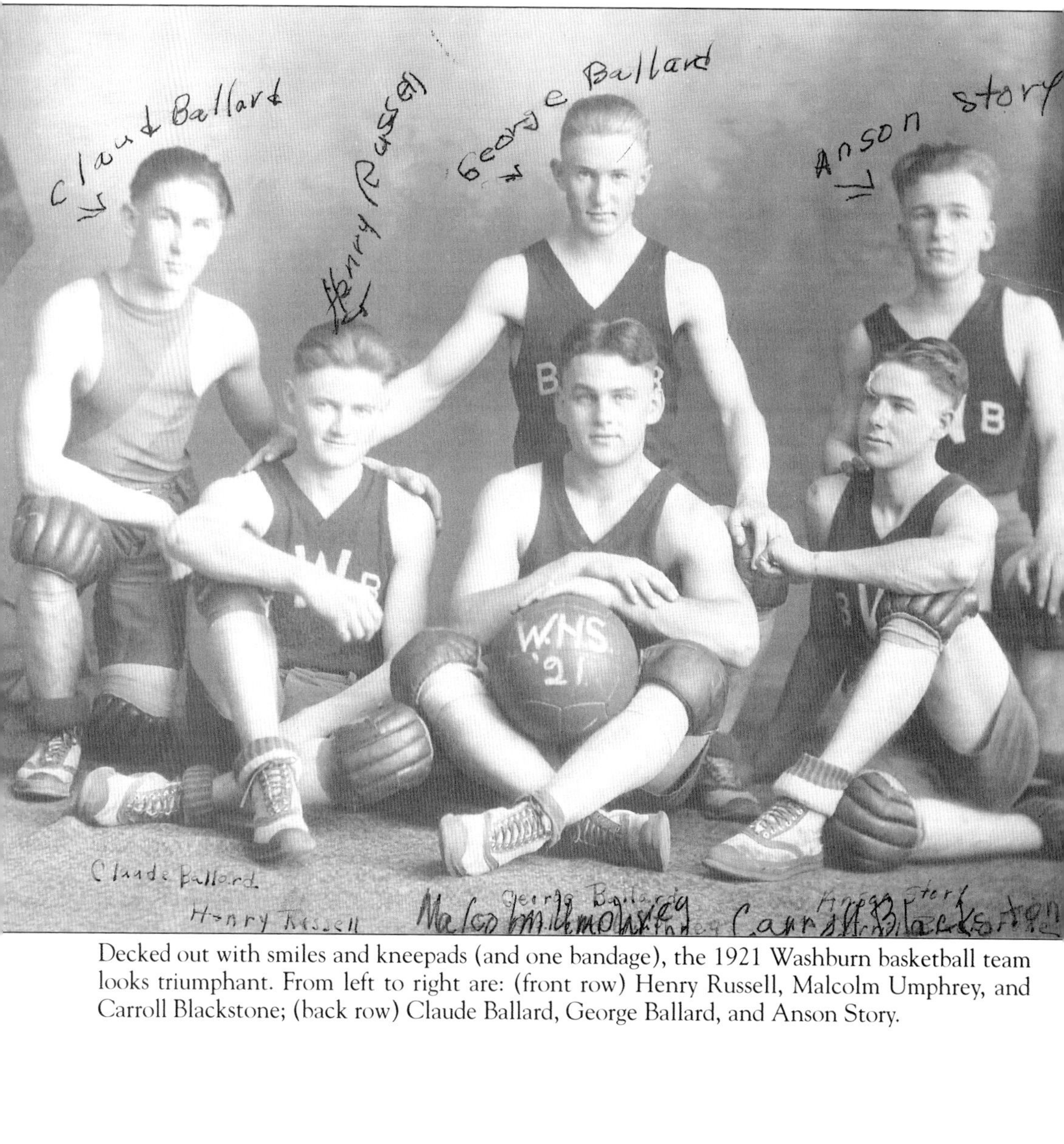

Decked out with smiles and kneepads (and one bandage), the 1921 Washburn basketball team looks triumphant. From left to right are: (front row) Henry Russell, Malcolm Umphrey, and Carroll Blackstone; (back row) Claude Ballard, George Ballard, and Anson Story.

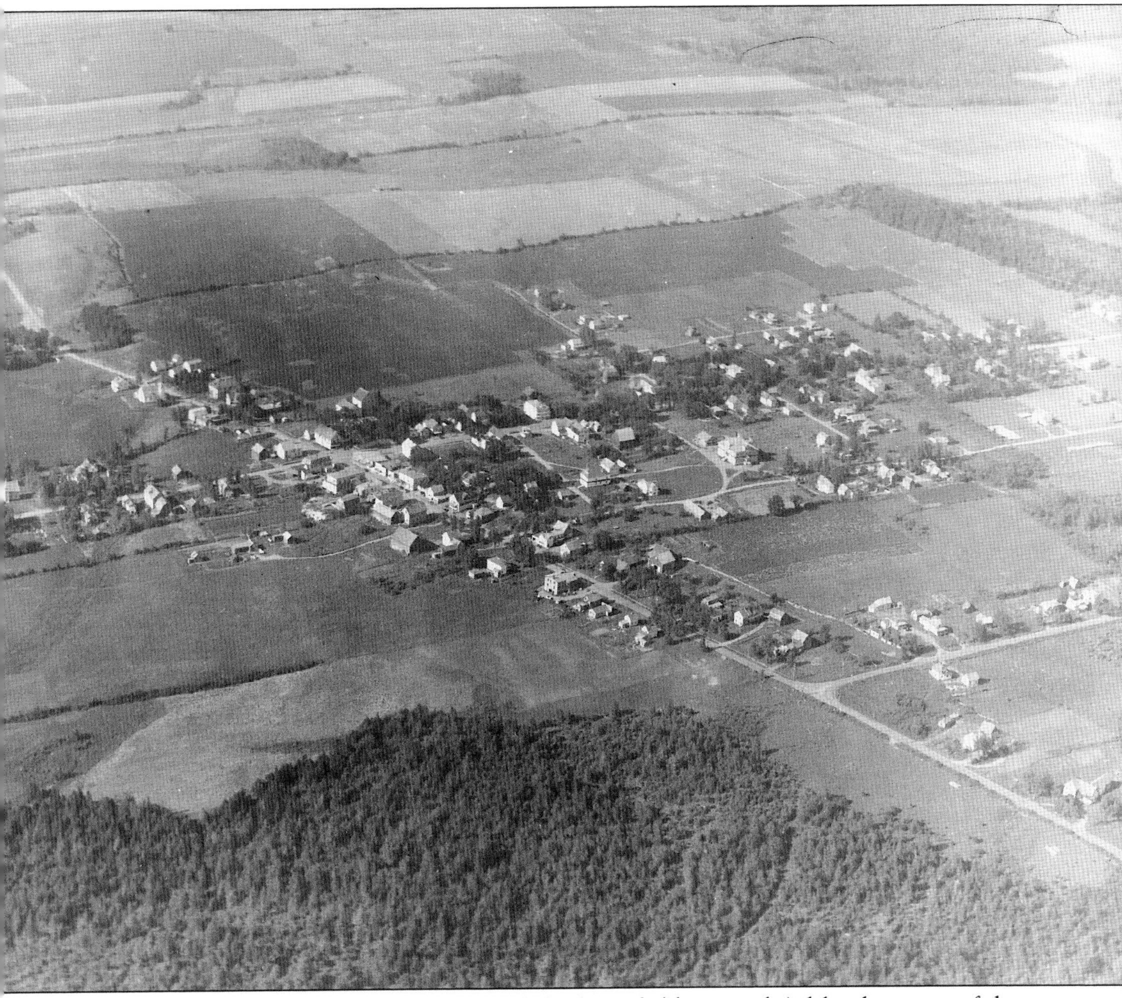

The rolling hills, the thick stands of trees, and the large fields around Ashland give proof that this quiet, rural area in 1927 is a hometown where neighbor knows neighbor, and life is good. Incorporated in 1837, thousands of acres of woodland separate Ashland and Canada.

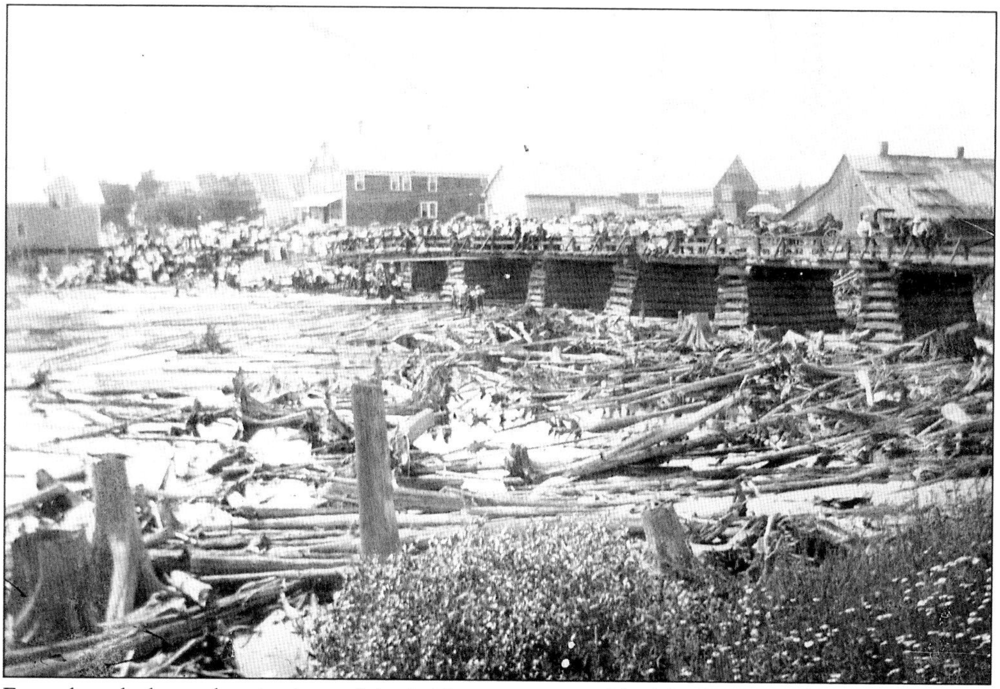

Even though the under pinnings of the bridge appear unstable, Mapleton residents take no heed as they watch the jammed log pile.

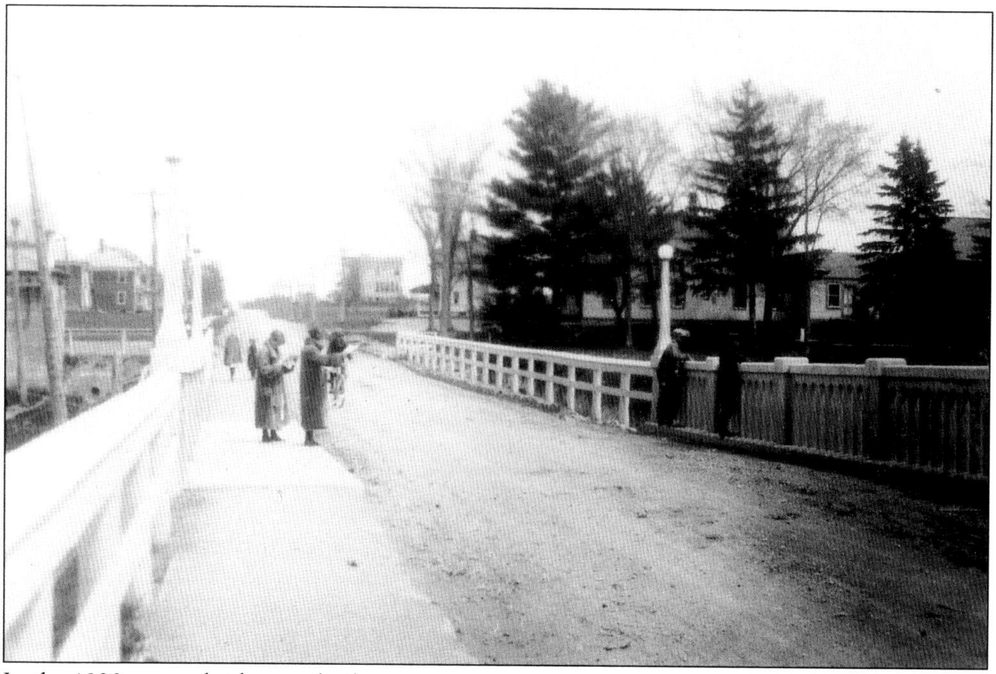

In the 1920s a new bridge was built.

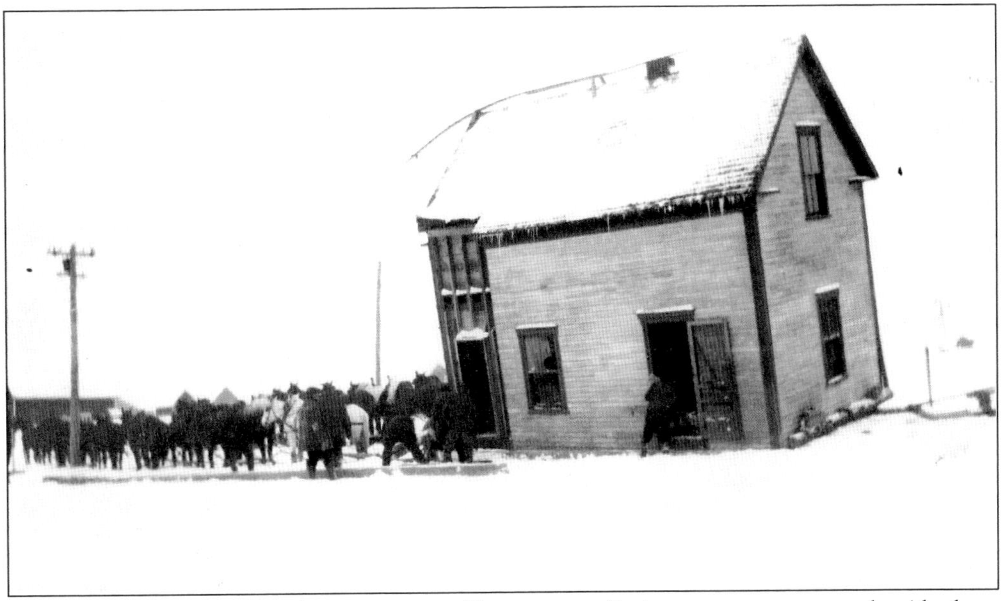

Moving a house in 1917 took manpower and horsepower. Easier to move on snow, the Abraham Crouse home was moved from its former location in Crouseville to the Lake Road, 3 miles away.

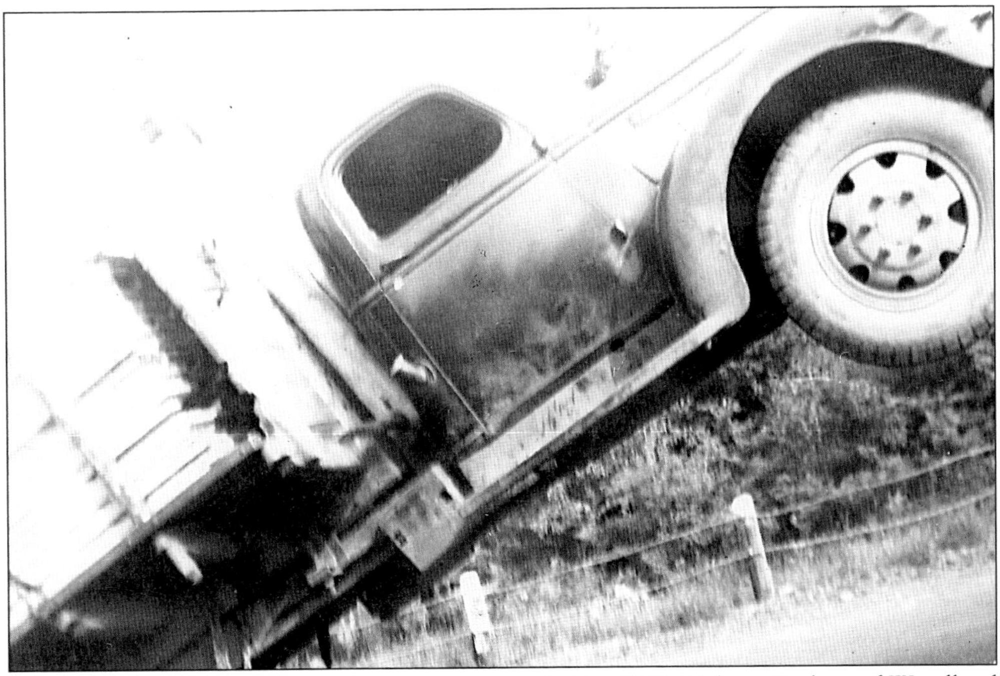

At times the enthusiasm for work goes a step too far! In 1939 Hjalmar Carlson of Woodland loaded his truck with lumber from a building he had torn down and was to redistribute. The load, however, was too heavy and tipped the cab skyward.

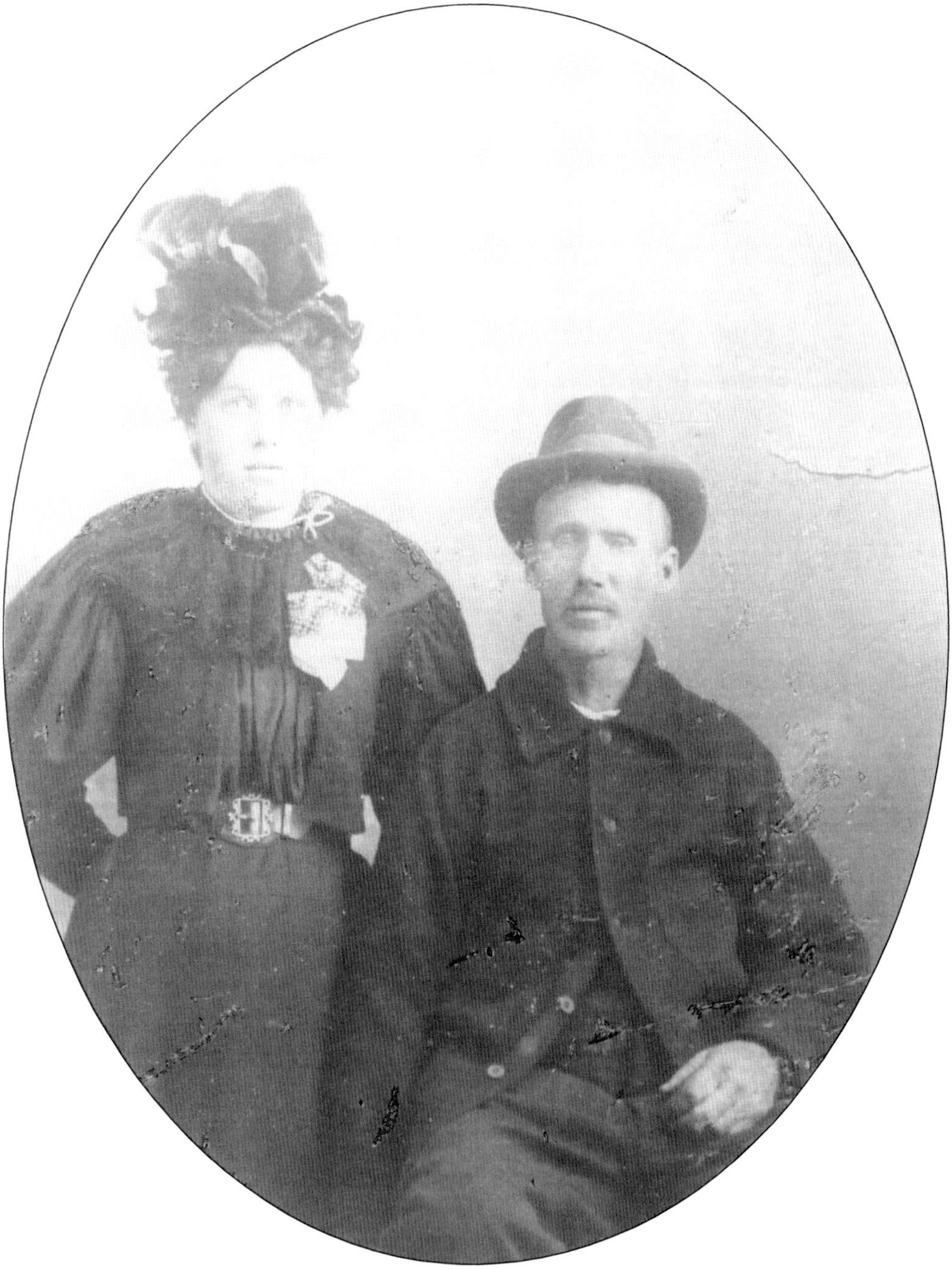

James Cochran (right) went down to the stream in Woodland to watch the first delegation of the Swedish people arrive. His daughter Ada (left) wrote down that when he returned to the house he said, "They look just like us."

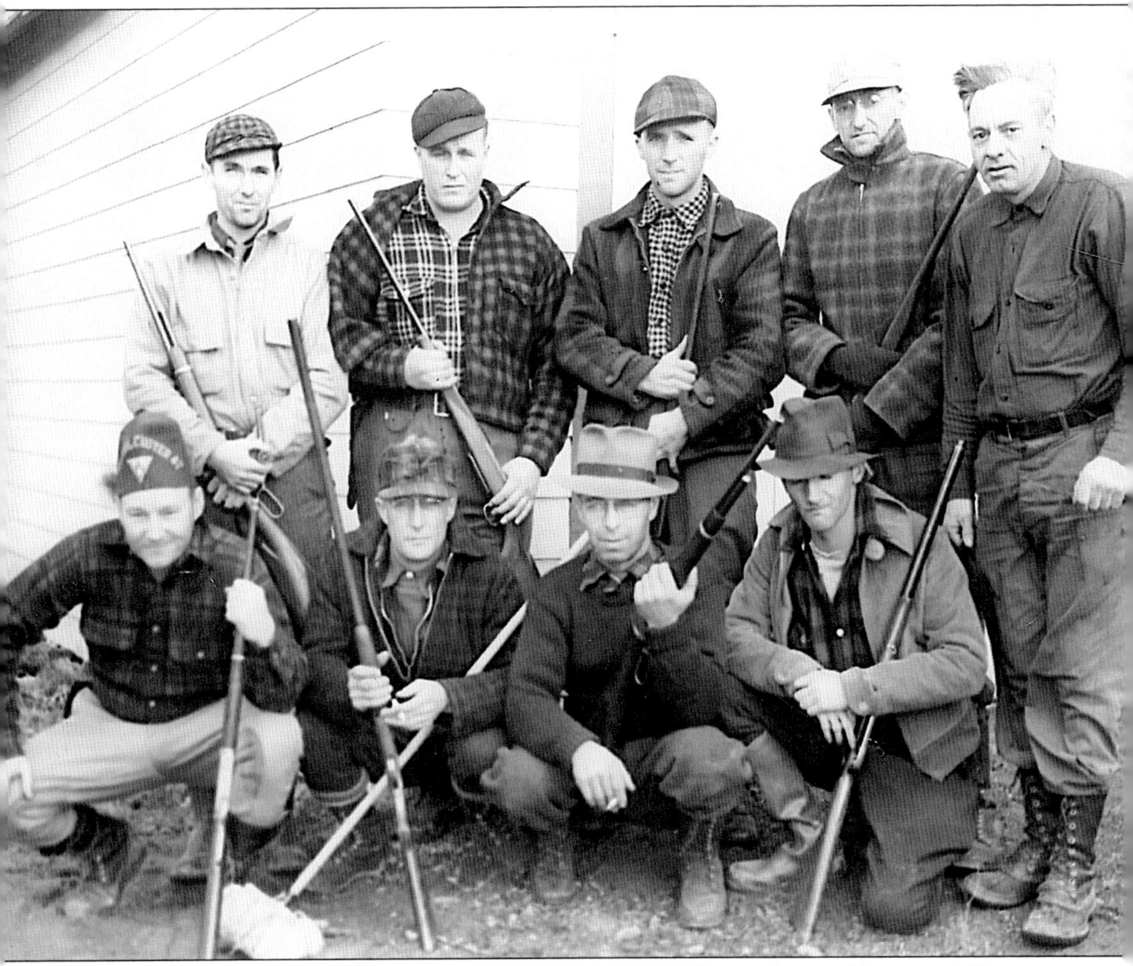

Looking forward to a hunting trip at Big Lake in 1940. From left to right are: (front row) Harry Drake, Arthur Jordan, Charlie Carlton, and Herb Jardine; (back row) Jasper Jardine, Claude Hemphill, Ralph Crouse, Harry Rand, and Carroll Bates.

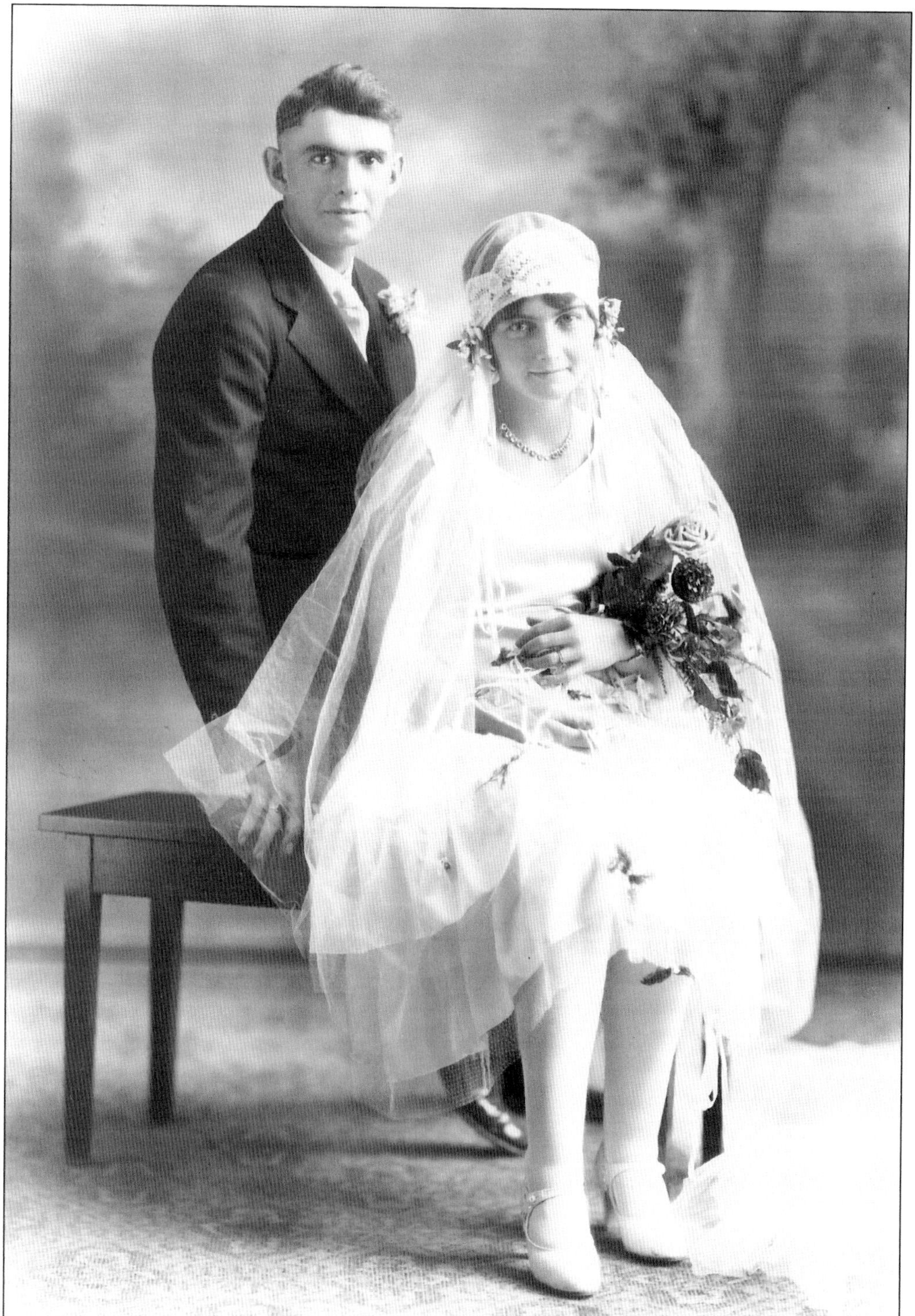

Resembling Miss America in her 1925 wedding dress, Lillian Russell became Mrs. Arthur Plissey. The two became a farming family and had two children, Verle and Judy.

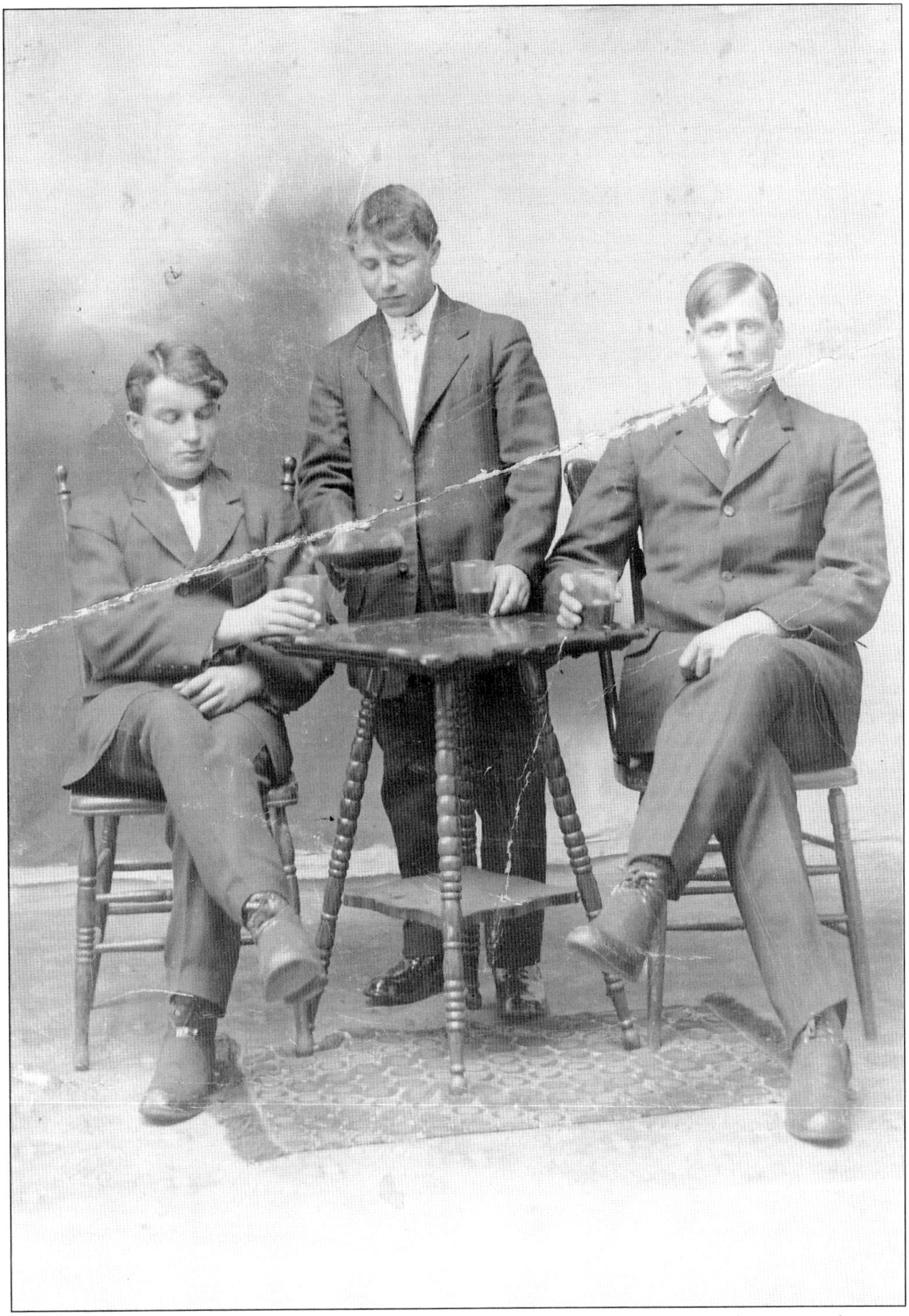

After working in the woods all winter, these three cousins dress up, relax, and enjoy civilization in this 1912 photograph. From left to right are Israel Vallaincourt, Hubert Gagnon, and Ernest Madore.

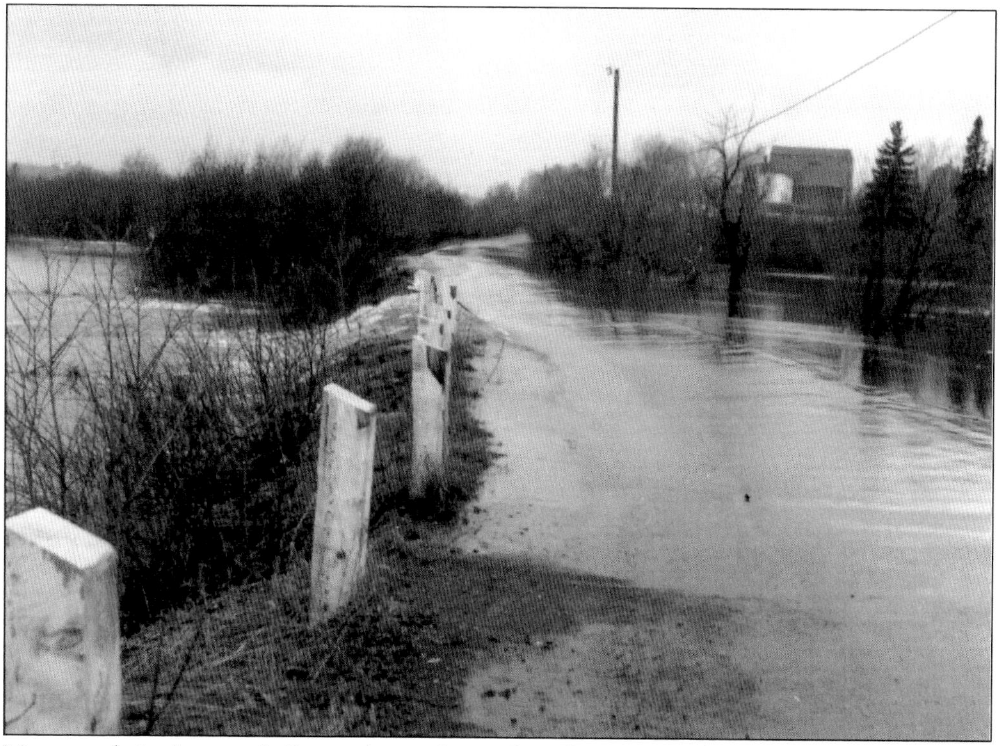

Most people in Aroostook County know the truth in the saying, "if you don't like the weather, wait a minute." In 1955, however, the weather however took a turn seldom experienced. Hurricane Edna caused many serious washouts and blackouts. This photograph is of the flooding on the Gardner Creek Road. Ken Duncan's farm buildings are on the rear right.

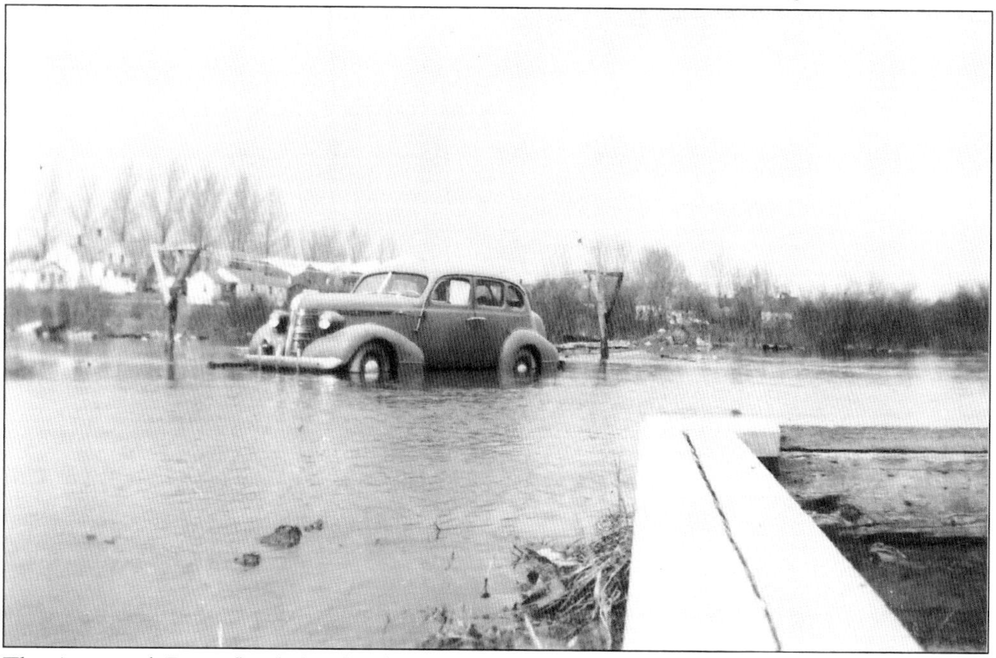

The Aroostook River flooded its banks in the spring of 1945.

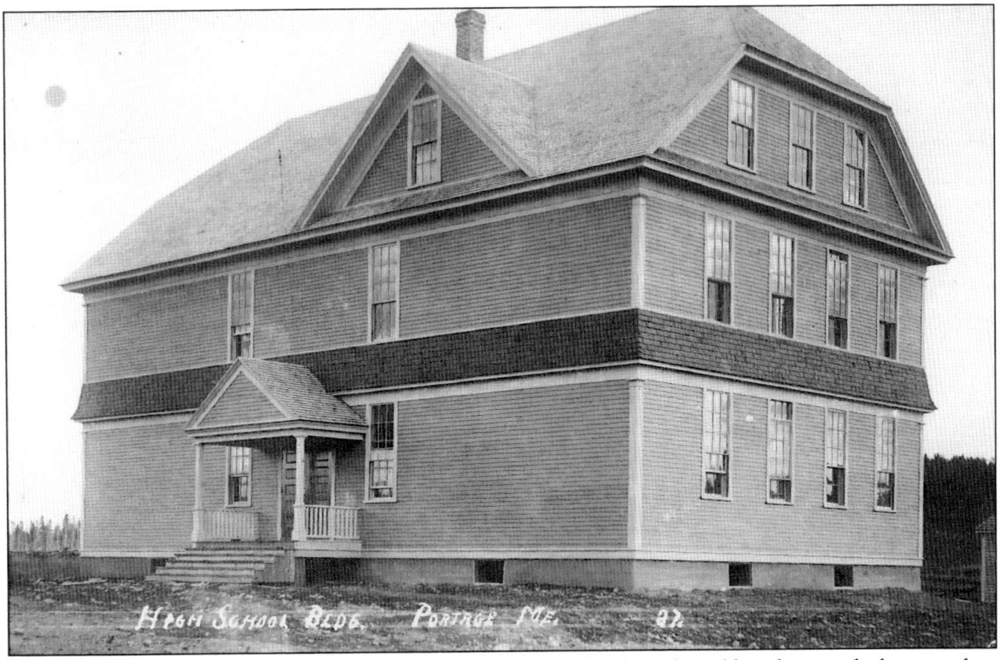

As population dwindled, this high school at Portage Lake found itself without inhabitants, but in 1916 it flourished with the voices of students resounding in its hallways.

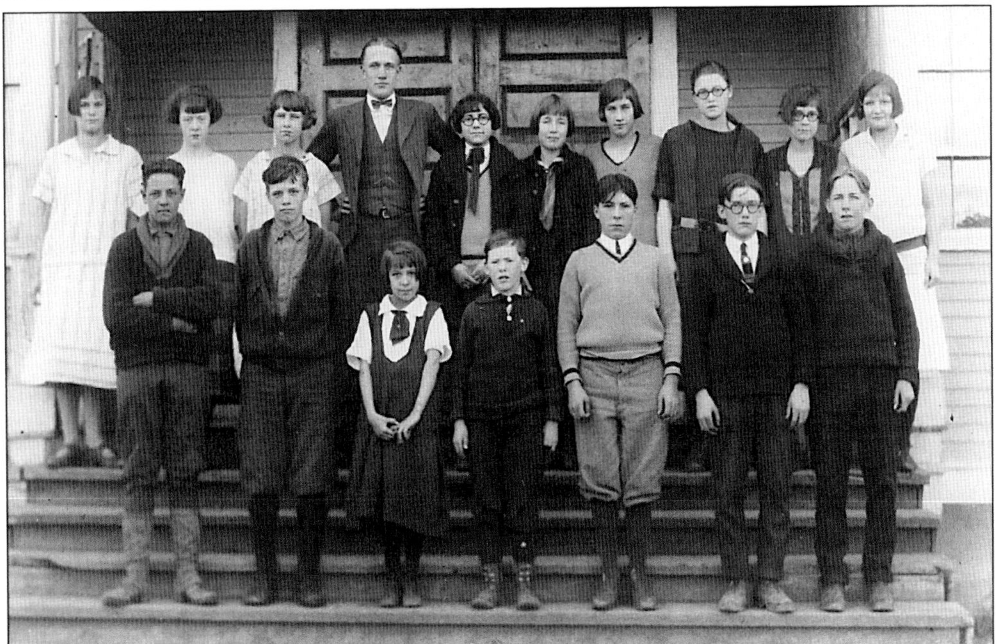

Although students now travel 10 miles each day to Ashland for their education, in 1926 the high school boasted 16 students and only one teacher. From left to right are: (front row) Herbert Stevens, Eddie Randall, Cecil Alward, Bonnie Condon, Vassar Tanguay, Frank Lee, and Arthur McCormack; (back row) Evelyn Pinette Johnson, Minona Wilcox, Winnie (?) Stookford, Mr. Andrews (teacher), Sylvia Tanguay Snead, Grace McCormack, Eunice Sutherland Davenport, Marion Pinette Hathaway, Isabelle Paradis, and Lucy (?) Kirkpatrick.

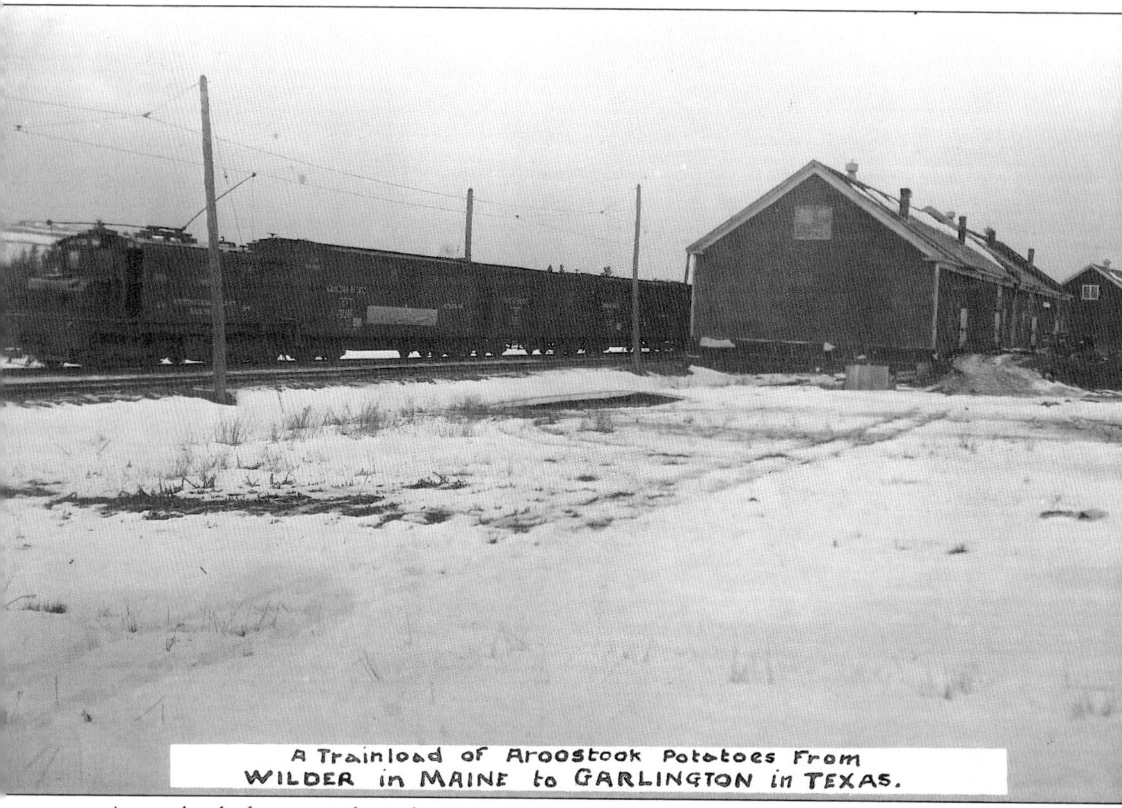

A trainload of potatoes from the Gene Smith potato houses leaves Wilders Siding in Washburn for Texas via the Aroostook Valley Railroad. Later both storage facilities burned.

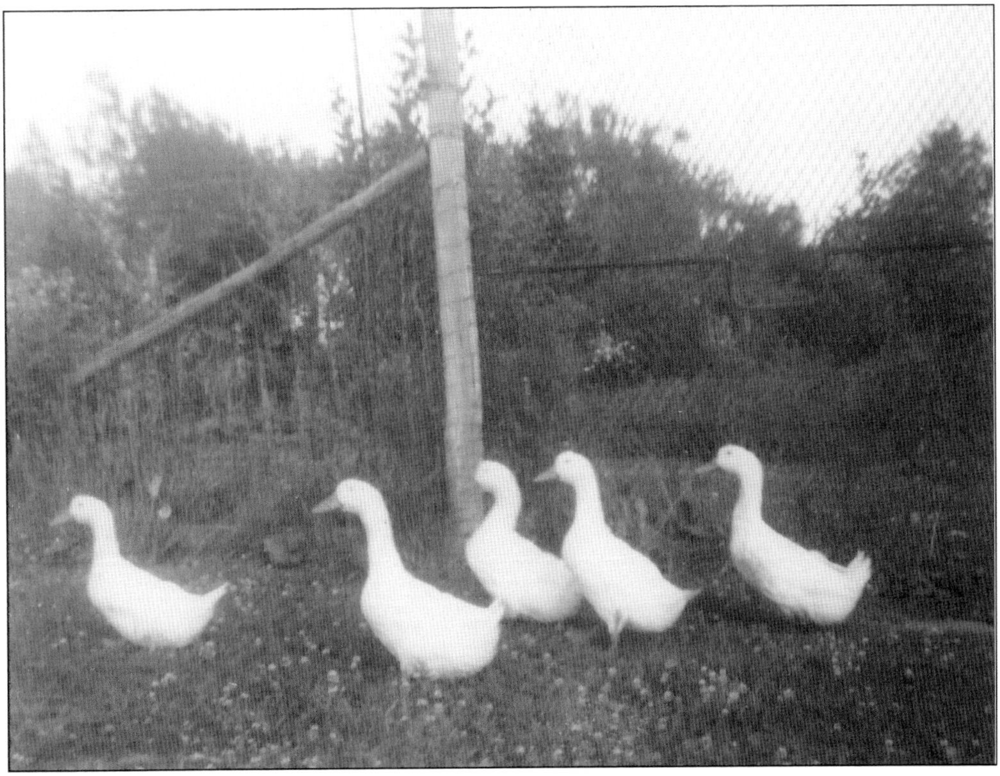

Frequently, horses and dogs, and many times cows, were given names by their owners. In 1948 Aurele Gagnon of Portage Lake went a step further and named his geese! Quacker is leading the way, with (in order) Winken, Blinken, and Nod following. Stupid brings up the rear.

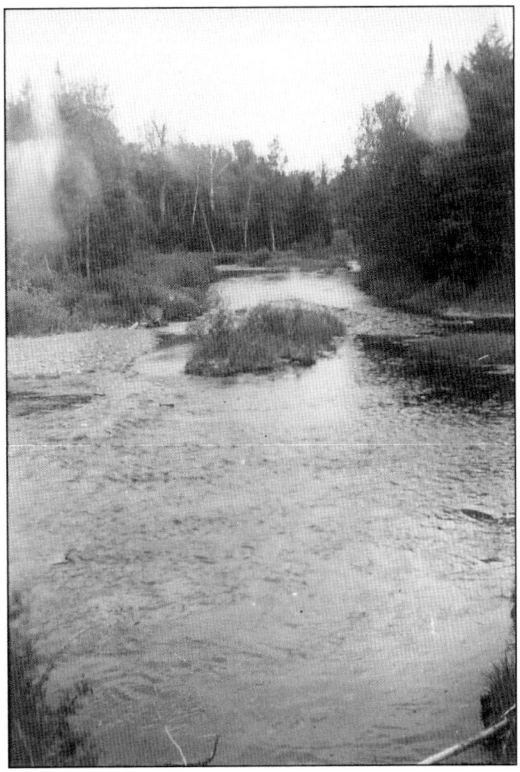

This photograph of the Machias River cannot be dated, but it was probably taken before the dam was built. Its pristine beauty is a reminder to hunters and fishermen and all nature lovers that little changes in the outdoor wilds of Central Aroostook.

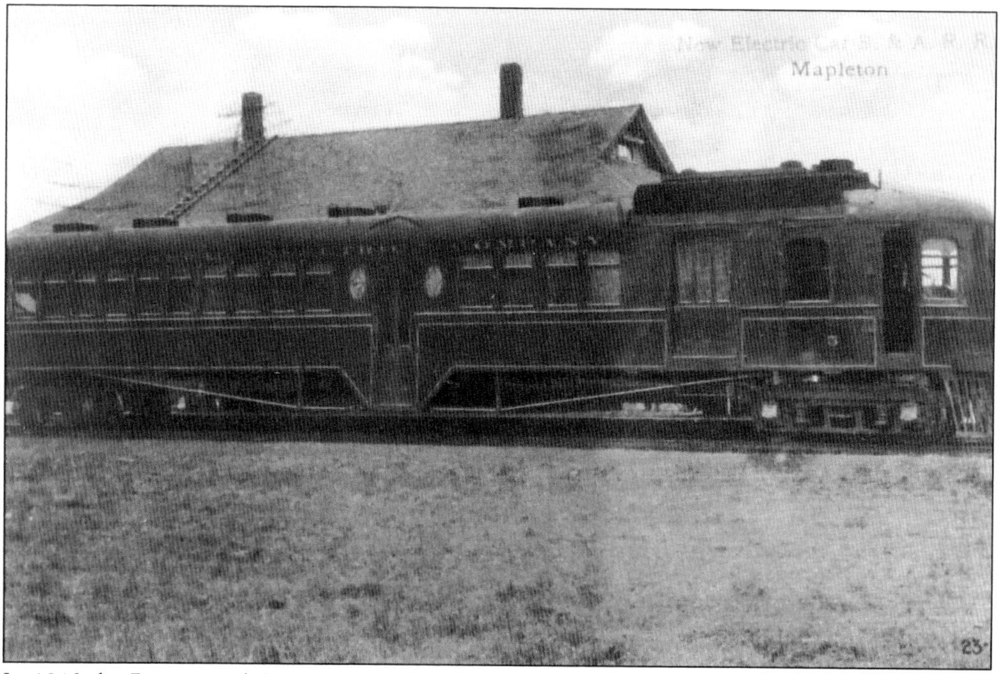

In 1913 the Bangor and Aroostook Railroad was persuaded by the townspeople in Mapleton to provide an electric car for their convenience.

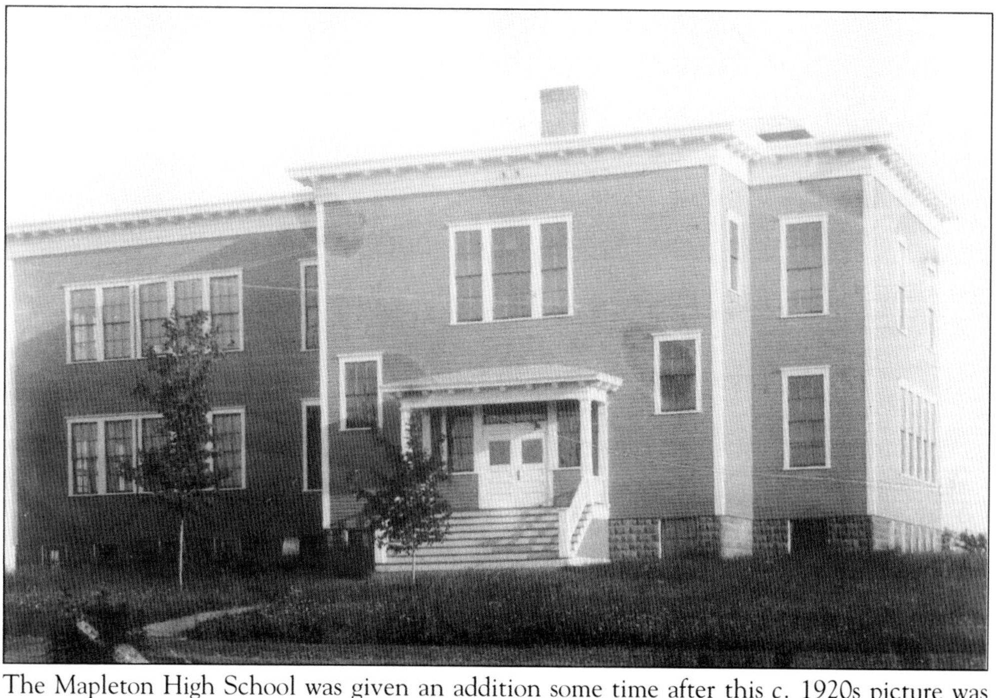

The Mapleton High School was given an addition some time after this *c.* 1920s picture was taken. The school later burned and was never rebuilt.

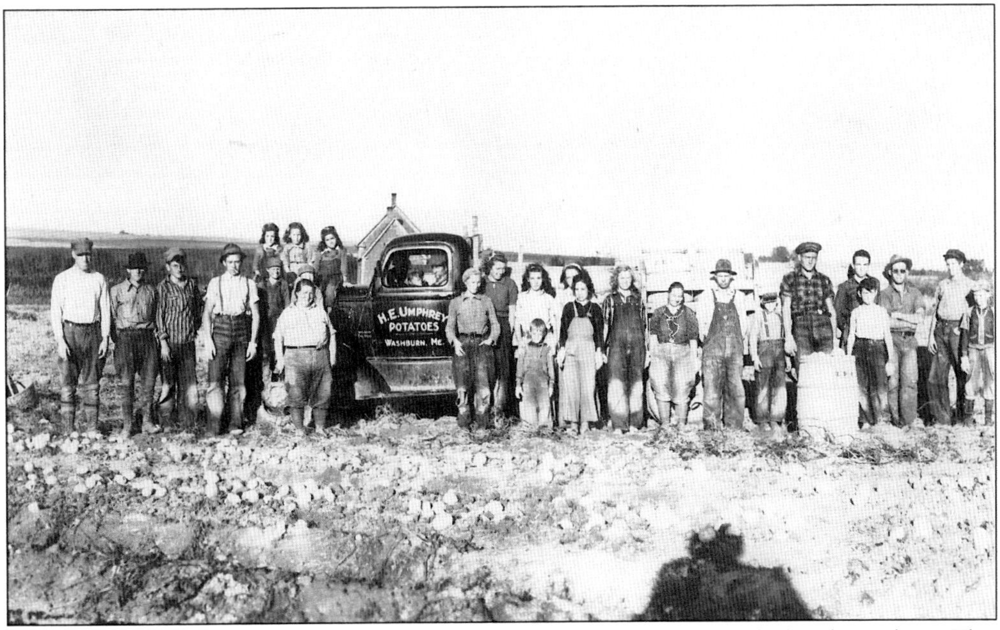

A glance at the knees of these potato pickers will attest to the hard work they have done. This harvesting crew was hired by the H.E. Umphrey farm in Washburn, c. 1939.

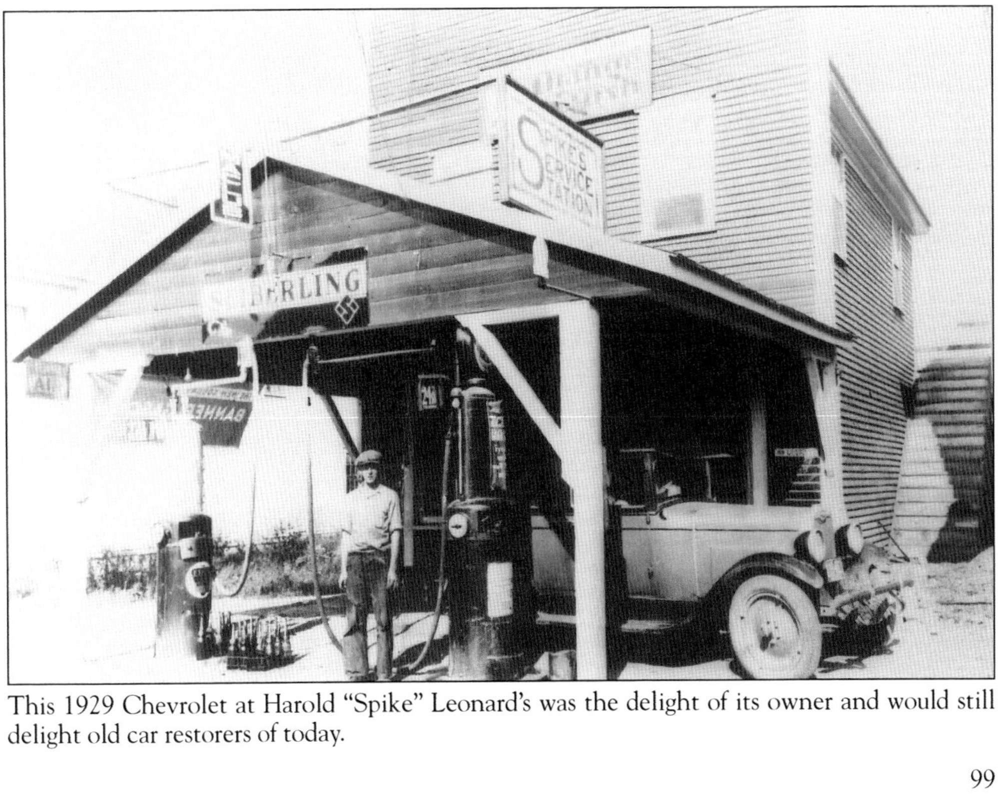

This 1929 Chevrolet at Harold "Spike" Leonard's was the delight of its owner and would still delight old car restorers of today.

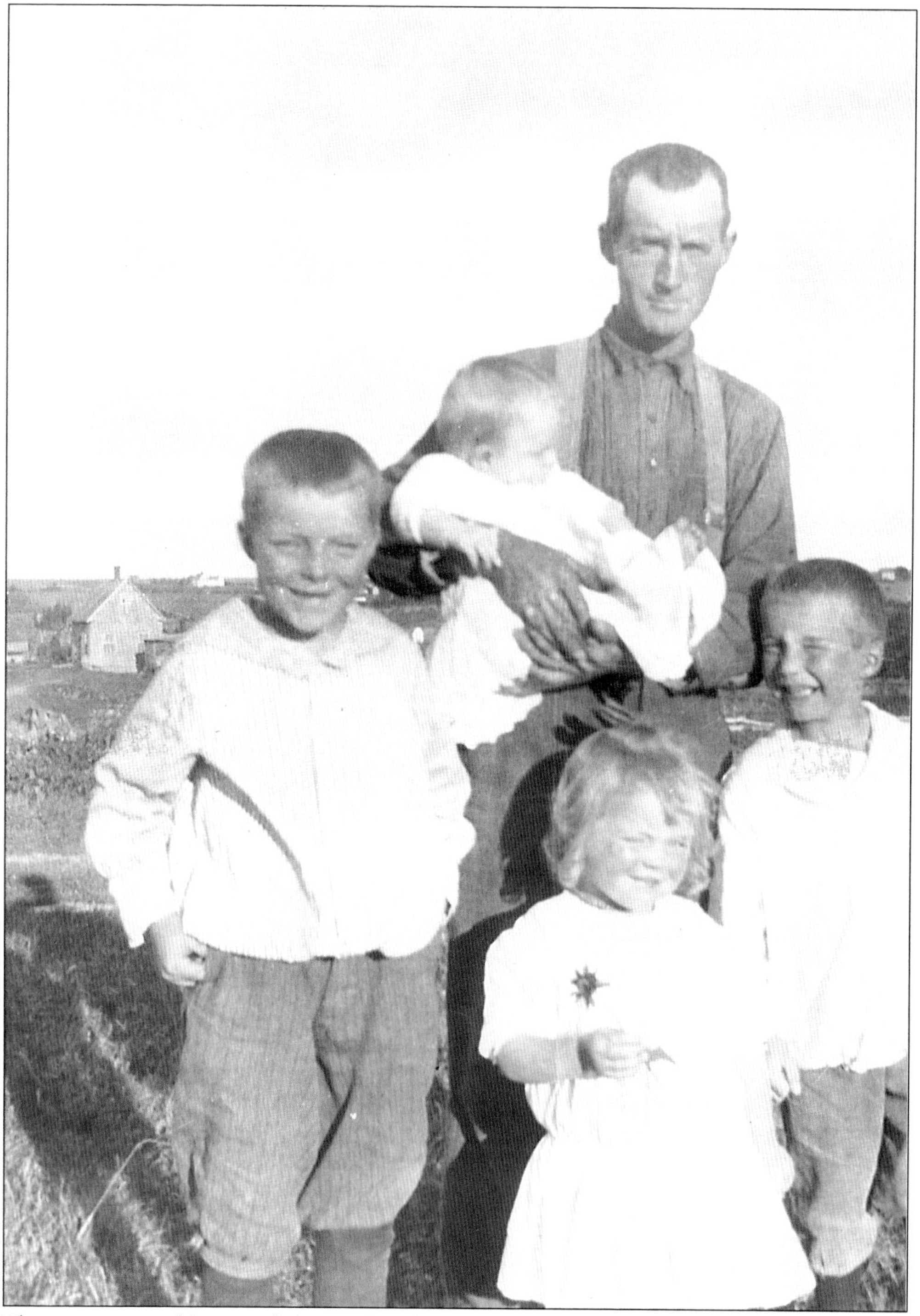

The remoteness of farms and the modes of travel of the day forced a strong reliance between family members in spread-out rural farms. The happy Russell family epitomize this. Father Charles holds baby Willard, while, from left to right, Jesse, Ella Mae, and Sullivan smile at the cameraman.

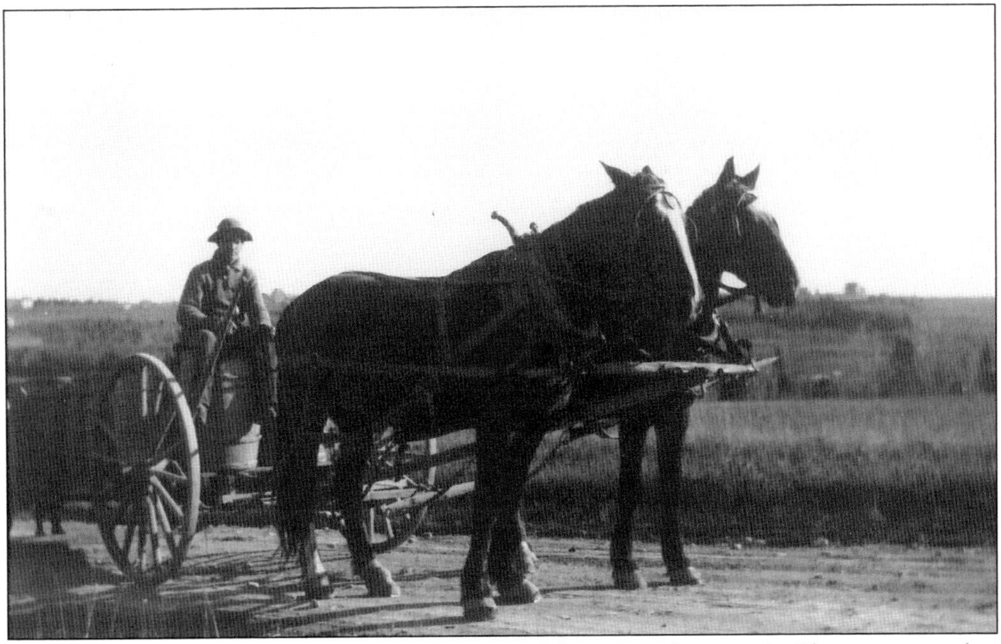

Note the two feet in the lower left-hand corner of this 1918 photograph. The story goes that Charles Russell was hauling potatoes to the starch factory and didn't know that three-year-old Bill hitched a ride. The horses are Prince (with the white face) and Frank.

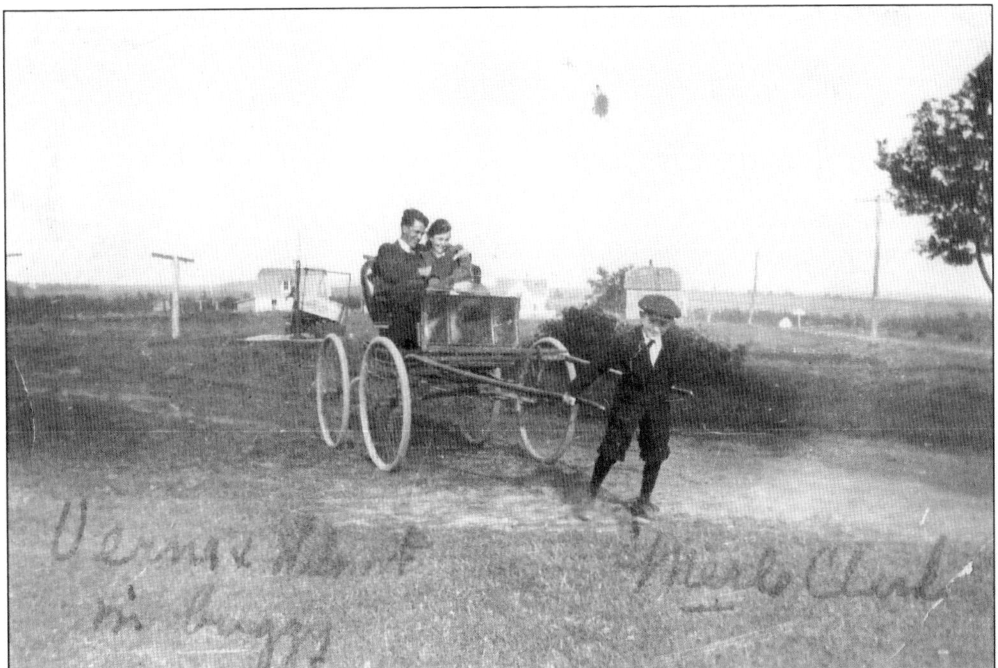

For the lack of a horse . . . Honeymooners Wilmont and Verna Churchill are being pulled to their destination by Merle Clark in this 1919 photograph.

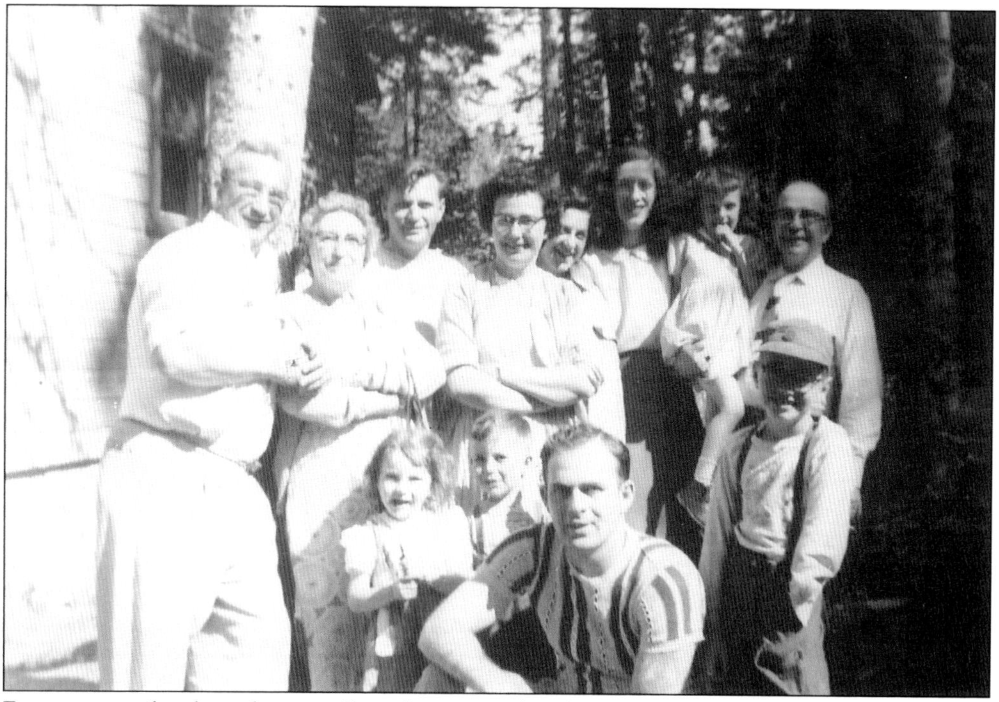

Easter meant family gatherings. First there was church to attend. Then came a big dinner of beans and partridge. That might not sound unusual, but Ernest Smart and Bill Eagle did not take the usual route to the Catholic church at Portage Lake. They swam, beginning at the camp directly across the lake and carrying their clothes in bags. From left to right are: (front row) Christie Smart, David Despres, Ted Despres, and Tim Eagle; (back row) Ernest Smart, Phoebe Smart, Bill Eagle, Bonnie Eagle, Del Despres, Flavie Eagle, Carolyn Eagle, and David Smart.

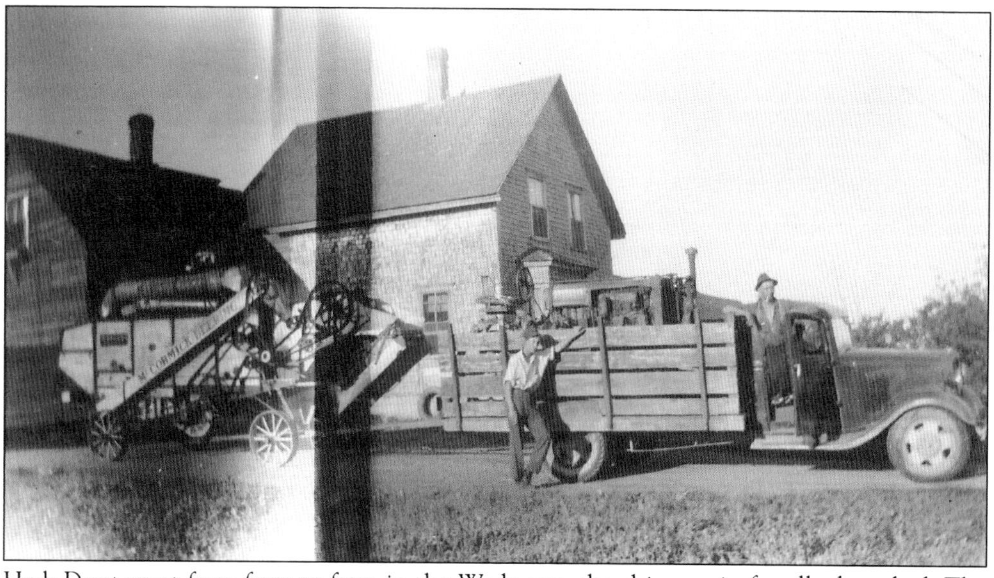

Herb Drost went from farm to farm in the Wade area thrashing grain for all who asked. The thrasher on back of the truck had old iron wheels.

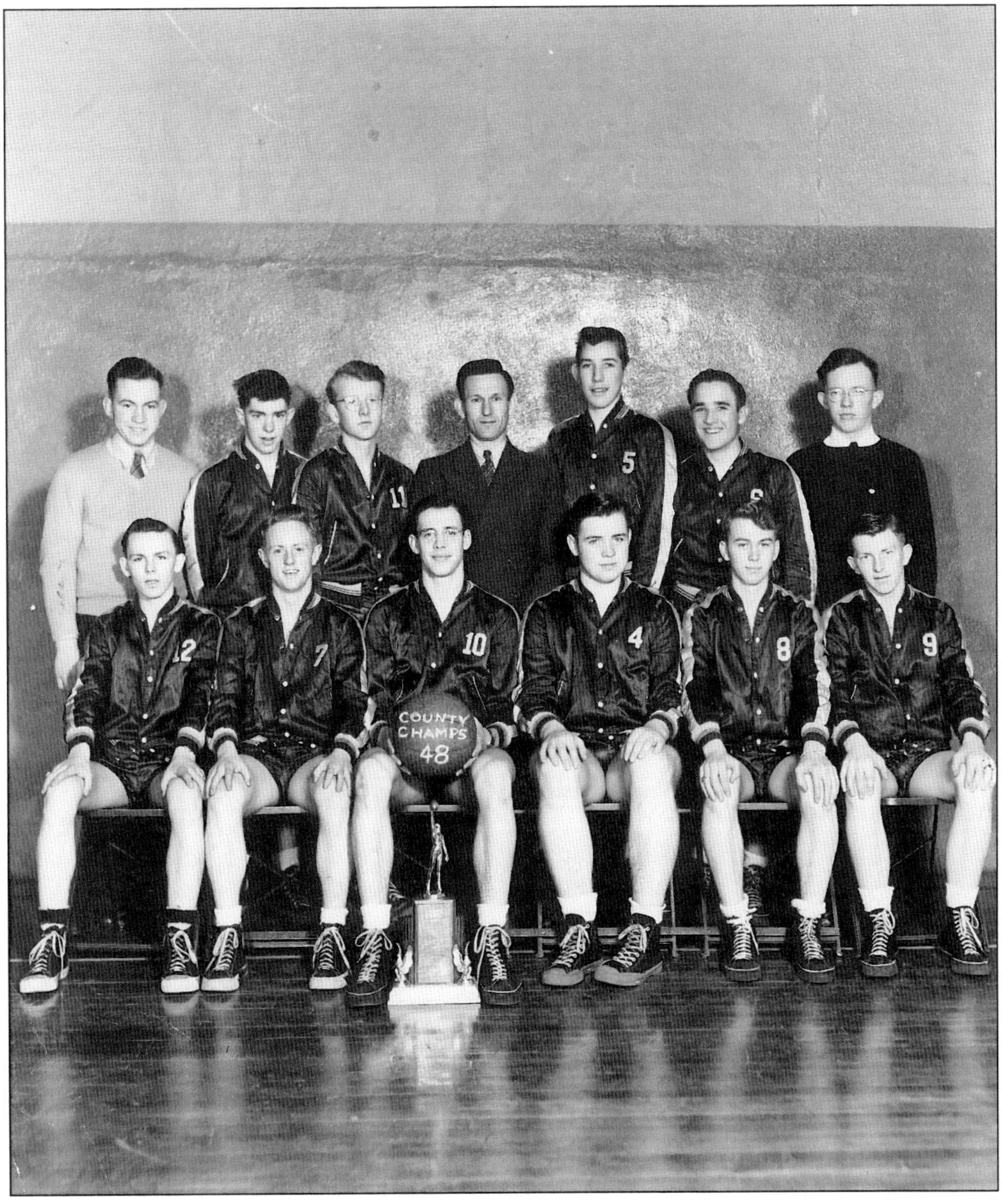

Washburn's 1948 County Championship basketball team. From left to right are: (front row) Harold Corey, Gerald McNeal, Everett Chamberlain, Bryce McEwen, Gary Umphrey, and Isaac Brewer; (back row) James Hunter, Dwight Sewell, Merlin Perkins, Coach Pauli, Philip Runstrom, Lloyd Blackstone, and Elke Woodman.

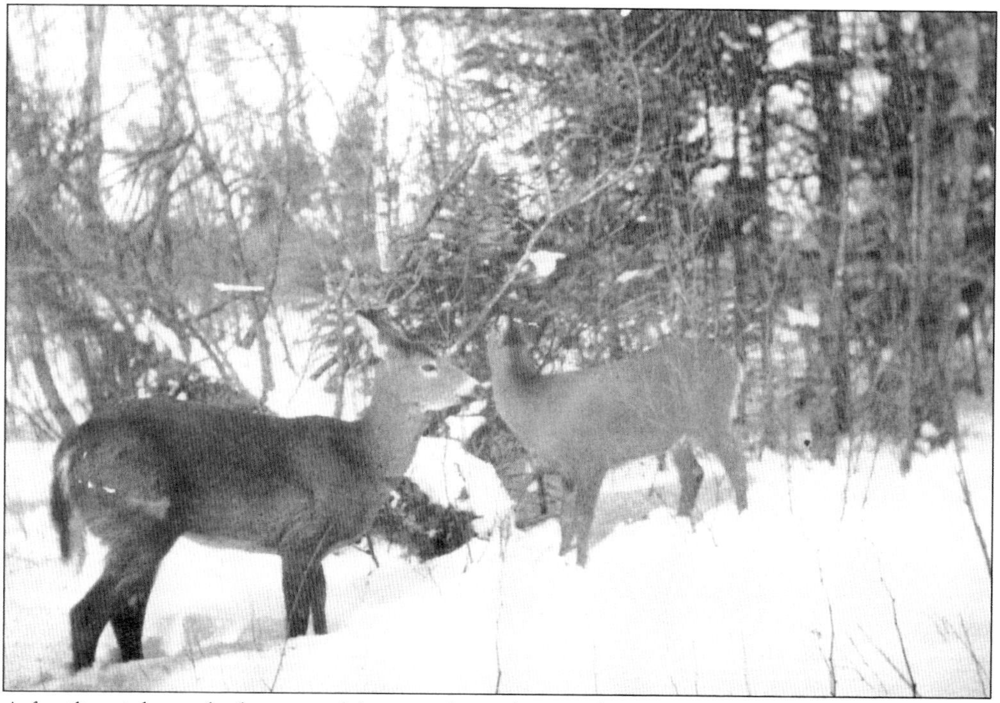

A familiar sight to the hunters of Aroostook are deer yards . . .

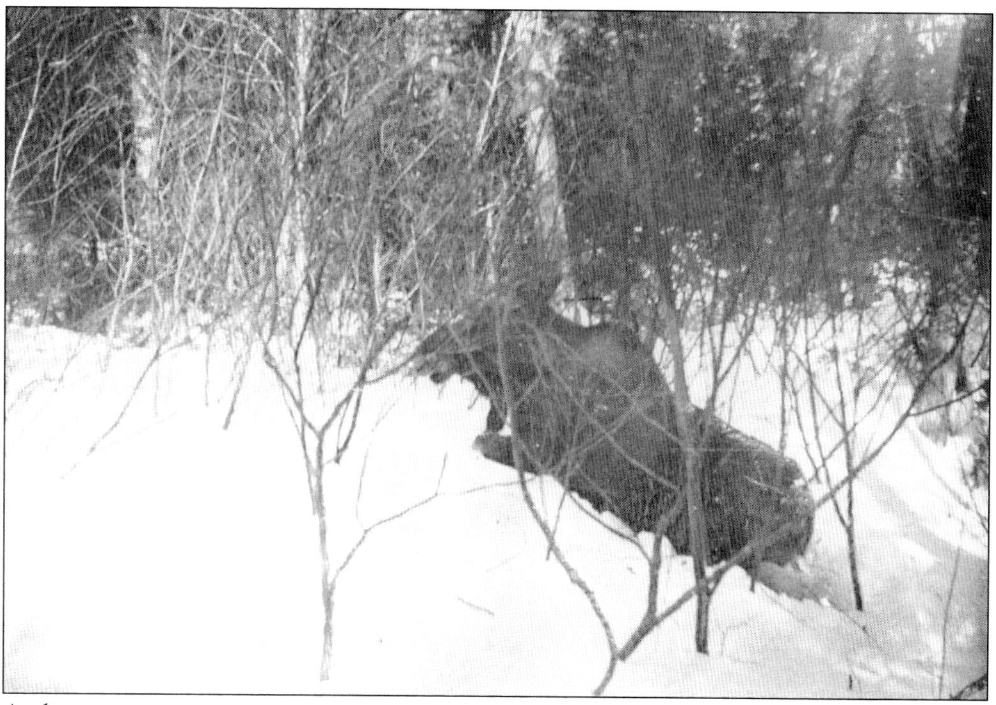

And moose . . .

Six

The Heirs and Heritage

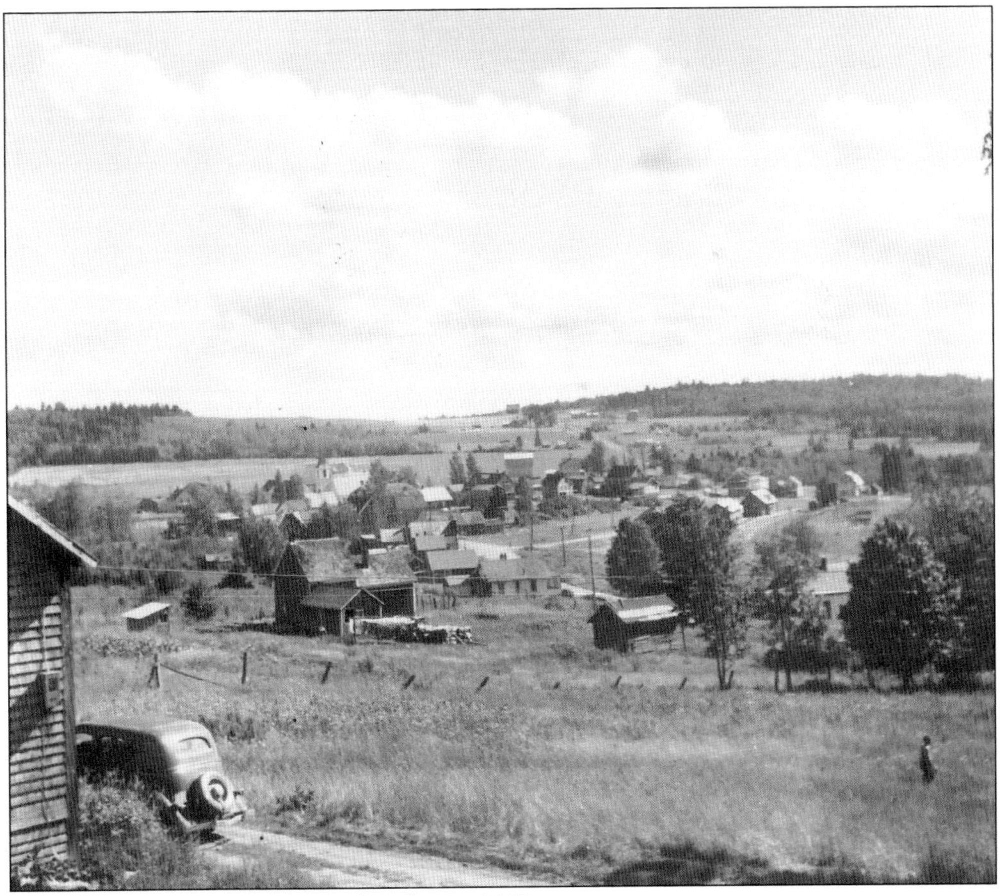

A view of the town of Portage Lake taken in 1939.

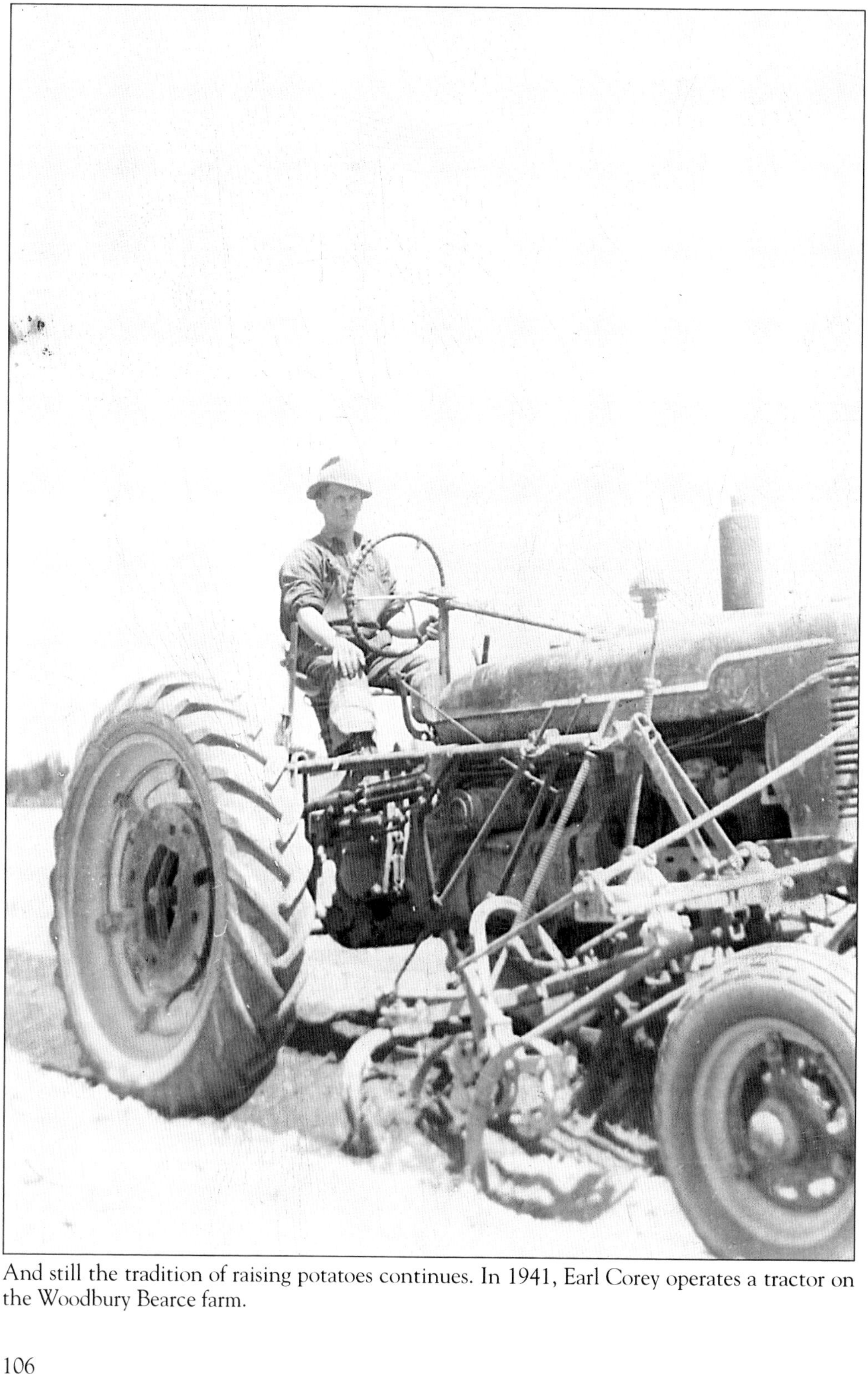

And still the tradition of raising potatoes continues. In 1941, Earl Corey operates a tractor on the Woodbury Bearce farm.

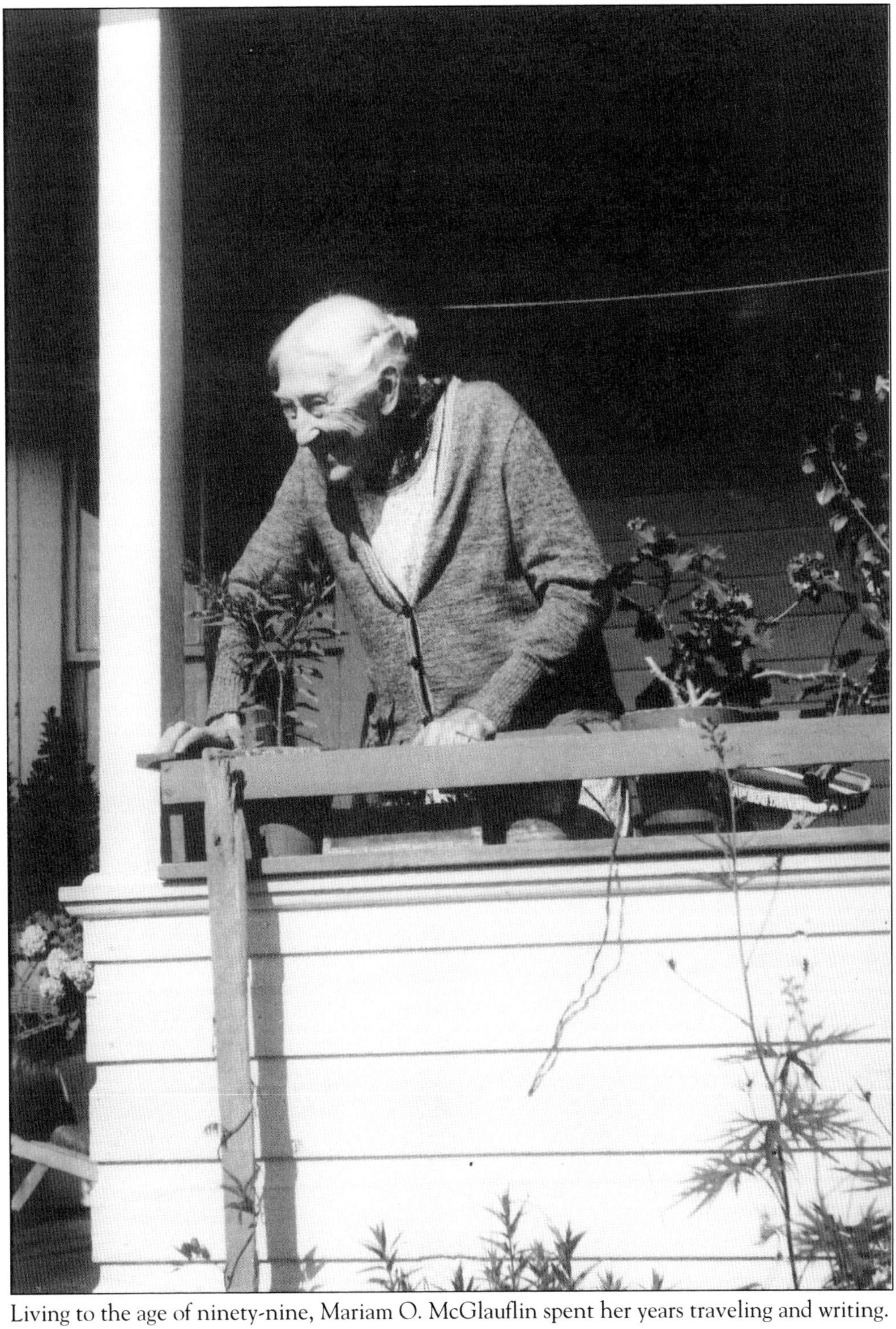

Living to the age of ninety-nine, Mariam O. McGlauflin spent her years traveling and writing.

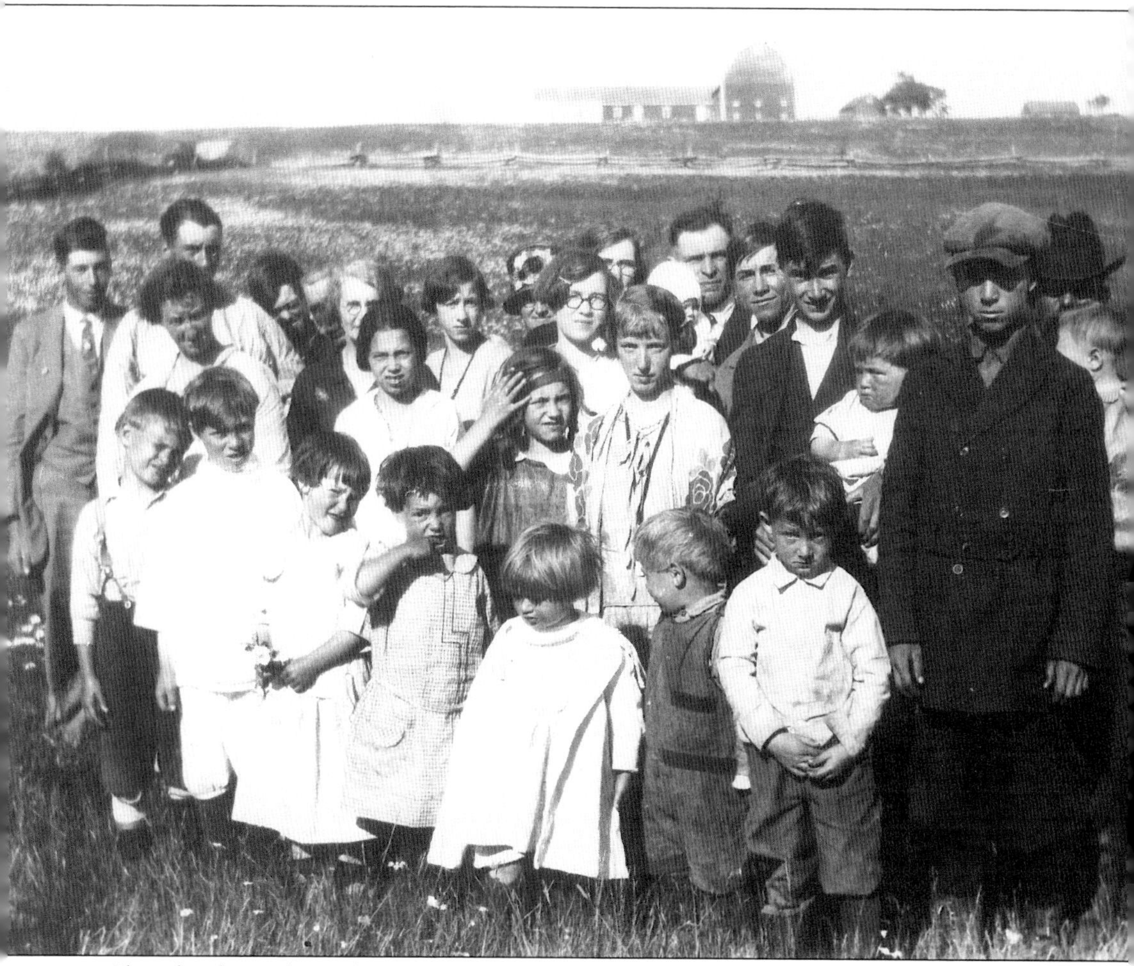

Close family ties have always been of great importance. Witness this family gathering in 1927 of the Wilcox, Drost, Bushey, Seward, and Ambrose relations. They are all cousins and live in Wade. Included in this photograph are Lillian Seward, Arnold Ambrose, Perley Drost, Herb and Leatha Drost, Gerald Seward, Bryon Drost, Beecher Ambrose, Henry and Beatrice Bouchey, Roy Wilcox, Sterling and Merle Wilcox, Elsie Drost, Roy and Henry Boucher, Addie, Mert, Hazel, and Laura Wilcox, Fern and Ruth Ambrose, Bill, and George Seward.

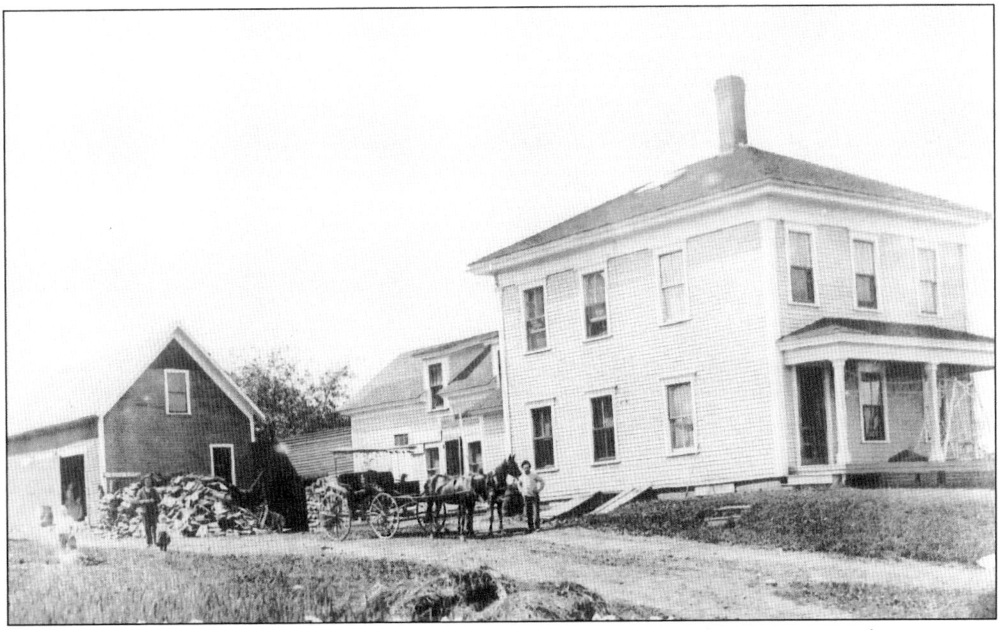

The Ed Smith house once occupied the land where Mapleton Hardware now stands.

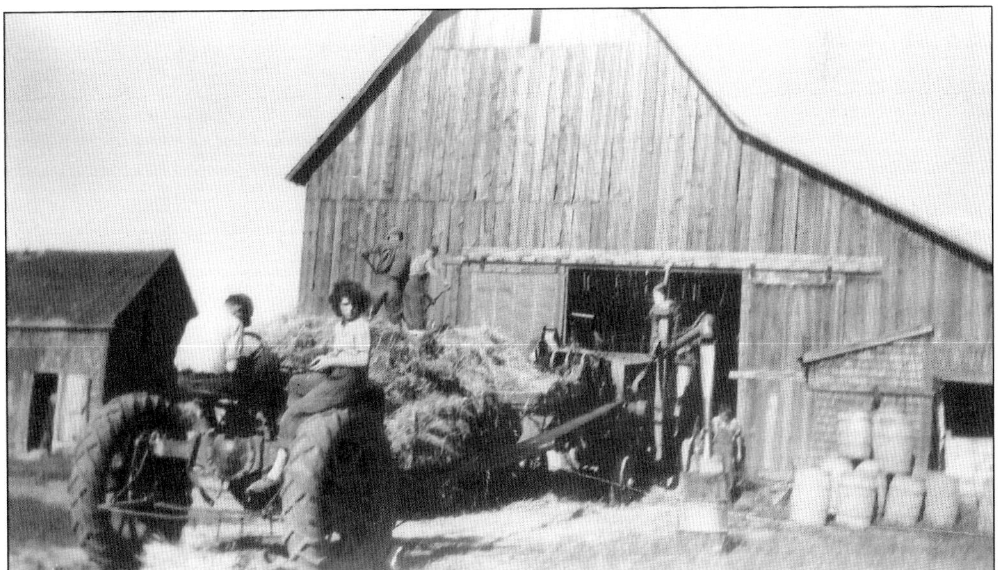

It's haying time in Washburn—while potato barrels wait a few weeks for their turn. Gloria Baker sits on the tractor wheel as Perley Drost sits in the driver's seat. On the top of the hay are Bill Baker (left) and Gerald Seward, and Herb Drost stands in the doorway.

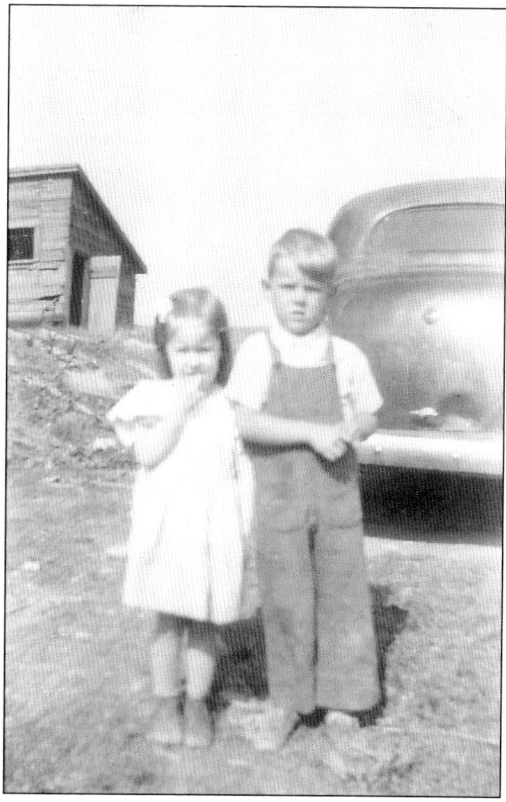

Family names are a tradition everywhere, but Carrie Corey and Cary Corey, cousins, share a grandmother and an aunt also named Carrie and Carrie.

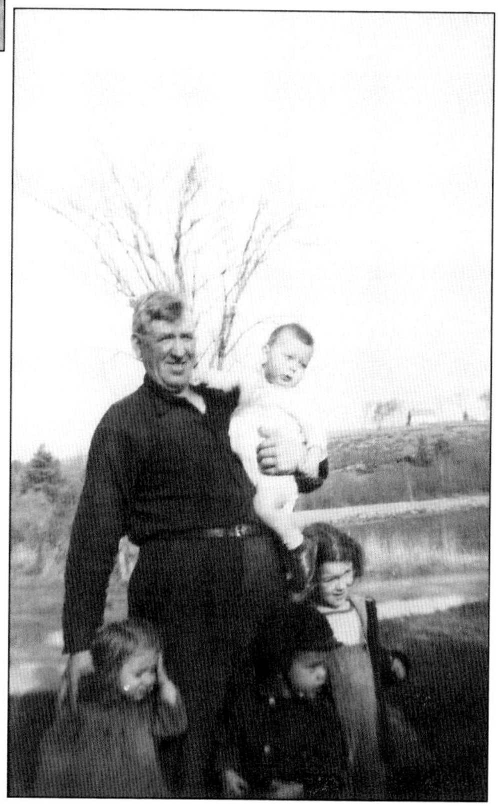

Braighton Alley in Castle Hill appears to be enjoying himself. He is shown in this 1953 photograph with his grandchildren; he holds Gary, and in front, from left to right, are Phyllis, Kenneth, and Sharon.

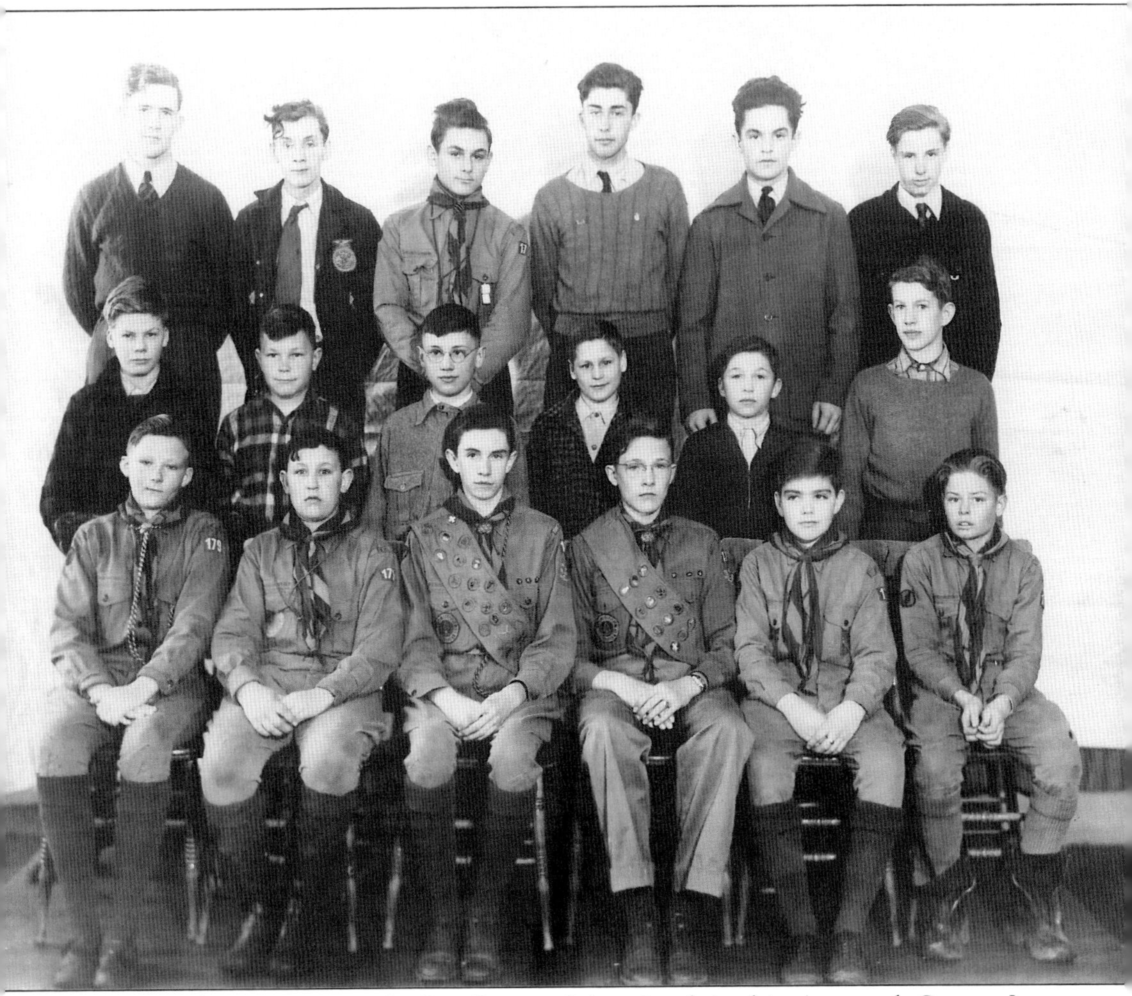

Always a popular organization, the Boy Scouts of America thrived in Aroostook County. In 1943, Troop 179, sponsored by the Donald Delnite Post 109, American Legion of Ashland, posed for a picture. From left to right are: (front row) William Harriman, Floyd Wakefield, Warren Aliot, Lynwood Harriman, George Sylvester, and Hutch Swett; (middle row) Carland Bartlett, William Savory Jr., Stephen Hews, Cecil Brown, Dana Hews, and Ralph Dumphy; (back row) Gerald Stevens, Reginald Tucker, Conrad St. Onge, Richard Blanchard, Audrey Chalou, and James Skinner.

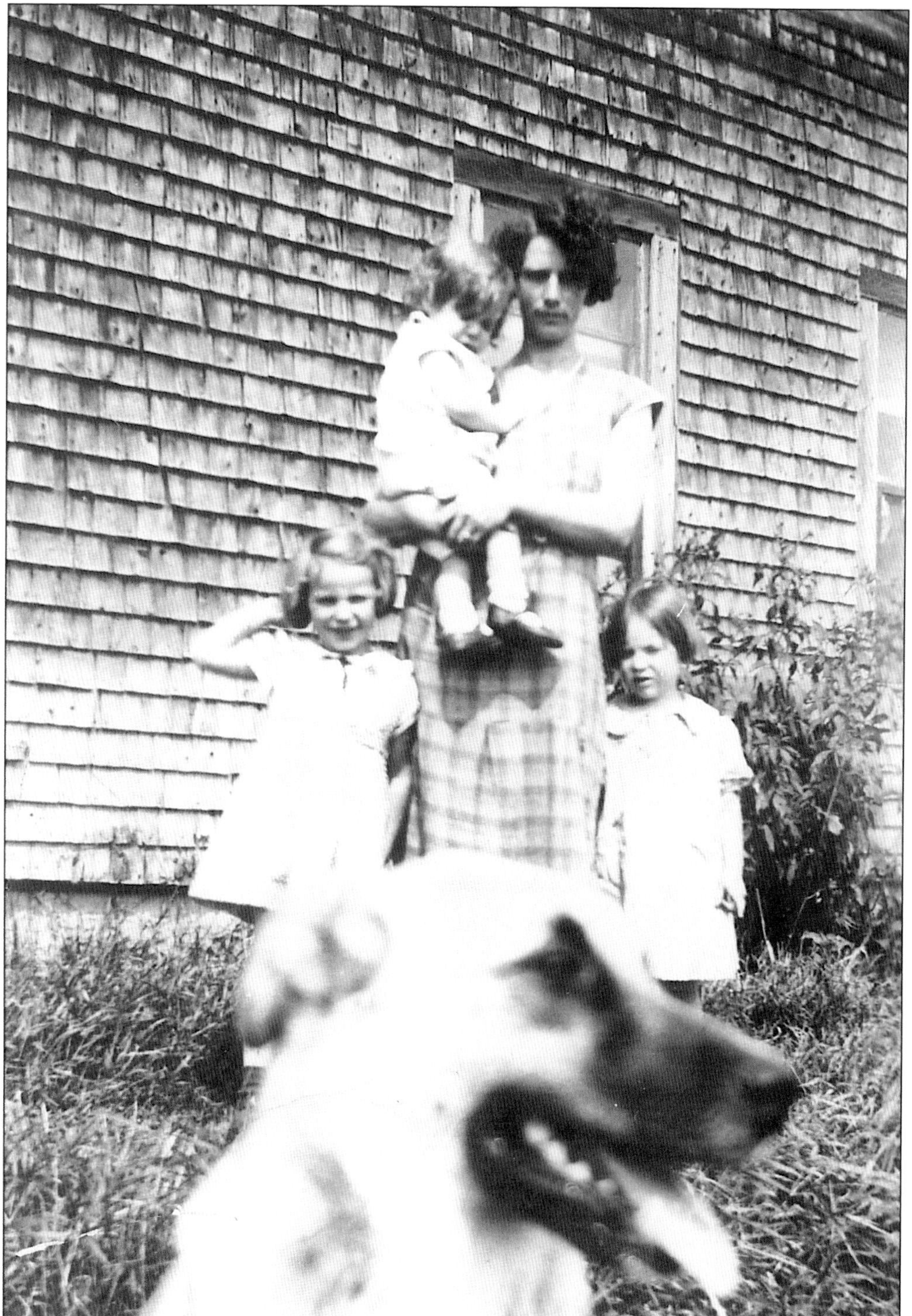

The house is gone now, but in 1936 on the Sloat homestead on Mapleton Road near Castle Hill, Elsie Clayton paused long enough from her chores to have her picture taken with her children. From left to right are Dolores, Athil Jr., and Darlene. Even King posed.

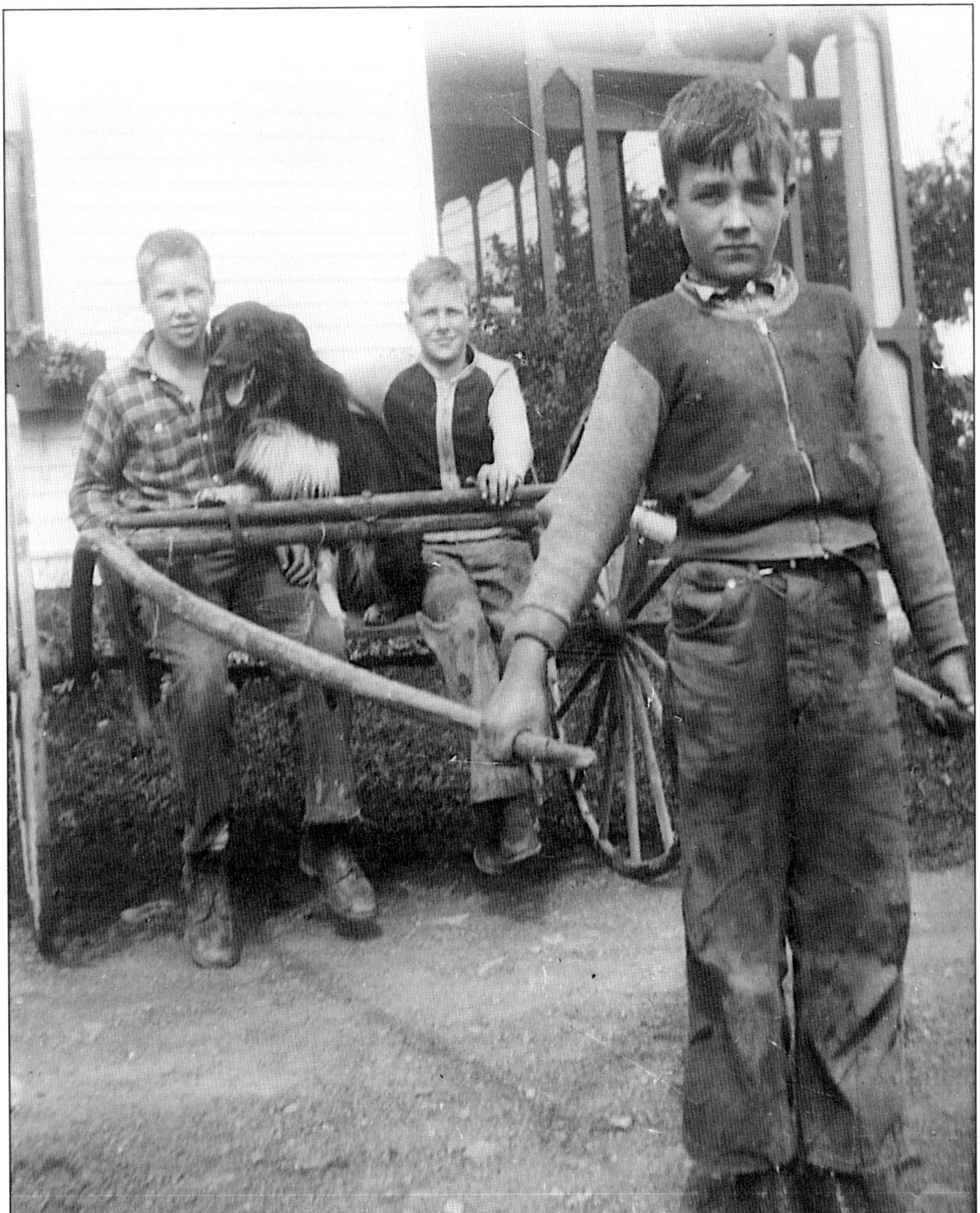

Riding in a pung from the "good old days," Bernard Blackstone, Shep (the dog), and Lloyd Blackstone are pulled by Lloyd Blackstone.

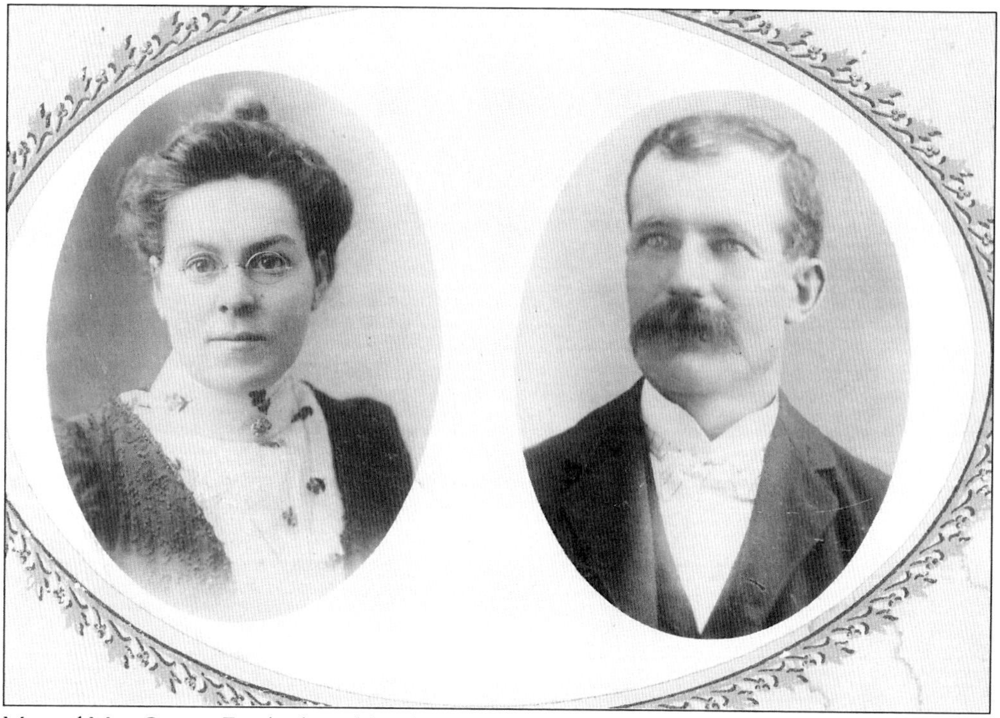

Mr. and Mrs. George Fox built and lived in what is now the Baptist parsonage in Perham. Their descendants still farm and have a trucking business in the same area of the original homestead.

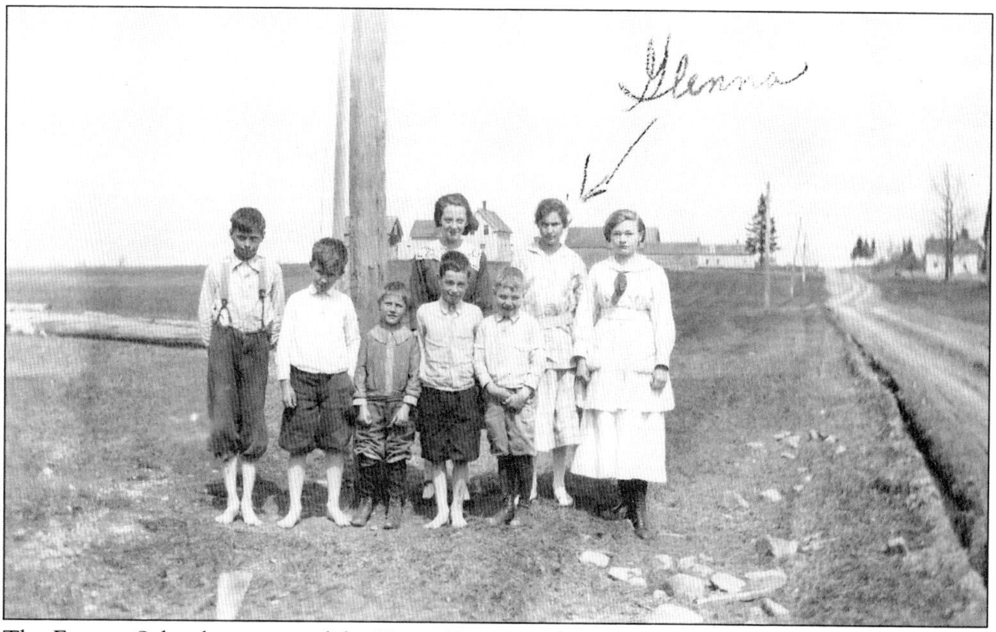

The Everett School was named for Henry Everett, whose house stands behind these students. From left to right are Donald Beckwith, Earl Whitehouse, Frankie Campbell, Harvey Wilder, unknown, Dorcas Campbell, Glenna (Estey) Blackstone, and Laura Roberts.

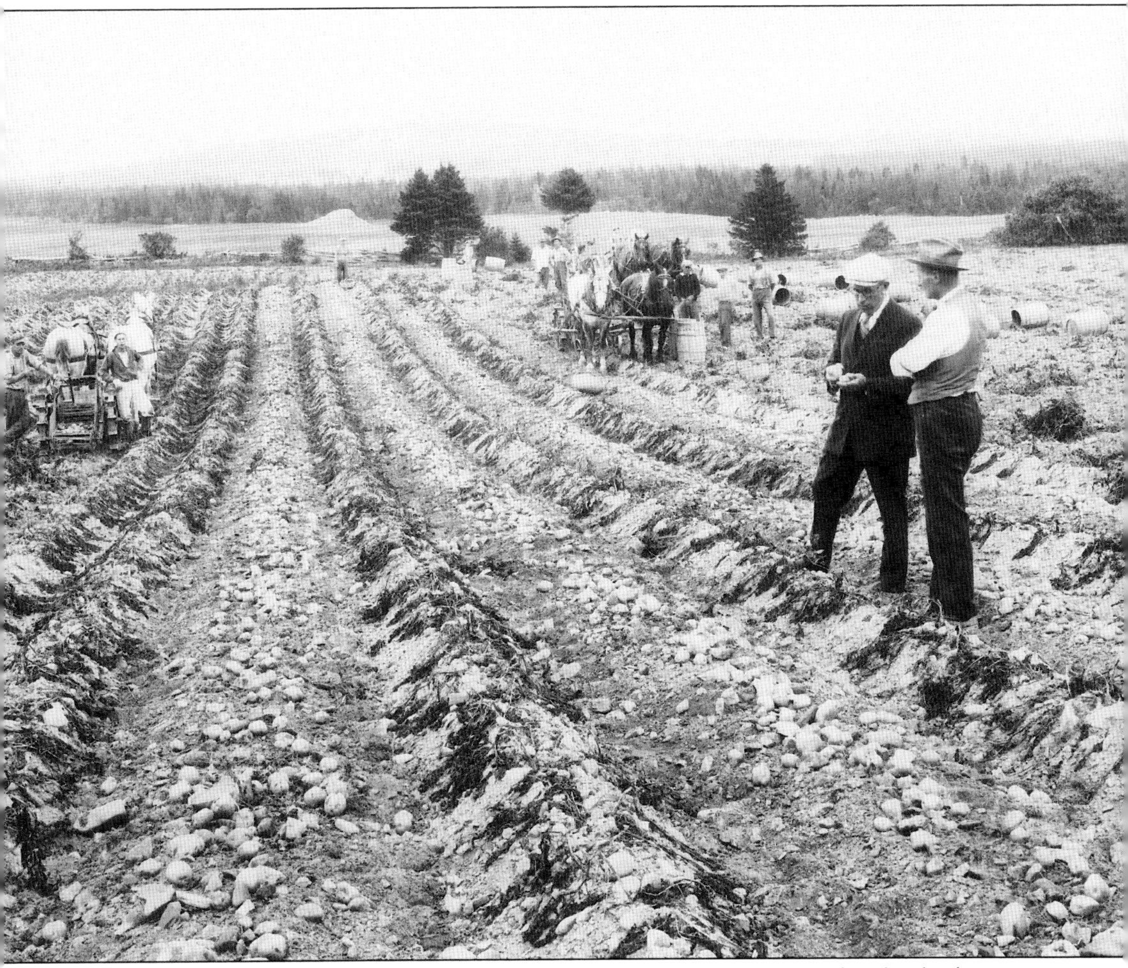

The Milton Smith farm is shown here in 1929 and is still is being farmed today by his son and grandsons.

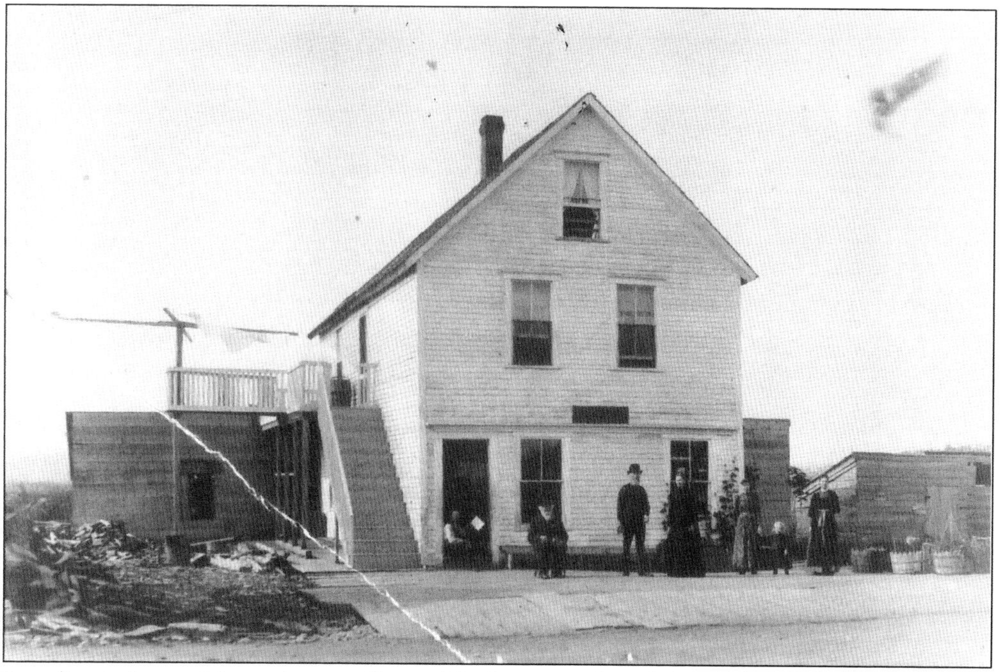

Standing in front of the early post office in Mapleton are, from left to right, Clifford McGlauflin, John Greenlaw, James McGlauflin, Mariam Greenlaw McGlauflin, Lula (McGlauflin) Keirstead, Fred McGlauflin, and Flora (McGlauflin) Searles. James was the second post master, and Fred became a game warden.

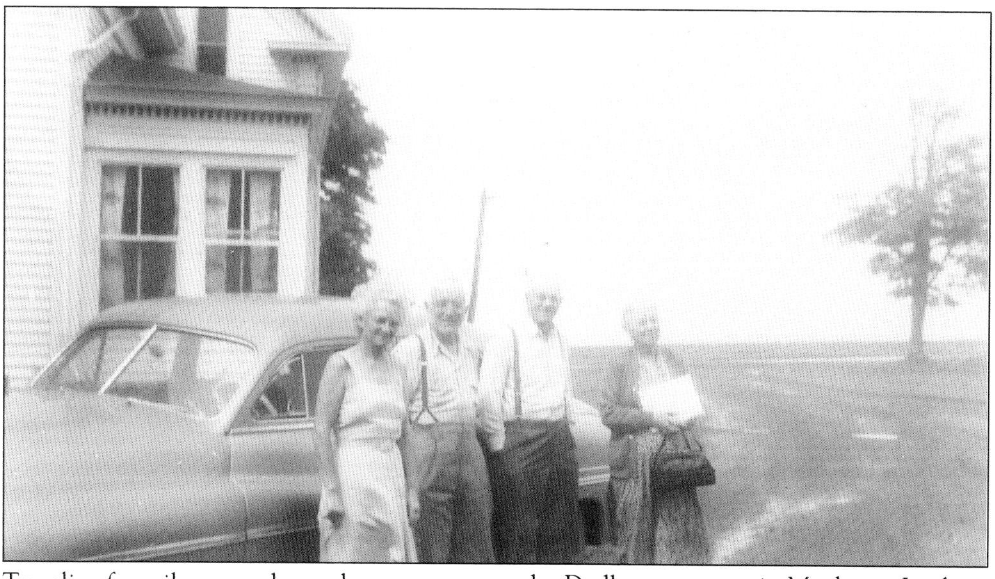

Traveling for miles around, people came to eat at the Dudley restaurant in Mapleton. Looking pleased and satisfied are, from left to right, Avis Dudley, Orin Higgins, Forest Dudley, and Susie Higgins.

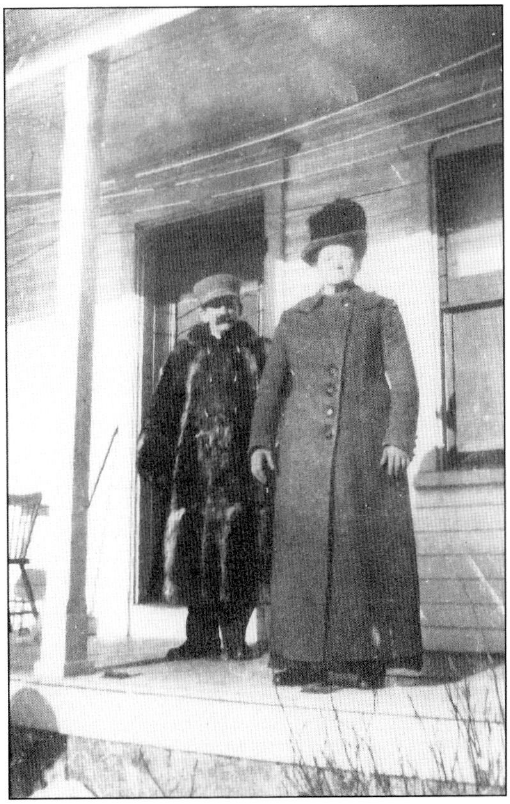

Henry and Loretta Everett, shown here in an early 1900s photograph, were the original founding settlers. The Everett District and the Everett School proudly bear their name.

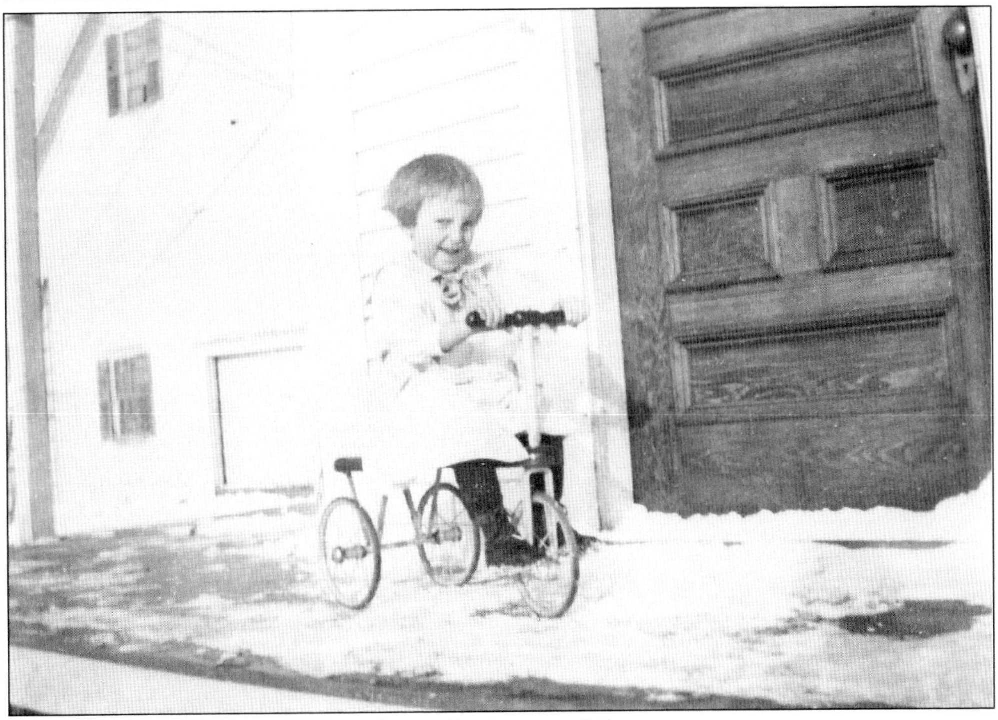

In 1916 Kenneth Estey conquers a three-wheel scooter bike.

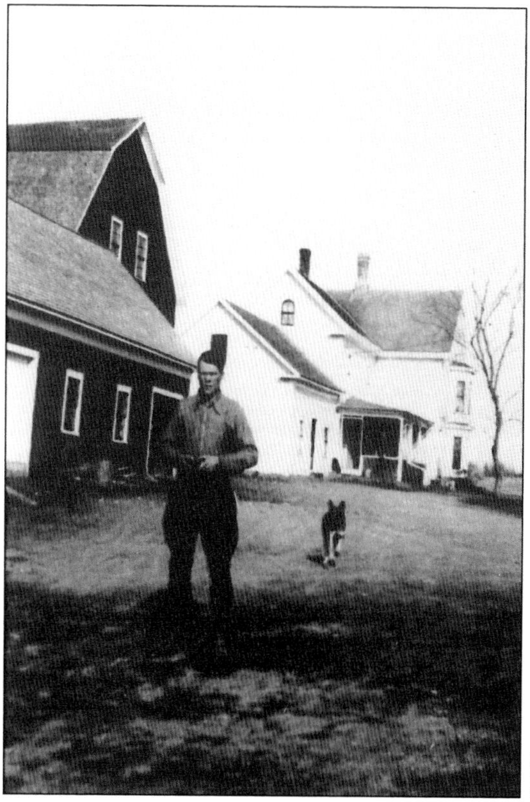

Although the dog appears to be heading home after a day in the fields, Gene Burns at the Glen Porter Farm in Masardis in the 1930s seems to be ready to go horseback riding.

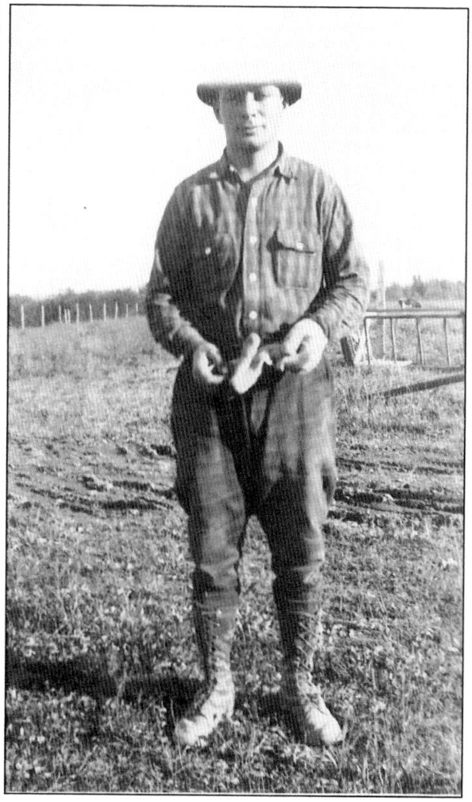

Knee-high, laced-up boots were the practical footwear of the day in 1932. Athil Clayton Sr., who worked for the Washburn School District for twenty-four years as bus driver and custodian, is right in style.

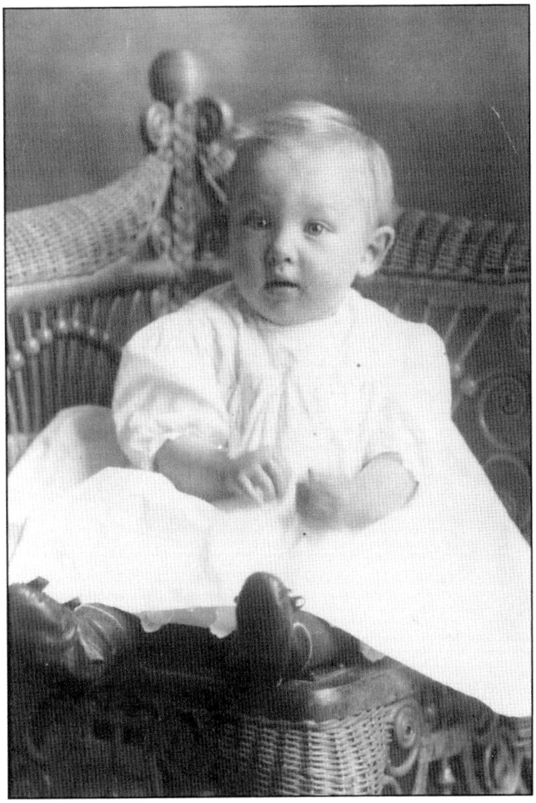

A farmer and carpenter for most of his life, Ken Harris (shown here in 1911) became a self-taught painter when he retired. Several thousand of his "Grandma Moses"-style paintings sold to all parts of the country.

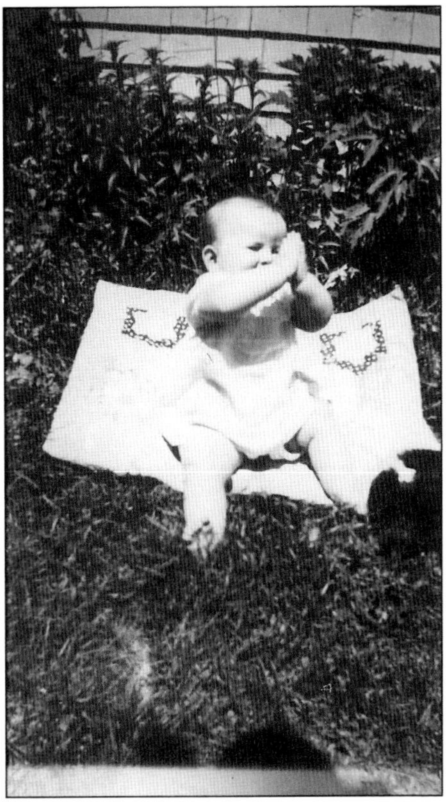

Autumn (Crouse) Creasey is on a picnic, either praying the good weather continues or playing patty-cake.

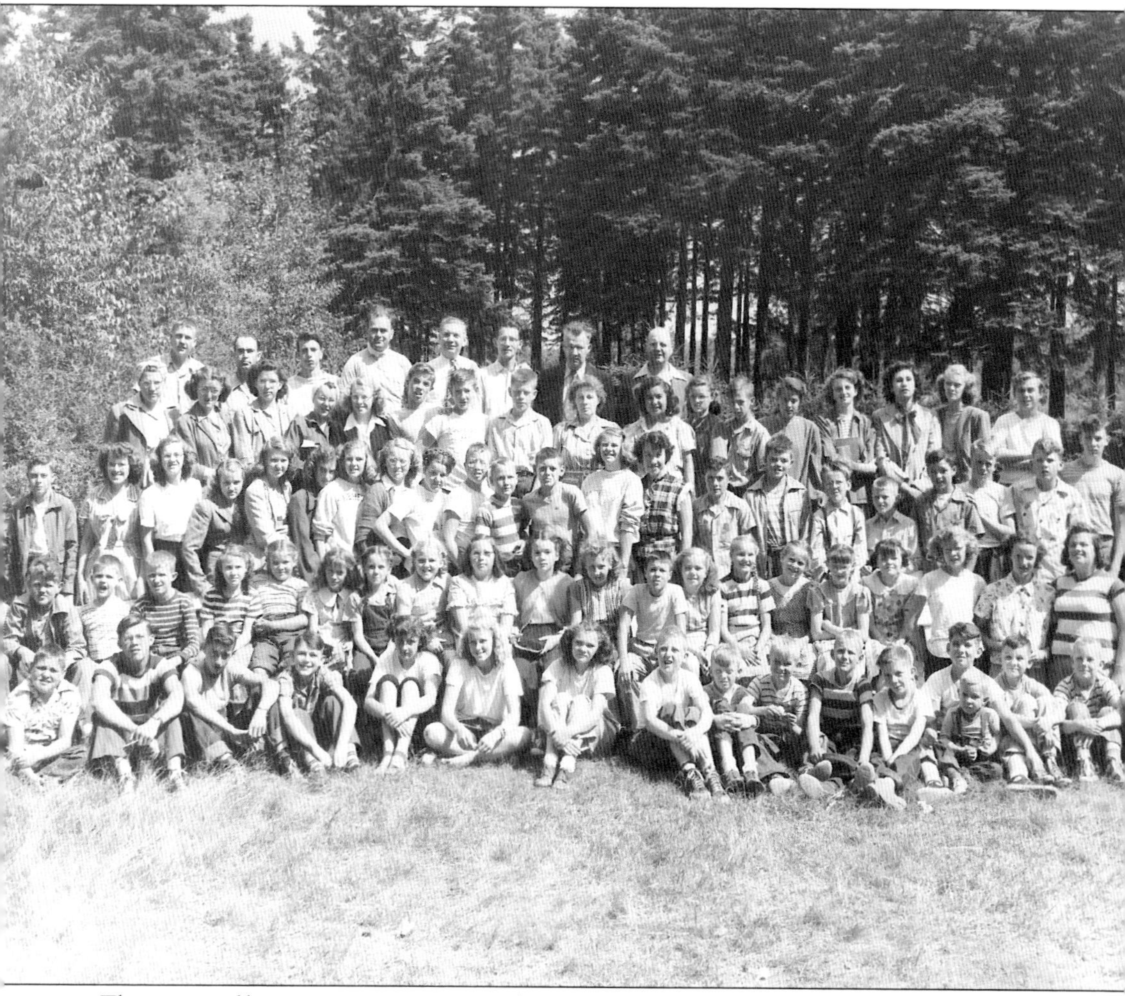

This group of happy campers were spending three weeks at the Advent Christian Youth Camp at Aroostook Valley Park, c. 1945.

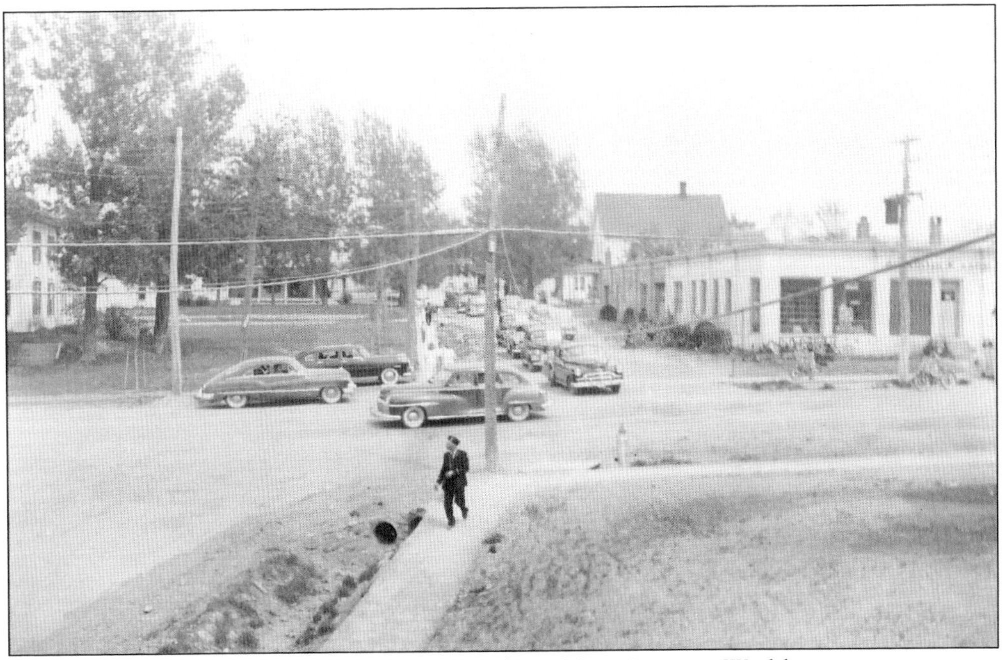

A Memorial Day parade in 1940 works its way down Main Street in Washburn.

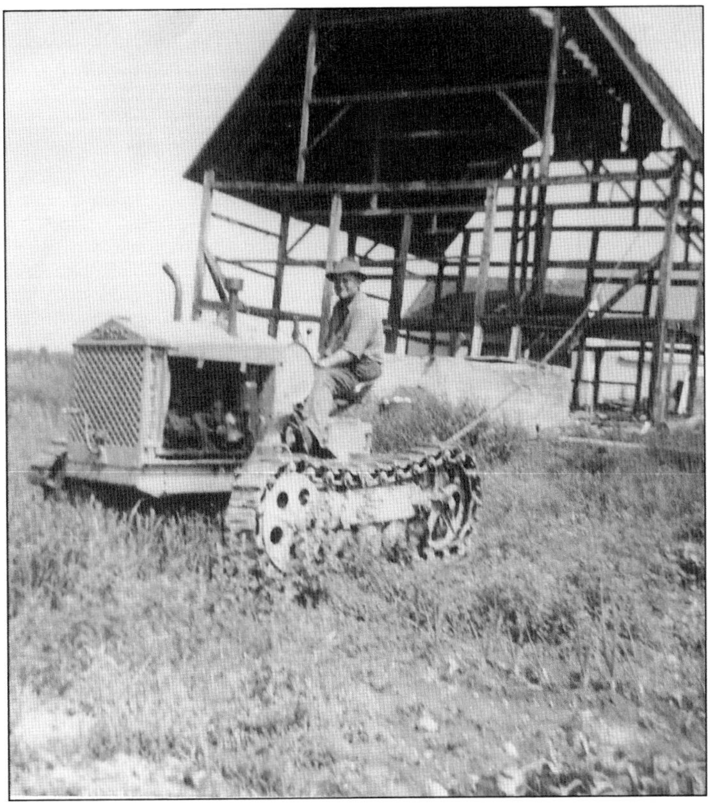

In 1947, Arvard Crouse found it necessary to pull down the old barn on his farm in Crouseville.

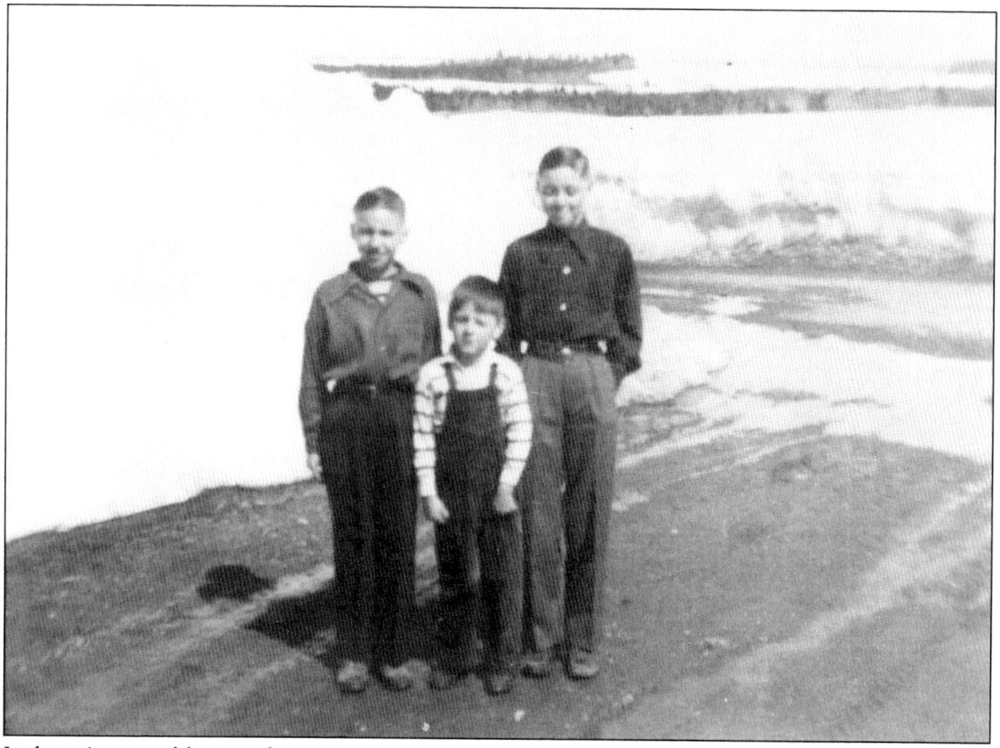

It doesn't snow, blow, or freeze every winter day in Aroostook County. On one Christmas day Gary, Mike, and Bill Cochran ventured out in shirt sleeves to measure the bank behind them.

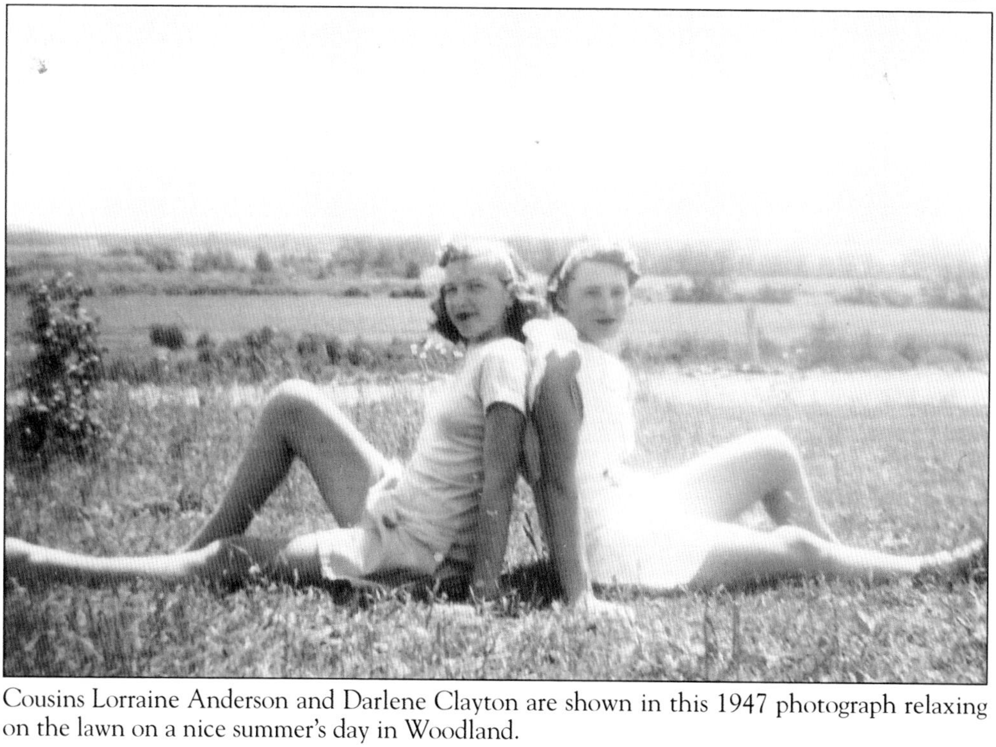

Cousins Lorraine Anderson and Darlene Clayton are shown in this 1947 photograph relaxing on the lawn on a nice summer's day in Woodland.

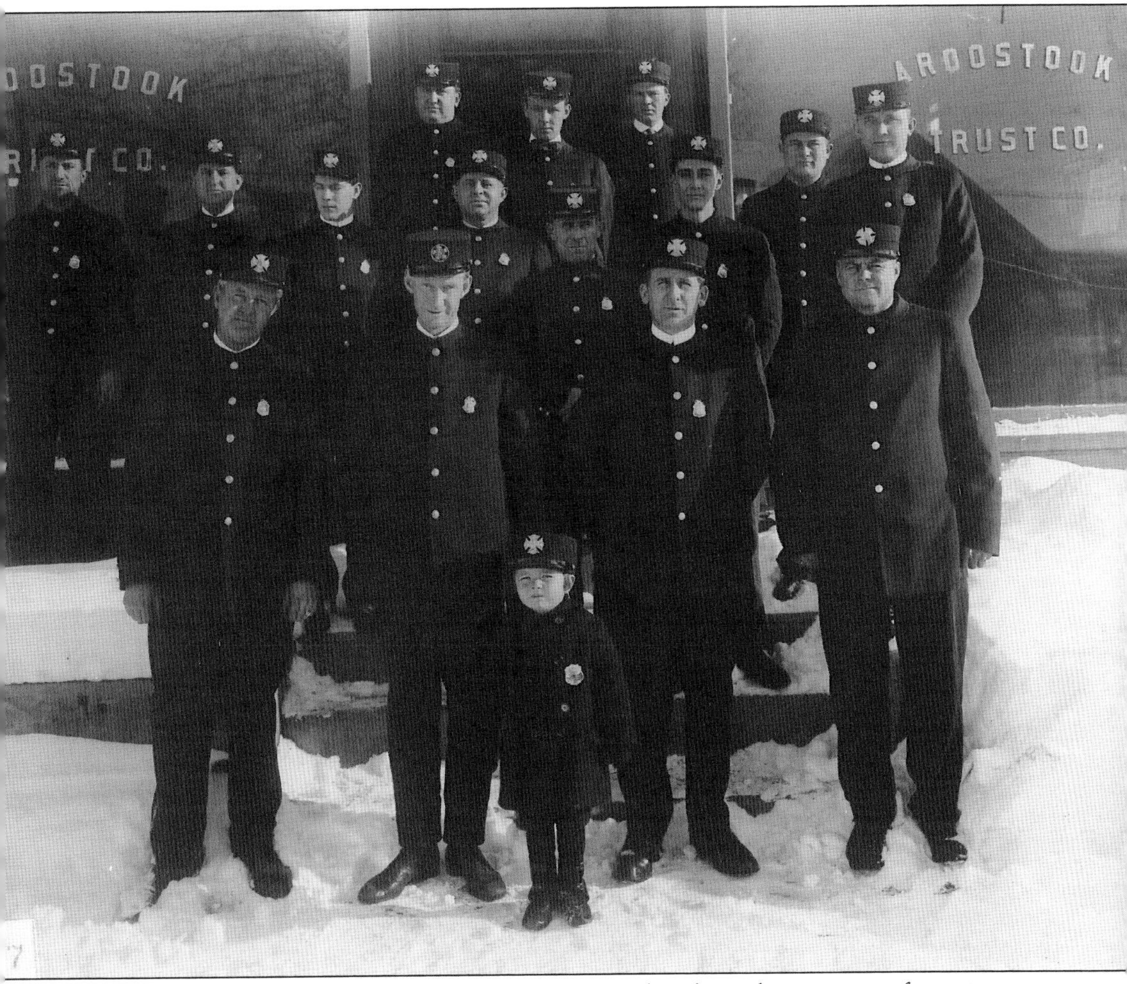

In 1916, the Washburn Fire Department took time from their busy chores to pose for a picture. Philip Carver (front) was the mascot, and looks as proud of his job as the grown-ups do. From left to right are: (front row) J. Woodside Doane, Chief E.W. Higgins, Henry Wilder, and Delbert Story; (middle row) W. Ballard, Guy Durepo, Amos Bagley, Vernon Wilder, Sam Eddy, Glen R. Cheney, Frank Carver, and Ernest Woodman; (back row) Charles Delong, Andrew J. Beck, and Woodbury L. Berce.

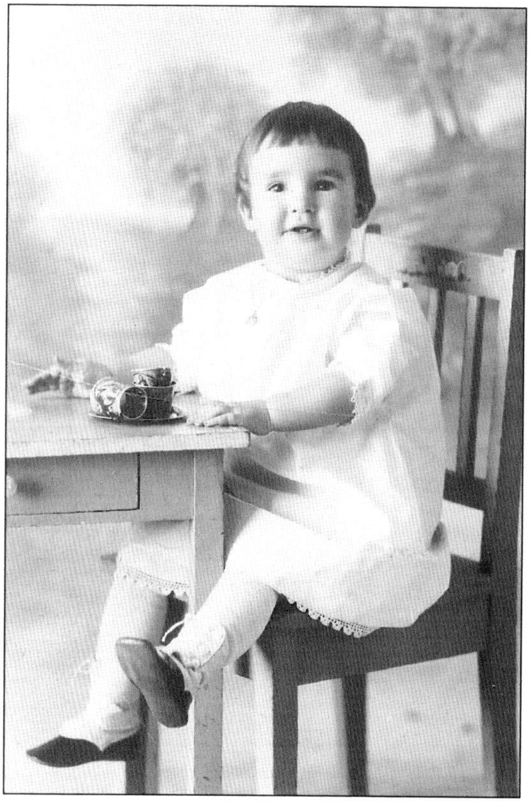

Phylis Churchill Allen helped her mother at the maternity hospital in Washburn. This photograph was taken in 1925.

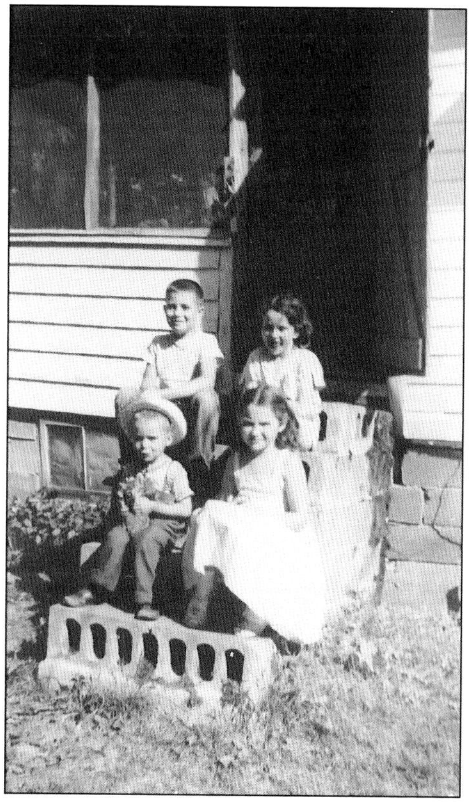

Smiling for the camera, these happy youngsters are, from left to right: (front) John Despres and Danna Kelley; (back) David Despres and Christie Smart. The boys went on to own a travel bureau and David worked for Senator Edmund Muskie, Senator Margaret Chase Smith, and presidential candidate Robert Kennedy.

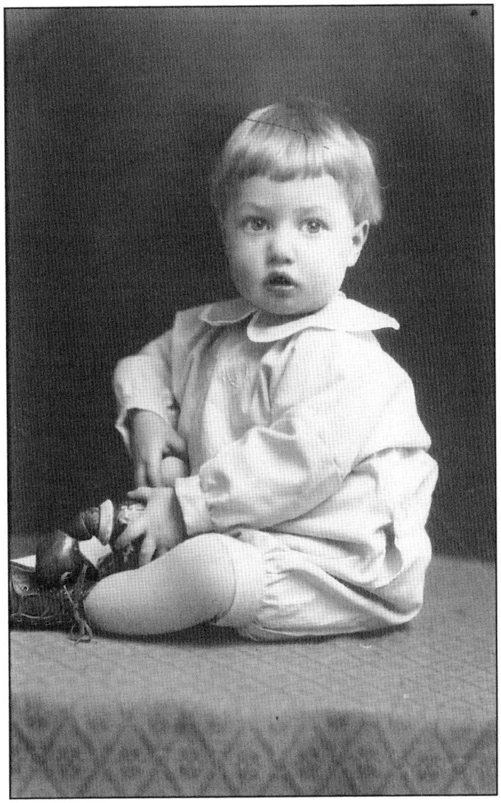

Gardner Sperry, shown here in 1929, made fire-fighting a life-long career and is the current fire chief in a neighboring community.

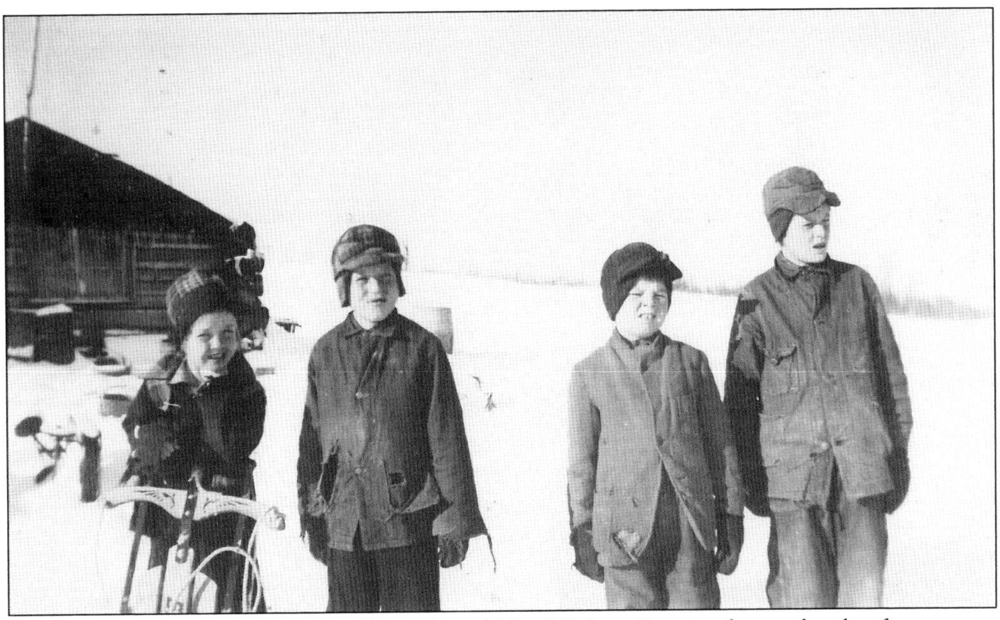

From left to right are Harry, Donald, Fred, and Lloyd Baker. Coming from a family of seventeen children, they became renowned in later years for "pitching in" and helping others, even taking time from their own work to do so.

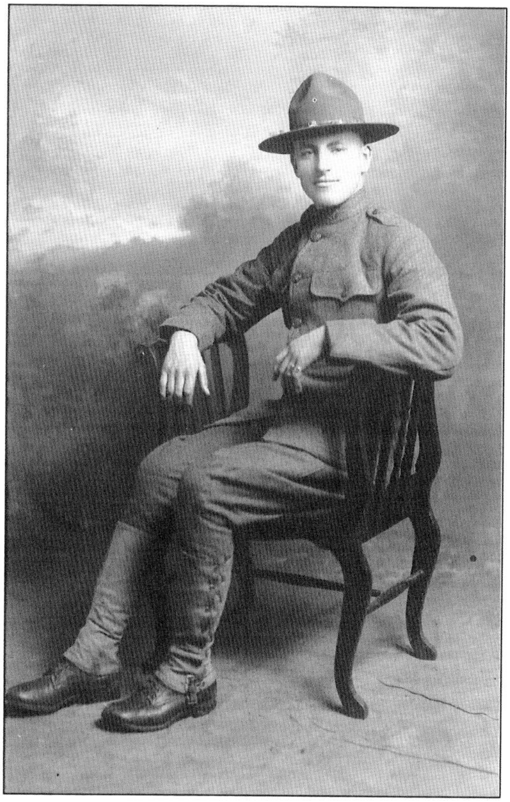

In 1916 Reuben Whitehouse lied about his age to enter the army. He served in France in the Medical Corps, picking up the wounded on battlefields.

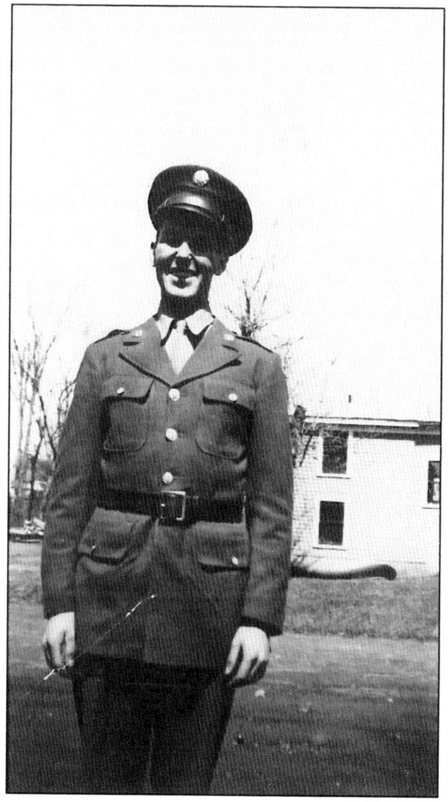

In 1941, Garold Alley answered the call of his country to liberate Europe. Over the next five years he saw action in five countries and was involved in three invasions. Returning home to Castle Hill, he brought with him many medals and citations.

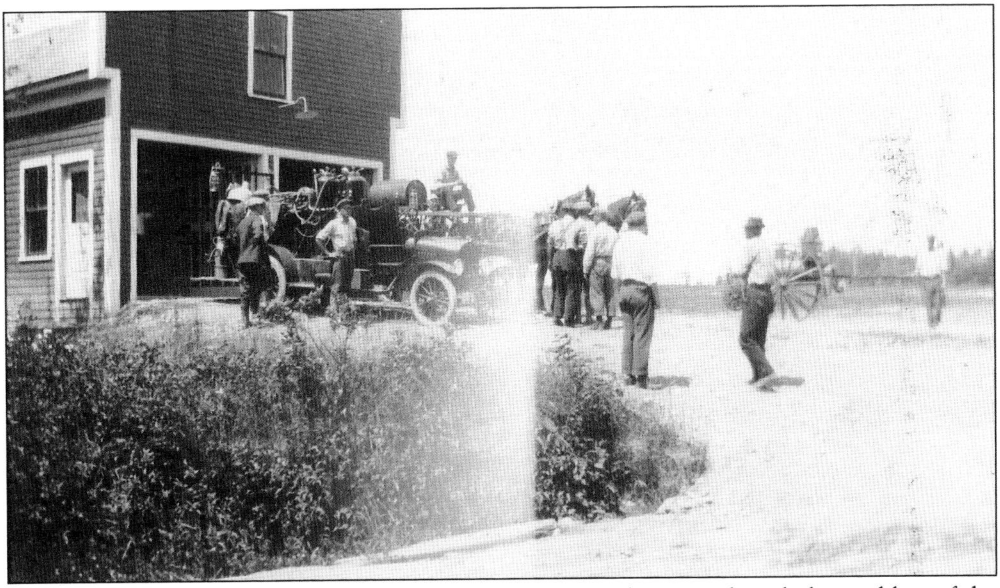

A 1922 photograph of firemen from Mapleton, who were always ready to help neighbors if the need arose. The horses were owned by Andrew Filmore, who also delivered the mail.

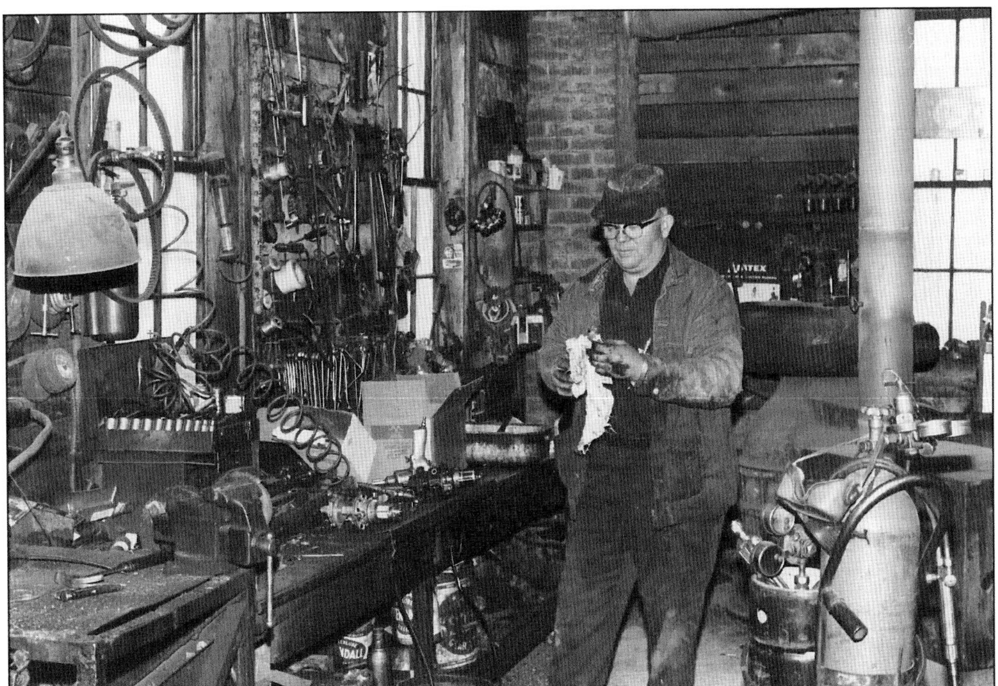

Ellsworth (Elke) Woodman in his first auto repair shop.

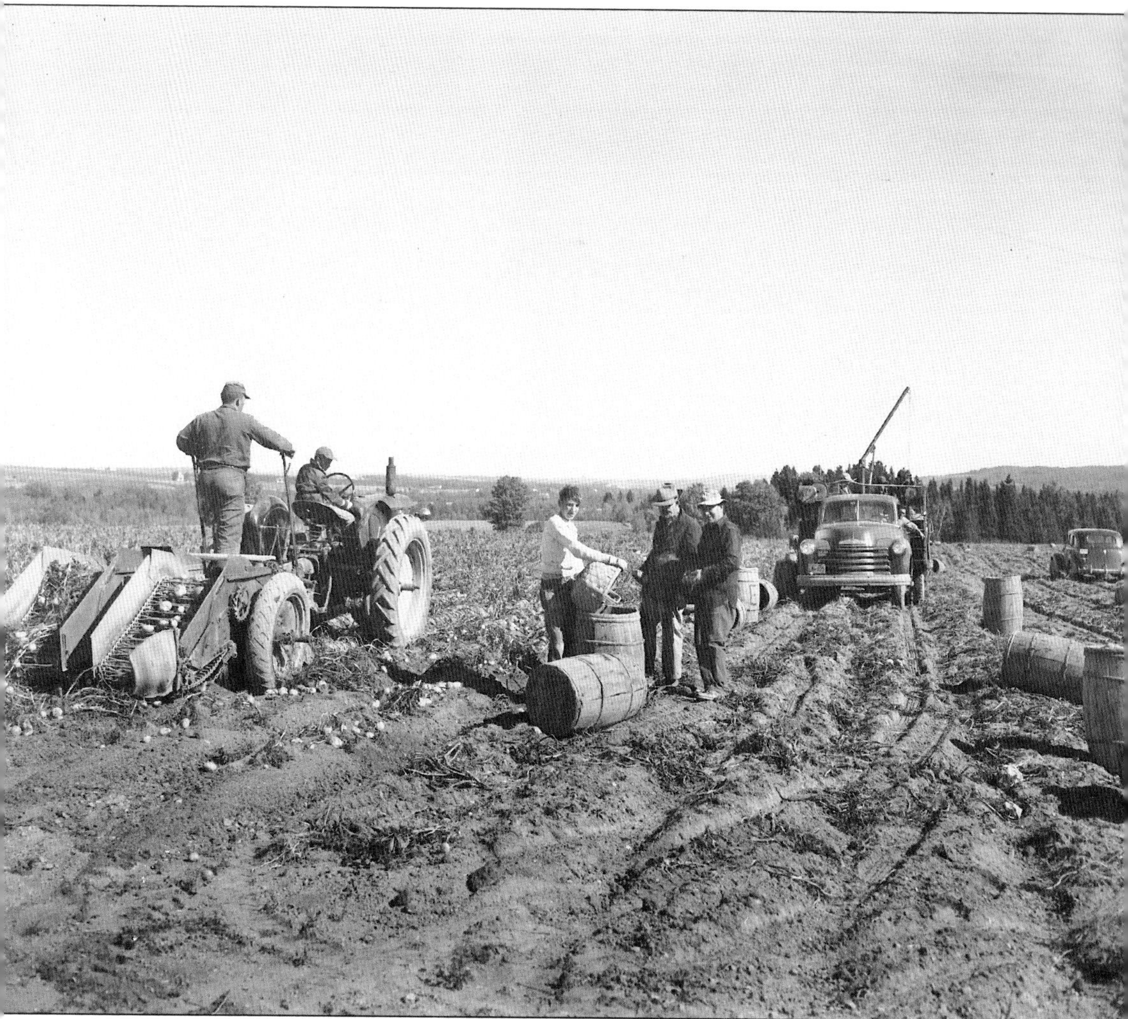

Picking "spuds" was back-breaking work, but the camaraderie was heart warming. In 1949, on the Tess Gould farm on the Mapleton/Castle Hill Road, a crew works diligently toward getting the crop from the field to market. Elke Woodman is on the back of the digger while Robert "Gum" Clayton drives the tractor. The picker, Sheldon Richardson, talks to Ira and Athil Clayton, and Liston Boyce drives the truck.